The Lives of the Piano

THE LIVES OF THE
PIANO

Edited by

JAMES R. GAINES

HOLT, RINEHART AND WINSTON
New York

Published by Holt, Rinehart and Winston,
383 Madison Avenue, New York, New York 10017.
Published simultaneously in Canada by Holt, Rinehart and
Winston of Canada, Limited.

Library of Congress Cataloging in Publication Data
Main entry under title:
The lives of the piano.
  1. Piano—History. 2. Piano—Construction. 3. Pi-
anists. I. Gaines, James R.
ML650.L58   786.2'1   81-47483
ISBN 0-03-057974-0   AACR2

First Edition

Designer: Jacqueline Schuman
Printed in the United States of America
10 9 8 7 6 5 4 3 2 1

Page 215 constitutes an extension of this page.

❧ CONTENTS ❧

OVERTURE

JAMES R. GAINES

This is a book made by men and women who have carried on a nearly lifelong love affair with the piano, and it is addressed to others who share that passion.

Why do we care so deeply? Each of the eight very independent, opinionated essayists in this book correctly perceives the instrument to be in some degree an anachronism—a weathered, somewhat perplexed traveler from another time whose purpose in our own is unclear. Its original virtues of melody and nuance seem echoes of old imperatives; its physical evolution has all but stopped. In the desire of some twentieth-century composers for its more percussive effects, there seems at times an underlying desire for a different instrument.

As I write this I am kept company by an eighty-five-key Steinway of late nineteenth-century vintage whose molds have long since been broken. It is, apart from the members of my family, my oldest friend; on dark nights and sunny afternoons alike I think of it that way, returning to it as one does to the closest of confidants. This piano's previous owner was my teacher in Dayton, Ohio, Donald C. Hageman, with whom I began to study when

I was about eight years old. I have heard many stories about the ordeal of child pianists given over to driven teachers, like the one Samuel Lipman describes in his essay. I can only be thankful that I was spared, that my parents had the foresight and intuition to send me to a man who taught me not only a great deal about musicianship and piano playing but also about the art of life.

My piano had been his when he was a boy. When I bought it from him—for fifty dollars—it had been standing neglected for years in an unheated cabin on his parents' farm. Its innards were rotted and its soundboard was badly cracked. A fine piano technician, Don had an entire Steinway action mechanism—antique but not beyond repair—stuffed in a closet in his house. We rescued the old piano's key bed, case, and iron plate. The rest had to be found, reclaimed, and, in a great volley of exciting packages, ordered by mail (new key facings, a pin block, lots of red and green felt, exotic tools). The project took over the family basement one year and our one-car garage the next. My father drove holes through the ribs of the piano and into the soundboard for the dowels that closed the cracks, and Don set the hammers on the shanks, but otherwise, with Don's patient supervision, the project was mine. I remember vividly the summer day I managed to prop the plate against the garage wall and spray-painted it. I had saved that job as long as I could, and I cannot imagine a more stunning sense of accomplishment for a twelve-year-old boy than was reflected in that glorious new coat of gold.

In the piano world, and in these pages, such experiences of joy and self-affirmation are everywhere: in the selfless, artful craftsmanship of a piano builder, in the welcoming warmth of a great teacher, in the delight and wisdom that come with overcoming one's limitations in the practice room, and in the resulting moments of exaltation in the concert hall. In such moments the piano is continually resurrected; it speaks as it has always spoken to the stirrings and strivings of the human spirit. The harpsichord and clavichord became obsolete when their singular voices came to seem insufficient to their time, when the piano's more urgent, dynamic sound drowned them out. But the piano's voice has adapted beautifully to its every passage, seemingly as well born to make tone clusters as to play twelve-tone rows. There is no supplanter in sight.

We celebrate here a phoenix—an instrument being habitually made new—and the people who have been charged at various times with its rebirth: inventors, builders, technicians, composers, and players. That we worry over its future is no indication that we love it less, but rather that we wish more than a glorious past for this most animate of inanimate objects, one whose lives will no doubt long outlast our own.

Among the many people whose dedication and whose love for the piano went into the making of this book, I would like to thank particularly Caroline Sutton, for her diligent and impressive picture research and for her patient persistence with the details of production, which made this book possible; Jacqueline Schuman, for her elegant design; Barbara Wood, for her expert copy editing; Jennifer Josephy of Holt, Rinehart and Winston and Daniel Okrent of the Hilltown Press, for their constant, steadying support. Finally I must thank the authors, not only for their musical and literary skills but for their gracious professionalism. It is their book, and I salute them.

James R. Gaines
April 1981

The Lives of the Piano

ANTHONY BURGESS

The Well-Tempered Revolution

A Consideration of the Piano's Social and Intellectual History

I, who earn my living by writing fiction and literary criticism, must, before opening the piano lid, present credentials for daring to summarize the social history of a musical instrument. I am called to the task, I suppose, by the voices of my ancestors, who were Lancashire Catholic with a fierce admixture of Irish. Living in a Protestant country which, until the Catholic Emancipation Act of 1829, forbade adherents of the unreformed faith to qualify for the learned professions, my family, which never lacked either spirit or talent, worked mostly in a field for which degrees and diplomas were unnecessary—that of popular entertainment. When my ancestors did not keep taverns, they performed in them or in that extension of them, the British music hall. My mother was a soubrette and my father a piano player. He would not use the term *pianist* of himself, considering that it ought to be reserved to artists who performed on the concert platform, to which he was never good enough to be elevated. His place was the orchestra pit. He worked in variety theaters but mostly in cinemas in the silent days before 1929, either alone or with a random

bunch of other musicians. He had, without being a virtuoso, as full a grasp of the capabilities of the piano as any professional performer I have ever known. He could switch from ragtime to Chopin; he was a brilliant improviser.

When, in about 1933, I wished to take up the piano myself, he gave me little encouragement. He had become embittered by the growth of mechanical music and the death of the cinema orchestra. Now, like his father before him, working as a pub landlord, he rarely touched the instrument that had been his livelihood. I taught myself the piano by discovering the position of middle C on the keyboard and in the printed music, and I traveled on from there. I never became more than a middling amateur, better at big chords than at nimble passage-work, but I did grow into a competent composer. A few years ago I composed a concerto (in a kind of E-flat) for piano and orchestra. It is dedicated to the memory of my father, whose craft brought him little money and a measure of hard work and suffering. It is too difficult for me to play, and it would have been difficult for him, who was always impatient with written notes. It was written for a pianist; both he and I have been merely piano players.

❧

An upright piano was part of the furniture of my father's house. It was part of the furniture of most lower-middle-class homes in the early years of this century. It was not always played; the minor profiteers of the First World War would install one as an emblem of mild prosperity and garnish its top with framed photographs and gewgaws. Sometimes, when there were daughters in the family, these would be given inexpert lessons on the instrument to justify the existence of the stool. This reversed the natural process of musical education. Oboists and bassoonists do not take to the oboe or bassoon because there happens to be one in the house. They hear the sound of the instrument at a concert or on a record or the radio and fall in love with it. If they are lucky, the instrument is imported into the home and the love affair is promoted under more or less expert instruction. Woodwind teachers, unlike the lady who has a card in her window that reads PIANO LESSONS $X PER HOUR, are usually professional performers. Myra Hess, a great pianist, used to complain about the prevalence of ill-taught and unenthusiastic young piano players. If, she said, the kitchen sink had had an arrangement of copper wires beneath it, whining daughters would have been led by the ear and made to play that.

The piano is the instrument that everyone knows. I have composed music for bassoon and bass tuba, yet I have never handled either instrument. There is no person alive in the Western world who has not handled a piano. It is familiar, but it is still fascinating. Young children hammer it, instinctively recognizing that it is a percussion instrument. When they discover that there is a sustaining pedal, they face the anomaly that fires the composer for it—the fact that a kind of complicated tuned drum can also, like the human voice, prolong its notes. The long keyboard, with its uncountable ivory teeth and regular pattern of duo-trio-duo-trio black keys, is soon recognized as presenting visibly

the entire range of pitches, from below the lowest note of the double bassoon to above the top note of the piccolo. It is not quite an orchestra, but orchestral music does not sound absurd on it.

More than any other instrument, it seems to make sound visible. The range of a flute or clarinet is not manifested in its appearance, since the mysteries of overblowing are involved in the making of its higher notes. The stringed instruments are mere stretched wire. The piano shows what triads and sevenths really are. The infant Grieg found out the dominant ninth by simply playing alternate white notes. The black notes make up the ancient pentatonic scale, on which any fool can play Chinese or Scottish music. Any fool can play two kinds of glissando. Anyone not quite a fool can be shown, in half an hour or so, how to play the three principal chords of C major. Of course, the piano is also the most difficult instrument in the world to master. The trombone is nothing to it.

Let us see what this instrument is made of. There is an iron frame, somewhat in the shape of a harp, laid against a wooden plank. There are tightly stretched steel strings screwed to the extremities of the frame. There are eighty-eight hammers to hit the strings. This is the simple basic structure, but in fact it is overlaid with subtleties that are triumphs of sophisticated technology. The hammers are not crude and brutal strikers; they are delicately fitted with felt-covered heads. The strings are, for the greater part of the range of the instrument, grouped in closely set threes, producing the same tone in triplicate. This makes for fullness of sound, a kind of orchestrality. A modern piano sounds fuller than one of the pioneer models chiefly because of this triple tuning to the same pitch—except in the lower regions, where two strings are enough, and, lowest of all, where there is but one long, thick, chiming cord of copper. The pioneer pianos were fitted with bichords, not trichords.

When attenuated softness is required, there is a mechanism for cutting off one string of the trichord. The printed designation for this effect is inaccurate: *una corda*, "[play on] one string." One is actually playing on two. This fossilizes the situation

Playing the piano was, alas, a good way to impress one's femininity on Mr. Right. The engraving at top is captioned with the words of the nostalgic listener: "How That Song Makes Me Wish We Were Back Again Where I Heard It First."

Some of the reasons for the piano's increasing popularity were that sound could be gotten out of it by the smallest child, some degree of accomplishment could be demonstrated for family and friends after even the most lax, dilettantish practice, and the mere presence of the instrument in the home was a sign of culture.

A pair of Elizabethans with a pair of virginals, fore-runner of the piano.

of the old bichordal piano. The restoration of tri-chordal fullness is shown, justly, as *tre corde*—"[play on] three strings." In the shifting between two and three there is that characteristic alternating of soft and full which gives the instrument its full name—*pianoforte*, or "quiet-loud."

Hammers strike the strings, then, but not with the uncontrolled vibrancy of nature. There has to be a mechanism for killing the sound at will. To stop sound suddenly there is a damper, a small piece of felt with a wooden reinforcement, which can lie against the strings and quell their vibrations. When we play a note, the hammer flies toward the strings and the damper automatically lifts off; the note vibrates as long as nature permits or art re-quires. The finger, having struck, stays on the key, and the damper stays away from the trichord. Re-move the finger, and the damper goes back to the strings and stops their vibrations at once. There are no dampers for the topmost strings, because these make sounds with very little duration.

The craft of using the feet, it is said, is almost as important as the art of the hands. When the right foot depresses the right pedal, the sustaining pedal, all the dampers are removed from their places of rest against the strings. Sound rings out even when the fingers are removed or shifted elsewhere on the keyboard. A chord of two hands can be played in

the upper, middle, and lower regions successively, and if the sustaining pedal is depressed, the effect is of an orchestral *tutti*. When the left foot holds down the left, or soft, pedal, a shifting mechanism prevents the hammers from hitting the entirety of the trichord or, lower down, bichord or unichord. It produces a thinning or muffling effect. On grand pianos it is usually the keyboard itself that responds to the touch of the left foot on the left pedal. The keyboard shifts slightly, taking the whole action with it. The hammers are gently moved off center, and we have the *due corde* effect which we call *una corda*. The foot is lifted from the pedal, and we are back to *tre corde*. It is possible to be a kind of virtuoso of the feet. Nothing betrays the bad am-ateur more than abuse of the sustaining pedal.

Once seen, examined, explained, the piano seems as rational as the wheel. But unlike the wheel, it

J. S. Bach in an engraving by A. H. Payne. Bach was a lover of the clavichord and harpsichord whose expe-riences with the pianofortes were not entirely happy.

came fairly late into human history. When it came, musicians were not long in wondering how they had ever managed without it. In a sense, it had always been there *in potentia:* its existence is implied even in the Old Testament, where there is talk of psaltery and dulcimer. The psaltery was a kind of primitive harp attached to a sounding board; the player woke the strings to life with a plectrum. This produced in time those keyboard instruments which seem to be, but are not, ancestors of the piano. Both the virginals of Shakespeare's time and the later, highly sophisticated harpsichord of Bach and Mozart are derived from the psaltery; there is a mechanism for plucking the strings. True, the perfecting of this mechanism—by which the depressing of a key leads instantaneously to the twanging of a wire—was slow to be achieved, and the piano owes much to it; but the quantum leap

to felted striking and singing prolongation needed inventive genius. If the psaltery was plucked, the dulcimer was hit with hammers; in this action there slept for millennia the concept of the piano.

The term *piano e forte* was applied to a musical instrument as early as 1598, but the instrument, invented by Paliarino of Modena, seems to have combined a virginals (the plural is awkward with a singular article; the Elizabethans called it a pair of virginals) with a small organ. This seems to have been a cumbersome way of attaining two opposite functions out of the same keyboard: attack and duration. The instrument has not survived, and we have learned about it late, from some letters discovered in 1879. The point is that the term—like *television*—was contrived before the thing itself. Musical inventors knew what they wanted, but they were slow in devising the peculiar machinery

The Bach family at morning prayers, from a painting by Toby E. Rosenthal. J. S. Bach's three sons—W. F., C. P. E., and J. C.—would show the enthusiasm for pianoforte composition that their father lacked.

of strike and release which we take so much for granted today.

Between the harpsichord and the pianoforte stands the clavichord. This does not pluck the strings with a quill; it pushes them with a kind of brass coin called a tangent. The pushing has to be gentle to prevent the strings' going out of tune. I have a clavichord, modern, Italian-made, and find it a very exasperating instrument. It is desperately quiet, a mere producer of whispers; but it has nuance, variety of tone, even vibrato. The harpsi-chord which I have in another room is, by comparison, a brash clatterer. Bach loved the clavichord. It is a very domestic instrument, suitable for playing to one's wife when the children are in bed. The neighbors will never complain about a midnight session; they will be quite unable to hear it. The player can hardly hear it himself.

🐌

In 1709 Scipione Maffei visited Prince Ferdinand de' Medici in Florence. The Keeper of the Prince's

A chamber group, ca. 1840, in a painting of the Cowper and Gore families by Zoffany. The instrument of choice was still the harpsichord, but its eclipse and the piano's rise were already in sight.

Musical Instruments was Bartolommeo Cristofori (1655–1730), and he appears to have made a kind of harpsichord with hammers instead of quills. Maffei wrote home about its possibilities, describing with some enthusiasm its capacity for alternating piano and forte, "the gradual diminution of tone little by little . . . a diversity and alteration of tone [of which] the harpischord is entirely deprived." This seems to have been the genuine prototype of our modern piano. It had a double lever to make the hammer fly fast and a check to prevent the hammer from bouncing. There were two strings to a note and a sliding device to achieve the subdued *una corda* effect. It was the apotheosis of the dulcimer. Cristofori called it a *gravicembalo col piano e forte*. His fellow Italians did not much care for the instrument, and Cristofori had to sustain himself by making harpsichords, reserving his invention for occasional private demonstrations. The interesting question is: What music was played upon it? I like to imagine that Cristofori was a composer himself and wrote pieces—post-baroque, pre-romantic—to exhibit the scope and range of a machine unhappy with harpsichord clatter or clavichord whispers.

Gottfried Silbermann (1683–1753) worked at piano manufacture in a country more amenable to musical revolutions than Italy. It is known that Frederick the Great of Prussia acquired several Silbermann pianofortes (Bach's biographer Forkel puts the number at fifteen). It is known too that Bach was unenthusiastic about Silbermann's instruments—weak in the higher register, action too stiff—and that it was Bach's strictures that made Silbermann labor at improvements. It is also known that Frederick summoned Bach to Potsdam and made him improvise a fugue, on a royally composed subject, on one or another or several successively of the Silbermann creatures. Out of this triple encounter—Bach, king, piano—came the *Musical Offering* but, so far as we know, no conversion of the aging composer to the new keyboard sound. With his *Well-Tempered Clavier* he exhibited the essential condition of the music that must be written for the piano—the availability of twelve major and minor keys, made possible by tempering or falsifying the natural scale—but it was left to his three sons,

Wilhelm Friedemann, Carl Philipp Emanuel, and Johann Christian, to develop the new music, based on free access from one key to another, which the new instrument craved.

The problem of musical composition may be expressed like this: How is it possible to achieve a piece of music which, without help from words liturgical or secular, can be of a length and weight commensurate with those of a piece of literature? One answer lies in the fugue or the passacaglia, which, as Bach *père* spectacularly demonstrated, could be of long duration and of an intellectual complexity and emotional profundity matching, say, Milton's *Lycidas* or Shakespeare's *Hamlet*. But a passacaglia, being a set of variations on an unvarying ground bass, is limited in key, and a fugue rarely travels beyond three or four closely related keys (say, A minor, E minor, C, G, D minor, F). There is not enough drama in either form. Drama was to come with the sonata, which the Bach sons pioneered and developed. The piano, with its capacity for alternating forte and piano, its ability to sustain long crescendos and diminuendos, its ability to *surprise*, was an instrument admirably suited for drama. With equal temperament and new devices for getting from one key to another, the sonata was, within less than a century, able to convey the range and variety of the novel or the narrative poem.

It is necessary to say something about equal temperament in relation to the piano. Tuning the instrument in such a way as to make it subtly out of tune with nature is a skilled art; the professional piano tuner was not long in coming after the instrument itself. The nature of his skill, and the cussedness of nature, can be demonstrated easily enough. Assume for the sake of explanation that the tuner starts with the lowest A of the instrument and that he moves up octave by octave and makes each successive A conform to the one before. With each jump of an octave the number of vibrations of the string per second doubles. If the lowest A has x vibrations per second, the ones after will increase their vibrations in the proportions $2x$, $4x$, $8x$, $16x$, $32x$, $64x$, $128x$. The tuner tunes the octaves first, then the fifths, in the manner of a string player. The tuning route goes from A to E to B to F-sharp

to C-sharp. C-sharp may (contrary to nature) be read as D-flat, and we can then proceed to A-flat, E-flat, B-flat, F, C, G, D, A. With each jump northward the vibrations do not, as in the case of octaves, double; they are multiplied by 1.5. If we multiply 1.5 by 1.5 again and again, we do not arrive at 128; the top A would be too sharp. To make the top A consonant with the bottom A, the tuner must cheat. He must make the fifths slightly flat. He must so organize his tuning for the rest of the keyboard that all semitones are equal (hence equal temperament). Nature does not acknowledge this democracy. Her C-sharp is sharper than D-flat, but in the tempered scale they are the same note. By means of this cunning adjustment the pianist has all the major and minor keys to journey through, whereas the old natural temperament—which many harpsichordists of Bach's day adhered to—did not permit travel to more than a few, the rest sounding out of tune.

What the new music suitable for the equal-tuned piano had to learn was how to get from any one key to any other, and as rapidly as was consonant with post-baroque drama. There were certain chordal devices such as the diminished seventh, which Bach had used, but only, often in quick chromatic sequences, for an effect of baroque brilliance. The same chord, which is made up of minor thirds, can be used for instantaneous moves from one key to another, sometimes very remote:

The first chord in each pair is always the same chord as far as its sound is concerned, though it can be seen that for the purposes of "grammar," the notations vary. Another chord, unknown to Bach and Handel, that was to be immensely useful to composers of sonatas was the augmented sixth, which in sound if not notation is identical with the

dominant seventh. It is this identity of sound that enabled Beethoven to indulge in dramatic "puns":

No baroque composer was able to move, by one step only, from the key of D-flat to the key of C—the nearest key in physical location but the farthest away in the key cycle. The equal-tuned piano became, with the development of the sonata and its wide-ranging capacity for sudden shifts of emotion, the instrument *par excellence* of the romantic movement. But first it had to serve the intermediate phase of the rococo.

What is the rococo? In music as in architecture, it is a mode of creation that rejected the complications of the baroque—complications that often appeared to twist the raw material (stone or sound) into patterns that strained the possibilities of the material to the limit. Rococo meant a fundamental simplicity—harmony instead of counterpoint—but a tendency toward surface decoration which, as with a wedding cake, went beyond the needs of sheer nutrition. Rococo can be vulgar. With Haydn and Mozart it maintained a tastefulness and a charm rarely betrayed into ostentation for its own sake. If the baroque in music served, at its most typical, the emotions of established religion, rococo presented an image of aristocratic stability, garnished with ornaments, prepared to employ set formulas and tags without apology—though with Mozart, such properties were miraculously transformed into the personal and idiosyncratic. It is not my purpose to evaluate the achievements of the great composers of the pianistic era but to consider the impact of the instrument itself on society. It was in the rococo period that the piano began to trundle its way through the Western world. We may associate the growth of its popularity, and the development of technique suitable for playing it, with Muzio Clementi.

William Beckford, the author of *Vathek* and the builder of the architectural folly called Fonthill—

Facing page: Portraits of two American families (*top,* the Schuylers, ca. 1824; *bottom,* the Hollingsworths, ca. 1870), in which square pianos figure as signs of feminine cultivation.

With the profusion of mediocre to poor piano music and instruction methods (*top left and right*) came a profusion of bizarre new modifications of the instrument itself. *Bottom*, inventor M. Schalkenbach demonstrates his "Piano-Orchestra," complete with electric motor, in 1862. In 1866 a piano was patented that turned into a couch and had closets for bed clothes and washing up. The stool turned into a workbox, looking glass, desk, and small set of drawers.

which fell down and was meant to—had a cousin, Peter Beckford, who was in Rome in 1767. There he heard a fifteen-year-old keyboard prodigy, son of the silversmith Clementi, and he bought the services of the boy for a term of seven years. Beckford had made his money out of Jamaican sugar and hence slavery, so this purchasing of a young white musician seemed to him a natural enough transaction. In London, helped by Beckford's wealth and influence, Clementi rose to the heights as a composer for pianoforte, as executant, and as cembalist (conductor at the keyboard) in the Italian Opera. It was as a piano virtuoso that he met Mozart in a kind of competition under the aegis of the Emperor Joseph II and earned the contempt of the greater musician as a mere mechanic, a show-off charlatan, skilled at playing thirds and sixths and octaves with great rapidity, but lacking taste, feeling, and expression. Yet, while Mozart wrote great music in many forms, Clementi specialized in pianistics; he showed the future directions of piano technique. Thirteen volumes of his works were published by Breitkopf in Leipzig.

Clementi's financial success as a virtuoso enabled him to buy his way into the British publishing firm of Longman and Broderip, which put out sheet music of great mediocrity but immense popularity among the now growing piano-playing public. In the firm was a young man named Frederick William Collard, soon to become a skilled manufacturer of pianos. Clementi may be said to have become the mediator between the piano as a structure and the piano as a producer of sound. The works of Mozart and Haydn and, later, Beethoven were for the most part beyond the capacities of the new piano-buying public. This public preferred the showy mediocre, the descriptive novelty (like "Pigmy Revels" and "The Enraged Musician"), the easy variations on Scottish melodies, to the profound and exacting sonatas of the masters. Érard in France (to which country the import of English pianos was not at the time permitted) promoted his own instruments with the same commercial fervor as Clementi and his colleagues in London. Some of the instruments made on both sides of the Channel exploited the extramusical with shameless commercial greed—

The first upright was built in 1800 by Matthias Müller, but the better models of John Isaac Hawkins of Philadelphia (*above*, one built in 1801) are the true ancestors of those played today.

"Turkish" effects such as pedals for cymbals and drums, even (with one of Clementi's models) a revolving cylinder that converted the piano into a music box.

The situation as regards the proliferation of the piano, its mass introduction into bourgeois homes with more money than taste, is similar to that of the guitar in our own age. The instrument is played as a glorified ukulele (popular in the twenties), not as a one-handed harpsichord. Its great exponents like Segovia are not followed; amateurs are content with minimal effects made spectacular through electronic amplification. There was, in the days of skiffle, a wholly mechanical guitar which, upon the pressing of buttons, gave a tonic, a dominant, and a subdominant chord. The popularization of an instrument has little to do with the popularization of great music composed expressly for it. The history of the pianoforte has nothing essentially to do with the history of great music.

Wolfgang Amadeus Mozart directing his last work, the *Requiem*, from a painting by Mihály Munkácsy. After Mozart came the Napoleonic age and the pianist hero.

Tireless in promotion of the piano and in a wholly healthy desire to make money, Clementi must not be totally written off as a serious musician. He produced a *Gradus ad Parnassum*, or series of technical studies, which Beethoven himself admired. There was a public for this, as there was for his charming but superficial sonatinas. Music publication became a big business. Breitkopf in Leipzig had invented a technique for printing music with movable type. Gottfried Christoph Härtel took it over but abandoned it for engraving on pewter plates. Clementi went to Leipzig to negotiate with Breitkopf and Härtel for British Empire rights to their publications. Publication and piano making went together, as though manufacturers of electric stoves should also be dealers in foodstuffs. Wher-

ever Clementi traveled he set up agencies for the importation of pianos and piano music—Moscow, St. Petersburg, Berlin. He was the most energetic of promoters.

He was not the only one. By 1800 the piano had become an indispensable piece of furniture in the homes of the genteel. In that year Matthias Müller created the first upright. John Isaac Hawkins of Philadelphia made an even better upright, the ancestor of the one we use today. Charles Jarvis, an immigrant Scotsman, set up his own factory in the same town. It is interesting to note that the division of function, or development of component specialization—usually thought of as Henry Ford's major contribution to mass production—began with the manufacture of pianos. By 1802 Broadwood in Lon-

François Gérard's painted tapestry of Napoleon in the throne room of the Tuileries.

of the piccolo. It also, on some models, goes down to a low C unattainable by any instrument of the orchestra. I played on such an instrument recently on BBC television; it was the piano favored by Oscar Peterson, who was on the program with me. Fortunately there was a masking device to make my bottom note the familiar A. Progress can go too far.

To the general public there are only three kinds of heroic musical executants—the singer, the violinist, and the pianist. The greatest of these is the pianist. He is on his own. He may be backed by an orchestra, but he can do well enough without. It may be significant that the rise of the pianistic hero belongs to the Napoleonic era. Napoleon himself had an Érard piano, though it is doubtful he ever played it (despite his early boasting of a perfect knowledge of compositorial technique). Beethoven is the first of the Napoleonic pianists, but to the uncultured public outside Vienna, he meant less than the now forgotten Daniel Steibelt. Steibelt was the first in the long line of traveling virtuosos whose technique and taste were less than perfect but who had a gift of showmanship and could play very fast and very loud. With him begins the cult of personality. He was a German with an English wife, who accompanied him on the tambourine. Johann Tomaschek, describing a Steibelt recital in Prague in 1800, writes: "The new combination of such diverse instruments so electrified the gentlefolk that they could hardly see their fill of the Englishwoman's pretty arm, and so it came about that Steibelt's female friend [Tomaschek apparently was doubtful of their marital status] was easily persuaded to give lessons on it. . . . Steibelt remained in Prague for several months and in due course sold a large wagonload of tambourines."

Steibelt, like many a pianistic showman after him—Liberace, for instance—knew his limitations and wisely kept quiet about them. When he played in Vienna, he made sure first that Beethoven was unlikely to be in the audience. He was well aware of Beethoven's supremacy in the pianistic field, and he did not aspire to rival him. He was content to travel widely, arrive late for concerts (unpunctuality

don was turning out 400 pianos a year, and the Érard factories in Paris were exporting madly to all the countries that were locked in Napoleon's Continental System. The instruments, though mass-produced, did not as yet settle to standardization of form. There were uprights that were made to look like upended grands and were called giraffe pianos. Some had the appearance of dressing tables, complete with mirrors. The Victorians, to whom ornamental excrescence was a necessity of life, produced gothic monstrosities. But by the middle of the nineteenth century the two major shapes had evolved to something like their final forms. All that had to be done was to extend the range from the limits inherited from the harpsichord. The piano now goes up to the high C just outside the range

Left, an Érard piano. *Below,* a drawing by Ingres, ca. 1815, of the family of Lucien de Bonaparte, whose daughters played the lyre and square piano and would soon be swooning to the performances and works of the romantics.

has always gone down well with frivolous music fanciers), and make money. Beethoven had music to write and did not move far out of Vienna. Had he chosen to cover the great concert circuits of the world, he would have shown up the charlatans. For it is he more than anyone who has provided the romantic prototype of the Napoleonic pianist—wide-eyed and wild-haired, a great smasher of pianos, a purveyor of storm and stress and fireworks as well as heartrending lyricism.

With the Napoleonic era came the birth of the romantic movement, in literature, painting, and decor as well as in music. Romanticism is best thought of as art that exalts the individual above the collective, emotion above reason, impulse above form. With Napoleon we have the first great instance in history of the victory of human personality over mere brash circumstance: the strong man, immensely gifted, more intuitive than intellectual, a believer in free will but also in destiny, imposes the images of his creative genius on inert traditional social forms and breaks them. The Napoleonic personality becomes, in the field of artistic endeavor, the Byronic. But the greatness of Beethoven cannot well be encompassed by a mere movement. To call Beethoven either classical or romantic is to limit his achievement. True, his work is the expression of the motions of an individual mind, but form is not crushed under their tempestuous impact. The Third Symphony, the *Eroica*, the supreme expression of the Napoleonic age, expands inherited classical sonata form. In the final works, especially the quartets, new forms are generated, but the principle of form is not denied. There is nothing of the rhapsodic about Beethoven. Beethoven is not Liszt.

It is in his impatience with the strictures of the rococo that Beethoven seems to show himself as a romantic. With him the piano seems to crack and strain under the weight of emotions too tempestuous for mere wood and wire to bear. Pianissimi alternate with fortissimi; fortissimi threaten the instrument with dissolution. Human emotion that seems to have its basis in moral struggle is almost too great for physical expression. The iconographs of Beethoven that young people wear on their T-shirts provide the popular image of the musician as

As this piano illustrates, makers bent on sales to the middle class often resorted to pandering to execrable taste.

he should be—torn, tormented, arrogant, aggressive, emotionally unpredictable, heroically muscular. Mozart will not do, nor will Haydn. Even Handel, who would hurl kettledrums in his rages, fails to fit the archetype. The ignorant public wants its musicians to be fierce and scowling and to have long, unruly hair. Or used to want them like that. Now it is prepared to listen to ordinary-looking young men and women as long as they have prodigious technique. But the Beethovenian image holds; it was transmitted to Pachman, and Paderewski, though not to Rachmaninoff, who always looked like a higher mathematician glooming over an equation.

In 1809 Mendelssohn was born, in 1810 Schumann and Chopin, in 1811 Franz Liszt. The age of the romantic piano was beginning. These composers remain, to the general public, more amenable than the gigantic Beethoven. They do not make his emotional, moral, and intellectual demands. They are capable of sentimentality. Mendelssohn wrote salon pieces that delighted Queen Victoria and

The piano, with the romantics, seems to become a monstrous aphrodisiac.

Prince Albert and were not outside their pianistic competence. Schumann produced albums of easy sketches for the beginner. Chopin can be difficult, but he sings to the heart. Liszt's pyrotechnics are beyond the amateur, but in the *Consolations* and *Liebesträume* he yields riches to the moderate technique. Chopin and Liszt, more than Mendelssohn and Schumann, sum up romantic pianism. They also provide something dear to the public heart: an aura of gamy eroticism. Chopin's affair with George Sand, Liszt's uncountable affairs with princesses, as also with Lola Montez, seem to rub off onto the piano itself. The piano, with them, seems to become a monstrous aphrodisiac. With Chopin and Liszt there was also a property nearly as thrilling as the erotic—a colorful nationalism, productive of, with the one, polonaises and mazurkas and, with the other, Hungarian rhapsodies. Here were two composers ready-made for Hollywood, though Hollywood has never done them justice.

The essence of romantic pianism has, to the general public, been best manifested in the piano concerto, wherein one brave and brilliant musician tussles with a gigantic force of strings, wind, and percussion. It is Cyrano de Bergerac fighting a hundred paid bravos. Alternatively, it is the piano taming the orchestra and teaching it the pleasing postures of subservience. As we may expect, it is not the finest concertos that have been the most popular. Beethoven's fifth, the *Emperor,* is insufficiently erotic; Chopin's two are indifferently orchestrated; the Schumann is slight, with insufficient hammering; in Brahms's first the piano seems an intruder (indeed, the work was first conceived as a symphony, and it sounds like it). The second Brahms is considered tuneful, though there is a regrettable lack of fireworks. It is only with the Russians Tchaikovsky and Rachmaninoff that the absence of show-off pianistics is excused by heart-lifting, if somewhat banal, melody and the pound-

Liszt at the Piano by Joseph Dannhauser (1840). Listening are Alexandre Dumas and George Sand, seated; the Countess d'Agoult, swooning on the floor; and, standing, from left, Victor Hugo, Paganini, and Rossini. The bust of Beethoven on the piano is also by Dannhauser, and a photograph of Byron is hanging on the wall.

THE WELL-TEMPERED REVOLUTION

ing of chords under the soaring of unison strings. As always happens, the epigone is preferred to the original, and the most popular concerto of the last forty years has been Richard Addinsell's Warsaw Concerto—not properly a concerto at all, since it has only one movement which, through the suspension of disbelief engendered by the film in which it was first heard, *Dangerous Moonlight*, nevertheless presupposes the existence of two others. Addinsell seems to have borrowed his main theme from four notes sung by Edgar in *King Lear*, which Shakespeare presents in sol-fa notation—fa-sol-lah-mi. Here we have secondhand Rachmaninoff, spurious emotion, banality difficult neither to hum nor, in a best-selling simplified version, to play on the joanna of a military canteen.

The public will always be given what it wants. It did not want the whole of Rachmaninoff's *Rhapsody on a Theme by Paganini*, but it did want the sentimental movement from it which inverts, in D-flat, the original violin motif. It wants the introduction to Tchaikovsky's first concerto but not the rest of the work. It wants a particular sound rather than a particular structure, and it likes that sound to be associated with cinema. A British film called *Love Story* introduced a pseudo-concerto called *Cornish Rhapsody*, and yet another, *The Dream of Olwen*, had an eponymous gallimaufry of arpeggios, runs, and simple aspirant melody. The piano became debased, a machine for conveying shopgirl emotions. It has always had this capacity for debasement, inseparable from its popularity. "The Maiden's

A rendering of Franz Schubert at one of his musical evenings in Vienna. Schubert carried a torch at Beethoven's funeral and died long before the great romantics were born.

Prayer" and "The Robin's Return" were written for it. The oboe and flute rarely sink so low. Some see its ultimate debasement in its exploitation as an instrument for jazz and its derivatives, but this is an attitude both snobbish and unrealistic.

❧

Before saying anything about the piano as a New Orleans whorehouse excitant or postcoital comforter, I must discuss the deromanticization of the instrument. Whatever jazz is or is not, it is not romantic. It tends toward dryness and understatement. There is no room for the languors of *Tristan* in it, except in the satirical form of the trio of Debussy's "Golliwogg's Cake Walk." The time of Debussy was also the time of rag. What happened with piano impressionism was a removal of the human element, a refusal to use the keyboard for imitating sobbing and orgasm or expressing Beethovenian aspiration and struggle. Jazz is also inhuman in that it exploits the animal rhythms of the blood and leaves out the cerebral cortex.

Debussy's two volumes of *Préludes* show what impressionism is about. He presents—in titles that appear at the end of the pieces, like afterthoughts— images of the natural world. Where people appear—like Mr. Pickwick or General Lavine or the girl with flaxen hair—they are reduced to paintings or puppets. The depiction of nature—fog or wind or a sea with sails on it—appropriately employs what seems far more natural to the piano-playing fingers than the structures of traditional music. Take, for instance, the whole-tone scale, which Debussy first heard in Javanese music at the Paris Exposition. It is pure color, and it is also pure pianistics. Play three notes on three black keys, then three notes on three white keys, and you have one of the two forms of it. It comes naturally. It is a scale but also a chord, and the sustaining pedal may be held down while it gurgles up the keyboard. It is natural to wish to employ all five fingers when playing a chord, and Debussy gives us not simple Mozartean triads but triads with added seconds and sixths. He often, as in "La Cathédrale engloutie," has whole sequences of these chords. They do not follow the traditional logical pattern (tonic followed

Top, a portrait of Anton Rubinstein by Ilja Repin (1914). *Bottom*, a caricature of Paderewski that ran on the cover of a World's Fair edition of *Puck* in 1893. The caption read: "A Peaceful Solution—at the next World's Fair Paderewski will play on all the pianos at once."

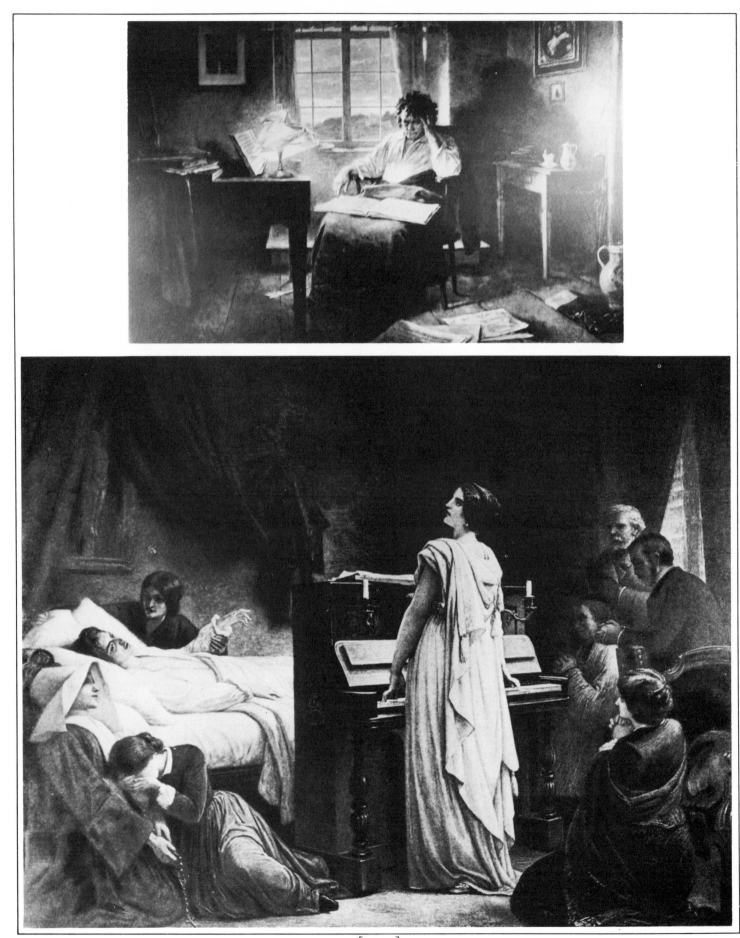

by subdominant followed by dominant and so on) but subsist as patches of pure color. Consecutive fifths and sevenths used to be banned, but in Debussy they are part of the basic language.

What we are encouraged to hear in impressionistic music is the entire spectrum, though often obscured by pedalic mist, of the harmonic series. It is into these component notes that the struck string naturally flowers. Increase of lip pressure on the metallic tube of the trumpet or trombone carries the player up the ladder of the series. The resonance of a note is a blur of its upper partials. Mozart as an infant is said to have fainted on hearing a trumpet for the first time; his ear was catching the whole range of the harmonic series in the note sounded and reacting in awe and fear. In the music of the past the upper partials were allowed to follow nature and merely be faintly implied. In impressionistic music there is explicit sounding of the partials, which contributes to the pointillist richness of the music of Debussy and his followers.

Some composers of music which, though not itself jazz, acknowledges the influence of jazz actually use the whole harmonic series as a cadential chord. The chordal sound of jazz and its derivatives is manifestly different from that of Beethoven or even Wagner, but it is close to that of Debussy. A common chord of C may have an A added to it and sometimes a D as well. A minor chord may have an added major sixth (E added to G, B-flat, and D, for example), thus implying agreement with Schoenberg's assertion that the minor scale and its chords do not exist in nature. Jazz pianism is essentially impressionistic. When Bix Beiderbecke put down his trumpet and wrote *In a Mist* for piano, he was paying one of the first jazz tributes to Debussy.

Early jazz kept to hymn-tune harmonies, but it was not long before impressionistic chords came in.

Facing page: Top, a portrait of Beethoven in his study by Paul Sonntag Berlin. *Bottom*, the *Death of Chopin*, from a painting by Felix Joseph Barrias. Romanticism continued well past Chopin's death in 1849, which was twenty-two years after Beethoven's death and thirteen years before the birth of Debussy, who, with other impressionists, would inherit the legacy of the romantics.

Melodically its rhythms were closer to those of speech than to the formalized patterns of traditional song. Certainly jazz piano insists on a new way of using the instrument. Its music defies traditional notation. It is far from easy to learn. And if it is harmonically impressionistic, it can also favor the dry, pecking sound of the baroque. Some jazz keyboard players have even gone back to the harpsichord. The sustaining pedal is not loved. The soft pedal might as well not have been invented. The pianoforte is, in jazz, a forte.

It must be admitted that jazz is not so popular as its tame derivatives. Jazz is gamy, earthy, and still has a quality of black deprivation as well as of African wildness. It began with brothel pianos but also with spirituals, street parades, and funerals, and no matter how refined by great sophisticates like Duke Ellington, it remains removed from music's mainstream just as its mastery lies beyond the technique of the traditionally trained pianist. It is the derivatives—show songs, commercial swing, and so on—that showered sheet music on the parlor piano from the end of World War I to the time of the rise of the guitar and the falling out of favor of the once indispensable domestic keyboard. This music itself was domesticated into the insipid and easy. Meanwhile lessons were taken, and there were newspaper advertisements beginning, "At first they laughed when I sat down at the piano. But when I began to play a hush fell on the room. I played the first movement of Beethoven's immortal *Moonlight* Sonata. When the last notes died away I was surrounded. I was nearly deafened by admiring voices. 'Who was your teacher? How did you get that beautiful singing tone?' I told them . ..."

For piano lovers like H. G. Wells, who did not have the time to learn the boring techniques of pianism, there was the pianola, about which the Prince of Wales, at a public dinner, made a joke. "A sick man had his body covered with paper, on which his doctors pricked the locations of his various ailments. When they had gone, he threaded the paper into his pianola, and it played 'Nearer My God to Thee.' " This mechanical marvel was, however, more than a kind of decorative treadled phonograph. The living masters recorded their

interpretations of the classics for it. A genuine pianist as opposed to pianolist could play duets with his betters. Stravinsky even composed for it. But the techniques of a less limited mode of recording and reproduction were improving, and the radio was joining the phonograph, often under the same lid, in rendering the piano (which now was considered as taking up too much space) more or less obsolete.

From the days of the virginals on, a keyboard instrument sat in the homes of the bourgeoisie and the aristocracy to sweeten life with an art never well understood (who can say what music is trying to tell us?) but curiously necessary. No home has ever been able to subsist, even at the most brutish level, without music. Now there is too much music, and none of it is homemade. There is no thrill in playing Beethoven's symphonies as piano duets when the works in their original form are ready to blast out of the quadrophonic engine. If, rarely, it is felt that the house is bare without a keyboard, this is more often powered by electronic impulses,

Facing page: A photograph of Debussy. *Above*, Maurice Ravel with Nijinsky in 1912, playing the score from *Daphnis and Chloë*. Debussy was more the impressionist than Ravel, but they shared the impressionists' belief in indirection. As the like-minded symbolist Stéphane Mallarmé put it: "To name an object is to sacrifice three-quarters of the enjoyment. . . . To *suggest* it—that is our dream."

THE WELL-TEMPERED REVOLUTION

An untitled painting by Sir William Orchardson, ca. 1920.

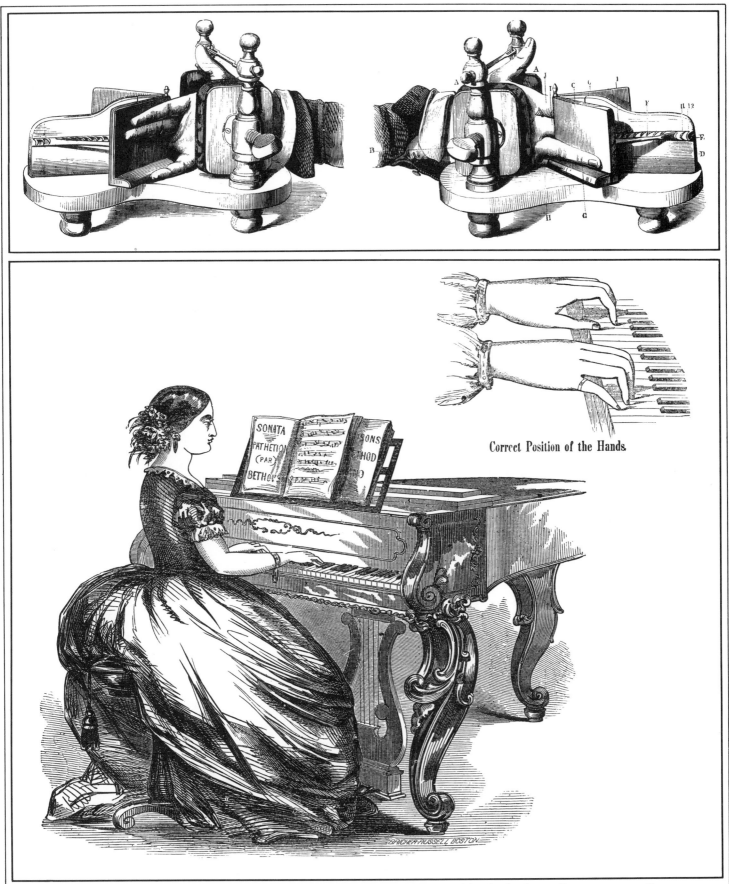

Correct Position of the Hands.

Top, one of many gadgets put forward to strengthen hands which in fact could cripple them. *Bottom*, a page from a more modest and less dangerous pedagogical system.

Above and facing page: Music lessons at a time when they gave the home its only musical sounds; now it has all too many, few of them homemade.

with ready-made chords and bongo drums activable at the touch of a switch. The piano is no longer a preserve of the amateur; it has returned to the professionals.

❧

Professional pianism has attained a technical excellence beyond the dreams of Liszt. Concert and recital programs exhibit an eclecticism that ranges from William Byrd to John Cage, with the late rococo and the romantic still, as in the nineteenth century, providing the bulk of the nourishment. To the average uninstructed listener who knows what he likes, the piano is an instrument for big chords, wide-ranging melodies, Chopinesque decorations. The contemporary composer brutally disregards these prescriptions, having decided that the piano is what children have always known it is—a percussion instrument. It is, of course, also an instrument for two hands capable of independent action, a multiple picture of a chromatic scale that does not exist in nature, and a gymnasium for prodigious leaping. The pushing of these four aspects of the piano to the limit accounts for much of the music written for it since, say, 1912—the year of Schoenberg's *Pierrot Lunaire*.

A kind of manifesto for the new way of using the

The PIANOLA

Advertisements for the player piano, including (*facing page*) Gally's Autophone and (*right*) Aeolian's Duo-Art. Thus began the trend that led eventually to electronic organs with built-in rhythms and ready-made chords.

piano appeared ten years after *Pierrot Lunaire,* when Paul Hindemith attached to his *Suite für Klavier* a series of "directions for use," which included "Take no notice of what you learned in your piano lessons"; "Play this piece very wildly yet strictly in rhythm, like a machine"; and "Regard the piano as an interesting kind of percussion instrument and treat it accordingly." This injunction was not meant too literally. It was not, for instance, intended to encourage the emergence of the "prepared piano" under John Cage. I once examined a Steinway in which steel bolts had been screwed among the strings and pieces of rubber inserted above and beneath them. I have heard, as items in Cage's percussive experiments, the strings hand-plucked, the keys banged with the elbows, and the iron frame struck with a kettledrum stick. I have seen Cathy Berberian seeming to vomit into the body of the open instrument, though actually merely using it as a resonating chamber for her voice. Cage has even exploited the silence of the piano, making the visual appearance of the player at the keyboard a focus for the attention of the audience while they listen to the fringes of silence—coughs, sneezes, passing traffic. All this may be interpreted as mockery of a great instrument, but the piano, a beast of burden as well as a king, can take it.

The fact that the two hands can achieve a measure of rhythmic independence led to experiments with tonal independence, as in Béla Bartók's bitonal works. Indeed, as Debussy demonstrated, the co-existence of a bank of black keys above an endless bed of white ones invites the simplest kind of bitonality, which Stravinsky exploited in *Petrouchka,* in which the key of G-flat major opposes but also conjoins with that of C major. Debussy's "Brumes" in the second book of the *Préludes* is essentially an exercise in this kind of bitonality. And the fact that the semitones on a piano keyboard are, contrary to nature, exactly equal makes the instrument ideal for dodecaphonic composition. The violin and cello

Facing page: Stravinsky with Ballet Russe colleagues Massine and Leon Bakst. It was in going beyond simple bitonality to discard most existing conventions of harmony and form that Stravinsky enraged the audiences of 1913 with his *Rite of Spring.*

do not hold with semitonal democracy, any more than does the open trumpet or horn, but the piano can do anything the composer asks with a tone row. It can leap in a single melodic line from the highest A-flat down to the lowest B-natural and then to the middle D-flat with grotesque agility:

The piano has always permitted clowning, from Haydn's middle C to be played with the nose up to Chico Marx's stiff finger chopping seasoned with glissandi. It has submitted to systematic detuning for Berg's *Wozzeck.* It will, with dignity, consent to be an unplayable monument, a piece of industrial archaeology, like the Gaveau upright that is one yard away from my typewriter—unplayable and beyond repair, but once the property of the great Parisian cabaret star Josephine Baker.

The firm Gaveau has disappeared, along with Pleyel and Érard, though the three names are kept alive by Schimmel of West Germany. Bechstein now belongs to Baldwin of America. The Jasper Corporation of Indiana owns Bösendorfer of Vienna and makes the Kimball, besides running Herrburger Brooks in England. Steinway is part of the Columbia Broadcasting System. Blüthner keeps itself to itself in East Germany. In Japan, at the biggest piano factory in the world, that of Yamaha, which also makes motorcycles, there is an annual output of 160,000 instruments for the home market and 41,000 for the rest of the world. From the Soviet Union the Estonia piano has been visiting the West—a solid artifact with an action made by Herrburger Brooks. The Chinese are working on piano manufacture. Despite those occasional sadistic competitions, sometimes televised in Great Britain, in which teams compete to see which can smash a piano to wood and wire most speedily, the creature that Cristofori invented (if it really was Cristofori) seems in no danger of dying.

❧

My final meditation is on the metaphysical significance of the piano or pianoforte or fortepiano or *Hammerklavier*. Was it mere accident that it arose in an era of European *Sturm und Drang*? Is it possible to think of Napoleon's wars with an accompaniment of harpsichord twangings or clavichord whispers? Music is different from literature in that it can extend its vocabulary only through technological innovation. The epics of Homer are fully winged literary art, but the music of that epic period is no more than harps and flutes. Shakespeare's *King Lear* could not be matched by Dowland or John Bull. It was only in the middle years of the nineteenth century that the resources of music—harmonic, structural, instrumental—had arrived at a pitch where literature could not merely be rivaled but actually overtaken. Think of a young Jesuit priest, Gerard Manley Hopkins, stirred by the news in the *Times* on a winter day in 1876, brooding on its story of the wreck of the *Deutschland* in the Thames estuary, wondering how the tragic tale of five drowned nuns, exiled from Germany under Bismarck's anticlerical laws, could be commemorated in English verse. The resources of the poetry of Wordsworth and Tennyson were inadequate for the expression of horror and hard-won reconciliation to God's will; Hopkins had, using sprung rhythm and head rhyme, to make poetry imitate Wagnerian music. Music had become the most expressive of the arts.

Wagner had much to do with the extension of music's capacity for expression. His art depended not only on the pushing of chromaticism to the tonal limit but on the invention of new instruments. The trumpet now moved with the ease of the flute; it was no longer restricted to the bugle calls of the harmonic series. Contrabass trombones, Wagner tubas, Parsifal bells, anvils, squadrons of horns and harps combined with complete woodwind families and an army of strings to convey the images of cosmic passion which his personal genius, and the inscrutable urgings of the *Zeitgeist*, forcefully dictated. It is possible, perhaps necessary, to view the piano as the keyboard counterpart of the new orchestra.

Because the function of this orchestra was, in the great music dramas, to depict the psychological turbulence that lay under the sung words, so the pianoforte served, in those contradictory lyrical musical monodramas called *Lieder*, to deliver the subtext of the melodized poems of Goethe and Grillparzer. The piano became essentially a medium for German *Innigkeit*. And yet the Germans did not invent it.

The irony is that Cristofori's fellow countrymen have never done much with the pianoforte. There are no great Italian sonatas or concertos, unless we except the achievement of Busoni, who, being of Alto Adige stock, was drawn naturally to Teutonic art. The French, exploiting the piano impressionistically and neoclassically, have deliberately avoided invoking the dangerous human depths which, in courage or folly, the Germans have courted ever since Napoleon shook them into a sense of nationhood. The piano, we may say, was invented for the benefit of the emerging German soul. It is the essential post-Napoleonic instrument, the reflection in miniature of the Wagnerian orchestra.

Under the Weimar Republic the piano was reduced and mocked. It was not raucous enough for the Nazis, and yet, with artist's insight, Charlie Chaplin in his *The Great Dictator* saw that it was a true voice for the brooding, inchoate dreams of an egomaniac like Hitler. Hitler used the piano only for its bass wires; with these the rebellious generals were strangled. In Visconti's *La Caduta degli dei (The Damned)*, it plays the *Liebestod* while Röhm's SA is massacred. In the postwar world its function is mainly historical: it feeds a romantic nostalgia with the concertos of the Russians or calls up the tortured and triumphant soul of Beethoven.

In Leonard Bernstein's musicalization of Auden's *Age of Anxiety*, the piano symbolizes alienation. "Confronted by the mass of the orchestra," says

Facing page: Top, a scene from *The Coconuts* (1929), one of many movies in which Chico Marx charmed with his antic piano playing. *Bottom*, the piano number in Busby Berkeley's *Gold Diggers of 1935*. The piano has, of course, suffered worse, and not only nobly survived but prospered, as it surely will do in the future.

Peter Conrad in his *Imagining America*, "the soloist . . . testifies to an existential division, the self's separation from reality. The piano plays beside the orchestra, and doesn't belong within it. The orchestra twice rebuffs it. . . . The piano is also excluded from the solemn optimism of the epilogue, which is the revelation of faith." That applies, however, only to the original version of the work, first performed in 1949. When he revised it in 1965, Bernstein allowed the piano soloist "a final confirmatory cadenza. . . . The way is open, but, at the conclusion, is still stretching long before him." The piano has become a lonely instrument playing febrile jazz, brooding, introspective, neurotic. It has outlived its romantic past.

It is necessary for us to shake ourselves out of this identification of an artifact with a historical period, with a national soul or a half-articulated metaphysic. Ultimately the piano is a most ingenious structure in which, under the hands of Rubinstein, or the single hand of a Wittgenstein, opposites are reconciled and acts of magic performed. The note begins to decay at the very moment of striking, but the illusion of durability holds. The instrument is a tuned drum, but it is also a human voice. Other stretched strings or vibrating air columns are competent to express a single aspect of the universe and the human life that tries to feel at home in it, but only the piano can attempt, in however miniaturized a form, the total picture. That is why it continues to deserve our homage and our wonder.

Portraits of two modern pianists and composers for the piano who, though entirely different, stand equidistant from the romantic past: *facing page,* Earl "Fatha" Hines; *right,* Glenn Gould.

Details of decoration on the underside of an eighteenth-century French harpsichord lid.

II

ANNALYN SWAN

Enlightenment's Gift to the Age of Romance

How the Piano Came to Be

"The pianoforte is the most important of all musical instruments," George Bernard Shaw wrote in the 1890s. "Its invention was to music what the invention of printing was to poetry." Most people realize that the piano has dominated music for the past 200 years. Few stop to consider, as Shaw did, the reason why. The piano is not just the great voice of the romantics: more than any other instrument in history, it has disseminated music on a scale once undreamed of. A self-reliant, one-man orchestra, capable of being turned out by the millions and played by the rankest of amateurs as well as the greatest of virtuosos, the piano grew up with the middle class and prospered as it prospered. By the mid-nineteenth century, 150 years after its invention in Italy, the piano could be found everywhere from the aristocratic salons of European capitals to British laborers' cottages and the saloons of American mining towns. Pianos entertained Turkish harems and German nobles, crossed the Andes by mule (a special hinged piano, which could be split down the middle, was made for the purpose), and rumbled westward in covered wagons. " 'Tis wonderful how soon a piano gets into a log-hut on the frontier," Ralph Waldo Emerson marveled. Like the printing press, as Shaw shrewdly observed, the piano took art away from princes and gave it to the public.

Shaw's comparison makes yet another point. Like the printing press, the piano is a machine—a brilliant, poetic-sounding machine, it is true, but nonetheless an "invention" in the fullest scientific sense of the word. The piano is even more a product of the industrial revolution than of the romantic era, and its origins lie in the Enlightenment's love of mechanical gadgets and intricate mechanisms. It came to maturity with the advancing technology of the nineteenth century, which gave its eighty-eight hammers and dampers—and the more than four thousand minutely regulated moving parts that connect them—their critical responsiveness to the player's touch. It owes its unprecedented popularity, furthermore, to the factory methods and mass marketing of the industrial age. The piano's story, in short, is as much that of a mechanical as a musical marvel.

Unlike the organ, which dates back to Roman antiquity, the piano is a relatively recent invention. An amalgam of percussive and string instruments, it is descended distantly from the archaic psaltery, which was plucked; the dulcimer, whose strings were struck with mallets; and the monochord, a primitive, one-stringed Greek instrument with a movable bridge to establish pitch. During the Middle Ages keyboards came to be attached to such early instruments to facilitate performing. On fifteenth-century organs, for example, slides that had been pushed in and out of the various pipes were replaced with keys, often up to a yard long and three to five inches wide, in direct and monstrous proportion to the instrument. (Organists did not really play their instrument; they attacked it, with clenched fists covered by leather gloves.) By the 1400s the two main stringed keyboard instruments of the Middle Ages—and the piano's two direct ancestors—had come into existence: the clavichord and the harpsichord.

Compared to the modern piano, the clavichord seems a child's instrument. It is essentially nothing but a monochord made into a polychord—the earliest had ten strings—and fitted with keys. The oldest clavichord at the Metropolitan Museum of Art in New York, dating from the late seventeenth century, looks like a wooden box (it has no legs) within which thin metal strings, as fine as beaten gold, are stretched horizontally across the keys. The action of the clavichord was extremely primitive. When the key was struck, a small metal blade or tangent at its other end bounced up and hit the string. Since the tangent remained in contact with the string as long as the key was depressed, the tangent simultaneously produced the sound and, by establishing the vibrating length of the string, determined the pitch of the note. There were no pedals, no dampers to silence the sound of the string (except for lengths of felt entwined in the nonvibrating ends of the strings), and few fancy cases.

As might be imagined, the clavichord was not a dazzling performer. Its voice was wonderfully soft and sweet, making a tender whisper of melody to beguile a sensitive musician's ears; if the player moved his or her finger on the key while it was depressed, a soft vibrato would steal forth to add a further tremolo of emotion to the performance. Yet the clavichord's sound was barely audible: by remaining against the string, the tangent "blocked" the sound even as it made it. Much of the clavichord's repertoire was written in simple two parts. On many so-called fretted clavichords, in which several tangents shared the same string, chromatic music was impossible; an A could not be played, for example, while the B tangent remained in contact with the shared string. Except in Germany, where the sentimental burghers of the seventeenth and eighteenth centuries wept and sighed to its tiny strains, the clavichord remained a crude, inexpensive instrument, akin to the "hack-brett" or primitive dulcimer of folk music and rural feasts. One seventeenth-century critic suggested that the best use for the clavichord was as firewood for cooking fish.

The harpsichord, in contrast, was an expensive, aristrocratic show-off. The descendant of the plucked psaltery, it became popular in the era of courtly music, when its fleet, brilliant voice quickly replaced the slow strumming of the lute as the all-purpose accompaniment. It was the consort of princes and kings. Both Henry VIII and Queen Elizabeth played the virginals, the small, horizontally strung harpsichord that could be found in almost every titled household of sixteenth-century England. Louis XIV retained a harpsichord professor on his staff; a century later, Prince Ferdinand de' Medici owned no fewer than forty of the instruments. As the king did, so did the lesser nobility; in sixteenth- and seventeenth-century England music was considered a necessary part of every gentleman's education.

The harpsichord's action was simple enough. When the player struck a note, a jack or wooden bar mounted on the far end of the key, positioned below and slightly to the side of the string, shot up. As it passed the string, a stiff crow's quill that jutted out from the side of the jack plucked the string hard; on the way down, the quill, mounted on a pivoting tongue, slipped around the string after faintly touching it. A damper attached to the

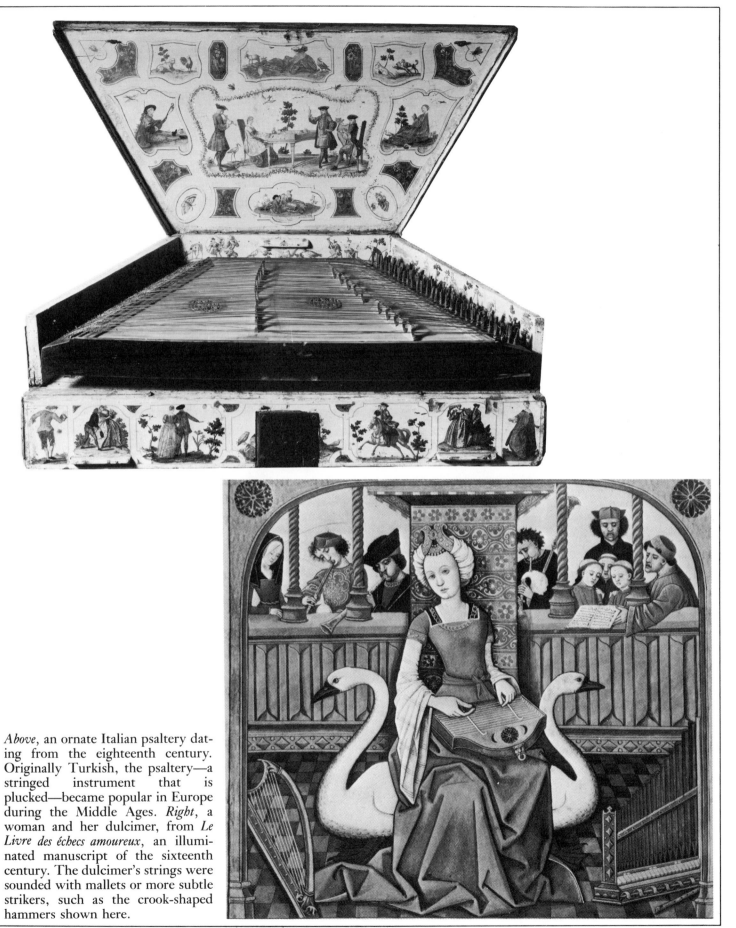

Above, an ornate Italian psaltery dating from the eighteenth century. Originally Turkish, the psaltery—a stringed instrument that is plucked—became popular in Europe during the Middle Ages. *Right*, a woman and her dulcimer, from *Le Livre des échecs amoureux*, an illuminated manuscript of the sixteenth century. The dulcimer's strings were sounded with mallets or more subtle strikers, such as the crook-shaped hammers shown here.

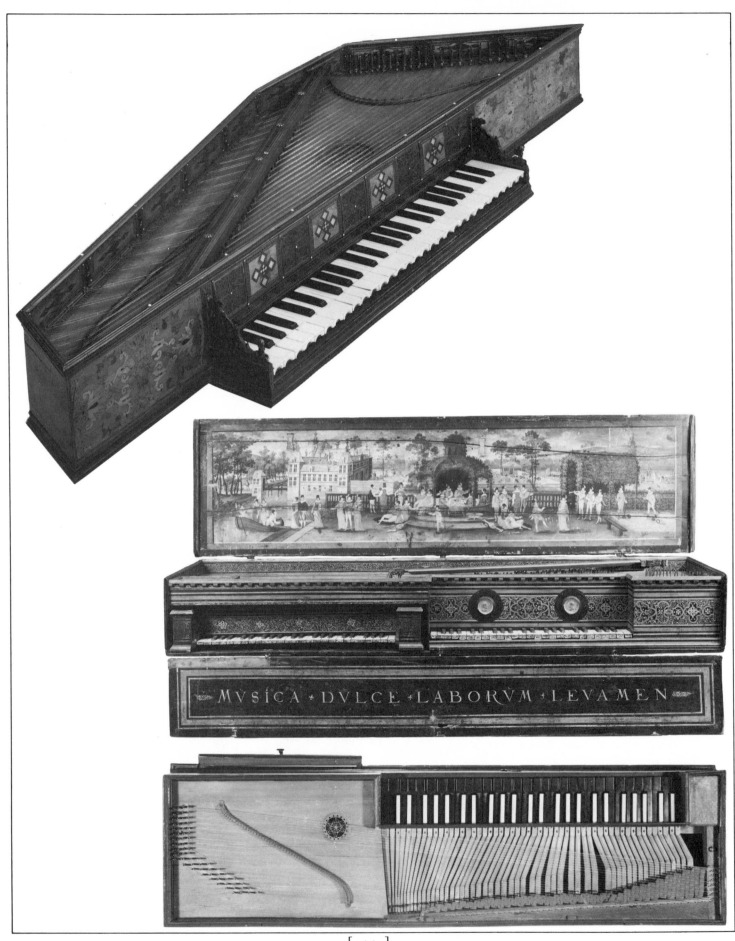

MVSICA · DVLCE · LABORVM · LEVAMEN

jack silenced any sound. Despite its seeming simplicity, the harpsichord was extremely expensive to buy and maintain. For one thing, it needed frequent requilling, a costly process. For another, only the Italian harpsichords were simple affairs with one keyboard and only one set of strings. The famous Ruckers family, which established Antwerp as the center of harpsichord making from roughly 1580 to 1670, made popular two-manual models, in which two sets of strings—commonly tuned to "unison" or standard pitch and operated by two different sets of jacks and manuals—could be coupled by the player to double the volume. Often

special stops were added to vary the timbre of the sound. A lute stop, for example, moved the jacks nearer the ends of the strings, thus creating a sharper sound when the strings were plucked.

In keeping with its aristocratic station, the harpsichord was an imposing-looking instrument—long and narrow, with a thin tail that jutted out to the rear and that contained the bass strings (as on a modern grand piano). By the late seventeenth century many German models were seven to eight feet long, and Shudi and Kirckman, the most famous of the British harpsichord makers, created powerful nine-foot models. The wooden cases, particularly

Above, a seventeenth-century engraving by Duclos of a French salon concert. One of the duties of a royal composer like Lully was to produce entertaining music for Louis XIV's salon gatherings at Versailles. *Facing page: Top*, an early Italian spinettina, made for Eleanora della Rovere in 1540. Such small, laterally strung harpsichords, also known as virginals, were especially popular in Renaissance England. *Middle*, a sixteenth-century double-manual virginals made by Hans Ruckers, the famous Flemish harpsichord maker. Often elaborately painted and carved, the Ruckers instruments were prized long after the demise of the harpsichord itself. *Bottom*, an eighteenth-century German clavichord. With its tiny tangents, or small metal blades, that struck the strings when the keys were depressed, the clavichord was the direct ancestor of the piano.

on Ruckers instruments, were often decorated with exquisite paintings by Rubens, Van Dyck, and Boucher (at a cost of up to thirty pounds sterling in the early seventeenth century). Most of the cases were beautifully finished. Elaborate veneers and inlays decorated the sides; ornate gilding was common.

The harpsichord, eminently showy yet capable of blending well with other instruments, perfectly suited both the collective music making of the Renaissance and the dazzling virtuosity of the baroque era that followed. Gibbons and Byrd, Rameau and Couperin all wrote gorgeously twined polyphonic partitas and toccatas for the harpsichord, and the intricately structured works of Bach in the next century remain the instrument's crowning repertoire. The age of the harpsichord was the age of ornamentation. Trills, turns, mordents, and appoggiaturas set off to advantage its clear, sharp voice and helped to prolong its brief sonority. Only the most skillful of players—those, perforce, who had time and money to lavish on their musical education—could master such fast, complicated music. If for no other reason, the harpsichord's repertoire would have limited it to the rich and noble.

No other instrument rivaled the harpsichord's supremacy in the sixteenth and early seventeenth centuries. By the end of the seventeenth century, however, there was growing dissatisfaction, particularly in Italy, with the harpsichord's lack of expressiveness—its inability to show sentiment, that most fundamental of music's charms. In Italy the founding of opera had sparked a new interest in the expressiveness of music and of the human voice; so had the emergence of string orchestras and of the glorious Amati, Stradivari, and Guarnerius del Gesù violins. By comparison, the harpsichord sounded increasingly wooden. "While all the other instruments have learned to sing, the clavier alone has remained behind in this respect," complained C. P. E. Bach, one of J. S. Bach's talented sons. At the same time musical taste was tiring of the somber counterpoint of the northern baroque. What was wanted, as Richard Steele put it in the London *Spectator* in 1711, was charmingly varied, expressive music—and the sort of instrument that could give it voice.

Appropriately, given the country's dominant role in the music of the period, the piano was invented in Italy. Scipione Maffei, writing in the *Giornale de Litterati d'Italia* in 1709, described a marvelous new invention—a *gravicembalo col piano e forte* ("harpsichord with soft and loud") made by Bartolommeo Cristofori, a Paduan harpsichord maker and caretaker to Prince Ferdinand de' Medici's instruments. Cristofori's instrument was not a harpsichord at all; it was, in fact, the first piano. In building it, Cristofori had worked out the three main principles that have guided piano makers ever since. First, he realized that in order to produce a tone that carried adequately the new instrument must have hammers that rebounded instantly after hitting the string; continued contact, like that of the clavichord's tangent, would produce a soft, dull tone. Thus, he reasoned, an "escapement" device was necessary that would trigger the hammer and then escape out of the hammer's way, allowing it to fall freely away from the string after hitting it. Second, he realized that the hammer, under the force of a strong blow, might jump up and hit the string several times. Some sort of "check" or preventive device had to be built into the piano to catch the hammer on the way down and keep it from rebounding. Finally, he realized that a damper, similar to that attached to a harpsichord's jack, was needed to clamp down on the string and instantly to silence any sound once the finger released the key.

The astonishingly sophisticated action that resulted can be seen in one of Cristofori's earliest extant pianos, which now stands in the Metropolitan Museum in New York. The hammers, covered with deer leather, are attached to elaborate double levers. When the key is depressed, the hopper, or first lever, jumps up and hits the hammer, which then hits the string with far greater force than the direct, shallow blow of the clavichord's tiny tangent. The hopper has two springs that cause it to

Facing page: A woman playing a Flemish spinet or virginals. In the early days of the harpsichord and clavichord, performers often remained standing while they played.

The changing of the guard: *below*, an aristocratic-looking Italian harpsichord of the seventeenth century; *right*, an eighteenth-century harpsichord by Jen Goermans, the Elder, which was later converted into a piano. *Facing page: Top*, a spare, simple pianoforte, ca. 1720, by Bartolommeo Cristofori; *bottom left*, its action; *bottom right*, Cristofori, who made some twenty pianofortes in all before his death in 1730.

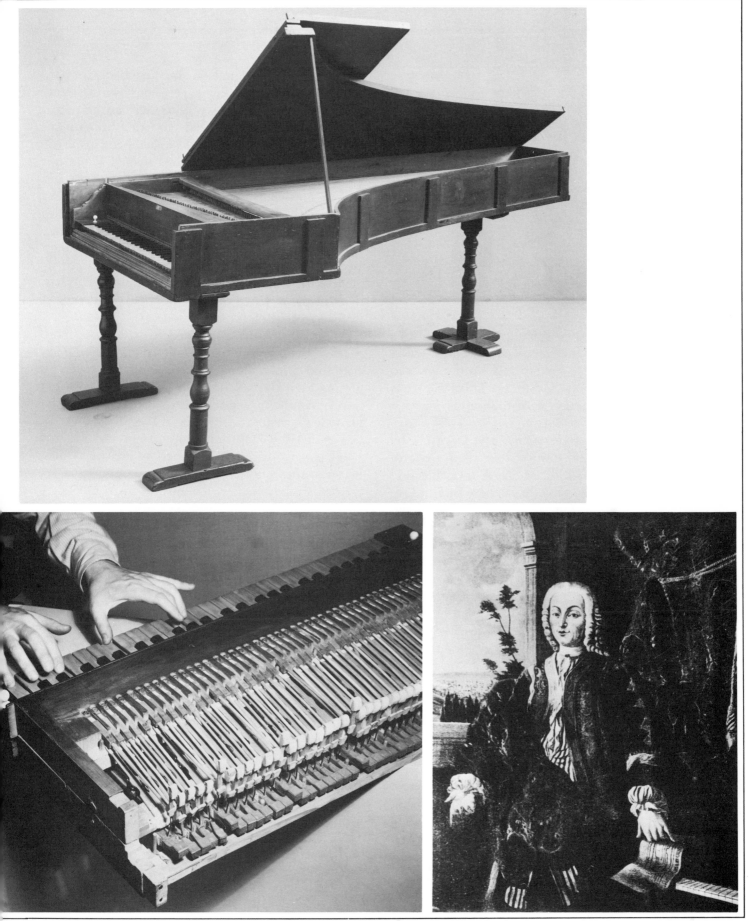

Advertisement for the piano's debut in Great Britain, at Covent Garden in 1767. Pianos rapidly became fashionable in both Britain and France.

jump back instantly after striking the hammer, thus clearing the way for the hammer's descent. Finally, at the rear of each key there is a leather-covered checking device; when the hammer falls back to its original position, friction with the leather keeps it from bouncing back up again.

Looking at Cristofori's piano, one is struck by how little it differs outwardly from a harpsichord. The plain black wooden case and four-octave keyboard are indistinguishable from those of a harpsichord placed nearby in the Met; so is the long, wing-shaped tail that juts out to the rear. The resemblance was deliberate. Until the end of the eighteenth century pianos were modeled as closely as possible on harpsichords—no doubt to assuage the qualms of cautious buyers who regarded the piano as a curiosity of dubious value. Even the quality of sound is much the same; the early piano's strings were as thin as a harpsichord's, and the tone sounds to the modern ear almost as bright and brittle.

Italy, with its traditionally conservative musical tastes, had never taken to the more elaborate harpsichords developed in the northern countries. Perhaps that innate conservatism kept the piano from taking hold there, or perhaps Italy had become culturally exhausted after its surge of opera. Whatever the reason, Cristofori stopped making pianos before his death in 1730 (he made some twenty in all), and few artisans continued after him. Instead, in the usual south-to-north flow of culture of the

time—Vienna bordered on the Venetian republic, and many northern Italians were employed in Dresden—the piano made its way to Germany. In 1730 an instrument maker named Gottfried Silbermann unveiled his first two pianos. He had been inspired, in part, by a creative eccentric named Pantaleon Hebenstreit, who had become famous after playing a giant nine-foot dulcimer, or stringed instrument struck with mallets, for Louis XIV at Versailles and gaining the Sun King's interest. Silbermann, who serviced Hebenstreit's instrument for his tours around Germany, tried initially to create an instrument with similar down-striking hammers. When that failed—it defied the laws of gravity—he turned instead to Cristofori's invention.

At first Silbermann seemed to have little more success than his Italian counterpart. J. S. Bach criticized Silbermann's early instruments severely, finding their trebles too weak and their actions too heavy. Yet the timing was perfect for the rise of the piano in Germany. The Peace of Westphalia in 1648 had ended the Hapsburg domination and inaugurated a new period of prosperity; artistic rivalry between the countless petty nobles and aristocrats created a ready market for musical instruments. A new middle class was also on the rise. Unable to afford the orchestras employed by the nobles, but eager both for entertainment at home and for the status afforded by musical instruments, the growing bourgeoisie also provided a ripe market. Finally, a cult of sentimentality had recently swept Germany, elevating the clavichord to new popularity because of its sentimental little voice. What better thing than an instrument that was expressive, like the clavichord, yet ten times louder?

To a remarkable degree, the piano's progress from the eighteenth century until today has been shaped by German craftsmanship and mechanical ingenuity. (Such great piano makers as Sébastien Érard, the celebrated Parisian inventor, and Henry Steinway, of American fame, were German-Austrian by birth.) By the 1750s pianos were being made throughout Germany—in the traditional wing shape or "grand" design, in large square models, and even as primitive uprights, or grands turned on end. By 1760 pianos had begun to spread to the rest of Europe. One of the first countries to benefit from the export of German talent was Britain, to which a group of German artisans from Saxony—dubbed the "Twelve Apostles"—fled during the Seven Years' War. The most successful of them, Johann Zumpe, soon began to make pianos based on a crude version of the Cristofori-Silbermann action. His design essentially abolished the complicated double lever, substituting instead a simple single lever that bounced up and hit the hammer directly. There was no escapement and no check. Zumpe's instruments were all square in design, no doubt in part because of the earlier popularity in England of the square virginals. The novel instrument made its public debut in London in 1767, during an intermission of the *Beggar's Opera* at Covent Garden. Crude as it was, it became the fashionable new curiosity, de rigueur in every up-per-class household. The French, then madly aping the British (who were considered the trend setters of Europe), snapped up "*les pianos anglais*" as soon as they crossed the Channel. One advertisement in Paris even offered to exchange a Stradivari or Amati violin for one of the far cheaper—but of course far more chic—pianos.

By the latter part of the eighteenth century, the piano's fortunes were rising fast. A measure of how fast was the change in musical tastes within the Bach family. To the end of his life, J. S. Bach continued to write music for the "clavier," without any dynamic markings. His son C. P. E. Bach, in contrast, loved the clavichord but always played the piano (not the harpsichord) in concerts, where greater volume was essential. C. P. E. Bach also codified the style of fingering, introduced by his father, that was to become standard on the piano.

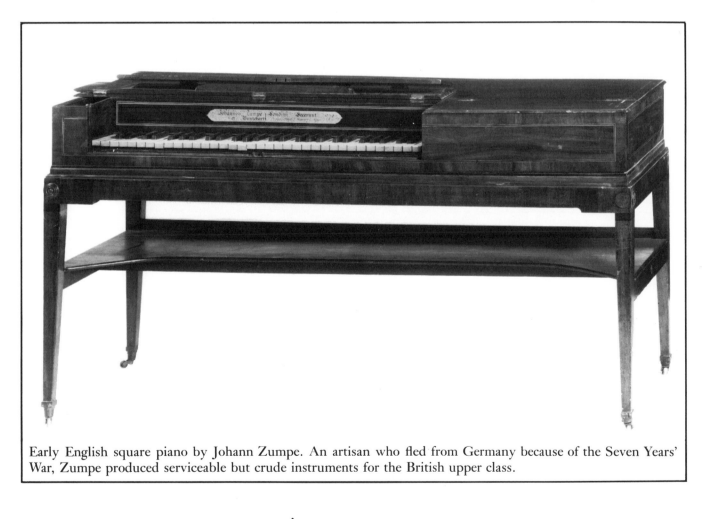

Early English square piano by Johann Zumpe. An artisan who fled from Germany because of the Seven Years' War, Zumpe produced serviceable but crude instruments for the British upper class.

Above left, Carl Philipp Emanuel Bach; *right*, his brother Johann Christian Bach (in a portrait by Gainsborough); *facing page*, their father, Johann Sebastian Bach. Although J. S. Bach never found a pianoforte to his liking, his two sons championed the new instrument; C. P. E. Bach codified fingering for it, and Johann Christian Bach, as Queen Charlotte's music adviser, helped make the piano the rage of the British aristocracy.

(Harpsichordists had eschewed the use of the thumb and the little finger, creating a hopping style that Beethoven later dismissed as "finger dancing.") As Queen Charlotte's music adviser, Johann Christian Bach, another son, influenced considerably the piano's rapid rise in England; as soon as it was known that he preferred the piano to the harpsichord, every court hanger-on scrambled for one. Bach subsequently gave the first public piano recital in England (the Covent Garden debut had been only a short entr'acte display) when he played a Zumpe square for a gathering of Dr. Johnson's famous Literary Club.

The battle between the harpsichord and the piano for musical dominance was far from won, however. The pianos of the period, particularly the English models, were sorry instruments. Their tone was often duller and softer than the harpsichord's; the wooden cases were so thin that the strings could not be pulled taut enough to produce resonant sound; and the hammers were too tiny to produce much in the way of volume. Zumpe's instruments were so light that they were delivered to their buyers on a porter's back. The single lever within the Zumpe models—derisively nicknamed the "mopstick"—was so poorly regulated that it often remained against the string after hitting it, thereby blocking the sound; or it rebounded again

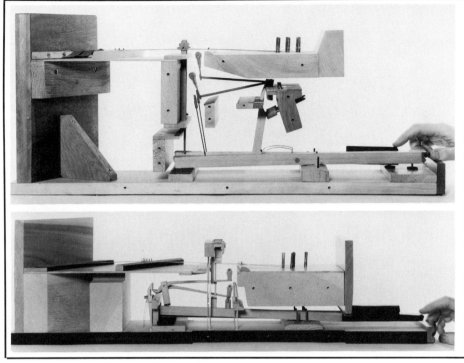

Models of the two rival piano actions that emerged in the nineteenth century, the English (*top*) and the German or Viennese. The English, a more powerful, heavier action, had an intermediate lever, based on Cristofori's original design, which threw the hammer at the string with great force. In the Viennese action, the hammer was mounted directly on the key. It lacked the strong blow and carrying force of the British model, but its action was more responsive to the player's touch, and its silvery sound was ideal for chamber music.

and again, making a dull, muddied tone. The harpsichord, meanwhile, fighting a desperate rearguard action, had grown increasingly elaborate. Often as many as twenty different tone combinations were possible, with the addition of more and more manuals and stops. In an effort to match the piano's expressiveness, Burkat Shudi, the English maker, even patented a device known as the "Venetian swell" that gradually opened and closed shutters on the lid to simulate crescendos and decrescendos.

The greatest drawback facing the piano of the period was not the harpsichord's strengths, however, or even its own weaknesses, but the fact that everyone treated it as a substitute harpsichord—the poor man's harpsichord—instead of as a unique instrument. Few performers of the day, all of them trained as harpsichordists, grasped that the volume of a passage could be varied from note to note and not just in contrasting sections, as on the harpsichord. Most played the piano with the same uniform touch that they used on the harpsichord; a soft stop was provided so that they need not master gradations of finger pressure on the keys. Many pianos boasted a harpsichord stop to blur the dis-

tinction still further. Until Muzio Clementi's hallmark piano sonatas were published in 1773, most composers wrote for the "clavier" and left the choice of instrument to the performer's discretion. Such music contained a few dynamic markings, but there was little true feeling for subtle tone contrasts, or the sort of sweeping, expressive melodic lines that could take advantage of the piano's possibilities.

What finally spelled the end of the harpsichord was the emergence of two new and far superior types of piano—the Stein piano of the so-called German or Viennese school, and the Broadwood piano of the English school. In the 1770s John Broadwood, who had taken over Shudi's harpsichord firm and who was convinced of the piano's eventual ascendancy, began to develop the "English" piano action. Instead of working with Zumpe's cheap action, he went back to Cristofori's version and streamlined it. He simplified the needlessly complicated intermediate lever and developed a simple screw to regulate the escapement. Broadwood strengthened the case and strings of his pianos to increase the volume and added half an

The two extremes: *top*, a Broadwood grand, with sturdy case and rosewood veneer finish, from 1827, and, *middle*, an 1801 Broadwood square; *bottom*, a fortepiano, or light Viennese piano, by J. A. Stein, dated 1780. Mozart praised Stein's instruments for their rippling action and smooth touch.

Title page of Muzio Clementi's seminal work of pedagogy. Clementi led an extremely successful life—as one of the two great early virtuosos of the piano, with Mozart; and, after retiring, as head of Clementi and Co., a piano-manufacturing firm in England.

action. A finger striking the key caused a little wooden extension or beak at the back of the hammer to catch on a *Prelleiste* or bouncing rail directly above it and literally bounce the hammer up at the string. To this simple action Stein added a check that kept the hammer from flying back against the string more than once.

Mozart, the first great virtuoso of the piano, played a critical role in the piano's ascension. He had grown up as a harpsichord prodigy, touring Europe with his sister and manager father. Early in his adult career he began to dabble with the pioneering Spath piano, a predecessor of the German Stein. Then, in 1777, he discovered the Stein piano. Its silvery, singing voice charmed him. So did its rippling action and its smooth, evenly regulated touch, which made it easy to shade from soft notes to loud. As he wrote to his father: "When I play vigorously, whether I leave the finger down or lift it up, the tone is finished the moment I sound it. I can attack the keys any way I want, the tone will always be even, it will not block, will not come out too loud or too soft or perhaps even fail to sound; in one word, everything is even." Eminently pleased, Mozart composed the rest of his keyboard music for the piano, becoming the first great composer to abandon the harpsichord completely.

In the closing years of the eighteenth century, the harpsichord vanished. Broadwood stopped making the older instrument in 1793; soon afterward the firm refused to accept any in exchange, claiming that "from their almost total disuse they are unsaleable." The last harpsichord prize was

octave each to the bass and treble; such an enlargement of the keyboard had previously been impossible because of the strain it would have placed on the case. He changed the knee levers that governed the *sostenuto* and *una corda* effects to the foot pedals that we use today, and he thickened the bass strings to provide a better tone. The result was a much more powerful, resonant instrument.

The Stein piano—or fortepiano, as the early German pianos are still called—was much lighter and mechanically simpler than the English model. Its action was based on a rather primitive design of certain eighteenth-century Bavarian pianos. The hammer was mounted directly on the key itself; there were no intervening levers, as in the English

Facing page: Bottom, the young Mozart entertaining a salon gathering in Vienna, in a painting by Gustave Boulanger. Mozart toured Europe with his sister and impresario father as a child prodigy on the harpsichord, but later became the first great champion of the piano. *Top left*, Muzio Clementi in later life, by E. Hader. *Top right*, the title page of his early sonatas for the harpsichord and piano. Composers neglected for some time to designate which instrument their keyboard works were intended for, or to indicate with dynamic markings any awareness of the piano's unique expressive capability. Clementi's later sonatas, for piano alone, marked the first music written for the new instrument that showed off its ability to modulate between soft and loud.

4 *Title-page of Clementi's Sonatas, Op. 1 (c. 1771).*

awarded at the Paris Conservatoire in 1795; by then the harpsichord seemed as outmoded as the old empire. Diderot's *Encyclopédie*, which had earlier dismissed the piano in a brief entry under the heading of "Harpsichord," now had nothing but panegyrics for it. Instruction books changed dramatically. James Hook's *Guida di Musica*, published in 1787, was described as an instruction book for piano *or* harpsichord, and Clementi's *Introduction to the Art of Playing on the Piano Forte*, published in 1801, addressed only the piano. As the turn of the century approached, the old guard was rapidly disappearing—Bach, Handel, and Rameau were dead and Haydn was in his sixties—and with them disappeared the harpsichord. The piano had won.

But which piano? Over the next few decades a genteel but earnest rivalry developed between the English and Viennese pianos—a rivalry based as much on national differences, it seems, as on the merits of the instruments themselves.

The English, the robust, mechanically inventive empire builders, preferred the far more powerful Broadwood piano. It had thicker strings, heavier and bigger hammers, and a sturdier action than the Viennese piano. It boasted three strings per note, instead of two as in the Stein, thus substantially increasing its carrying power. In the Broadwood the strings were braced for the first time against the case, an advantage that the Viennese piano lacked.

The Stein, in contrast, was the perfect instrument for elegant Vienna, that city of intimate chamber music soirees. For all its lack of power, the Stein had an unmatched clarity of sound and a distinctive sparkle and brilliance of tone. Since its action was not nearly as heavy as the English one, notes could be repeated much more quickly. Piano

---

Facing page: Top, an artist's depiction of the meeting in Vienna of two masters—Beethoven and Mozart—and by implication of a critical juncture in music history. *Bottom left,* a portrait of Beethoven, dated 1814. Beethoven called the old eight-finger playing style of Mozart and others "finger dancing"—and wrote music for which ten fingers were barely enough. *Bottom right,* the title page of the first edition of Beethoven's *Hammerklavier* Sonata, composed in 1817–18 and still one of the most demanding works ever written for the piano.

Top, John Broadwood, founder of the famous British piano-making firm. The modern grand owes as much to Broadwood's efforts to strengthen the piano and thus increase its volume as it does to Cristofori's original design. *Bottom,* French inventor Sébastien Érard, to whom the modern grand owes the double-escapement action.

Cartoon published in 1809, titled "Farmer Giles and his Wife showing off their daughter Betty to their Neighbors on her return from School," which mocks the piano's abuse by the middle class as a status symbol.

virtuoso Johann Hummel wrote of the Stein: "It allows the performer to impart to his execution every possible degree of light and shade, speaks clearly and promptly, has a round flutey tone, which, in a large room, contrasts well with the accompanying orchestra, and does not impede rapidity of execution by requiring too great an effort." The legacy of the Stein piano can be seen in the graceful, elegantly flowing music of Haydn and Mozart, in which, in deference to the Stein's fragile nature, there are no thunderous chords or huge crescendos. Never, perhaps, have period and piano meshed so well. The smooth cascades of notes matched the fleetness of finger and rippling style perfected by the Viennese and reflected exquisitely the filigreed taste of imperial Vienna—then, under its musician king Joseph II, the musical center of Europe.

Musical taste in the classical era was not, alas, everywhere on a par with that of Vienna, and piano music sank especially low. The piano was, after all, the instrument of the rising, not highly educated middle class, to whom the piano was a cheap status symbol (an English square could be had for twenty-five guineas in 1800) and a theatrical entertainment. After Empress Catherine of Russia signed a treaty with the Turks at the end of the eighteenth century, for example, and celebrated the event with a Turkish Janissary band, a Turkish craze swept Europe. The poor piano did not escape. Piano makers, inspired by the harpsichord's myriad stops, attached all sorts of exotic pedals to the piano—a bassoon pedal (in which a strip of wood covered with parchment was pressed against the strings to create a nasal sound), a cymbal pedal, a triangle pedal. Although serious pianists disdained such effects—

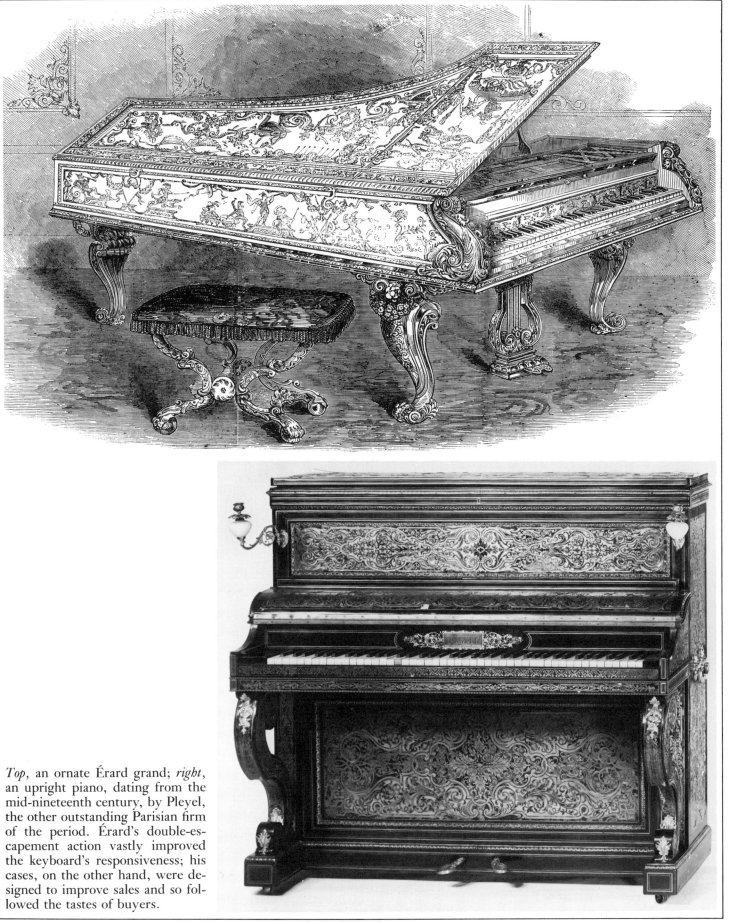

Top, an ornate Érard grand; *right*, an upright piano, dating from the mid-nineteenth century, by Pleyel, the other outstanding Parisian firm of the period. Érard's double-escapement action vastly improved the keyboard's responsiveness; his cases, on the other hand, were designed to improve sales and so followed the tastes of buyers.

Interior and exterior views of an iron-frame square piano by Boston piano maker Alpheus Babcock. Babcock cast the first one-piece iron frame in 1825, thus solving the problem of how to brace the piano against the greater tension of the strings.

Czerny, for example, called all superfluous pedals "childish toys of which a solid player will disdain to avail himself"—they proliferated. So did ornate new styles of pianos. The giraffe and lyre uprights, for example, which were popular in turn-of-the-century Vienna, were so encumbered with gewgaws and so topheavy with their towering cases that they threatened to topple over. One Thomas Kunz of Prague, obviously inspired by delusions of grandeur, produced the most extraordinary piano of all: it had 230 strings, 150 changes of register, and 360 organ pipes.

Needless to say, what was played on such instruments was often depressingly bad. Music publishers churned out prettily titled ditties with simple melodies and easily executed chords—mostly for the growing market of middle-class women who, as in Jane Austen's novels, cultivated the piano as one of their "accomplishments." In France most music was inspired by the popular opera arias of the day, and English taste proved as bad. "You won't believe how backward music still is here, and how one has to hold oneself back in order to bring forth such shallow compositions, which do a terrific business here," wrote Josef Wölfl, a virtuoso pianist from Salzburg, on a visit to London around the turn of the century. Even the Viennese had their vulgar streak: they adored the cheapest of waltzes and swooned over the gratuitous cannon firings and bird calls in otherwise unremarkable program music.

Piano making might well be designated "Before Beethoven" and "After Beethoven," for that great composer changed the future of the piano's development as much as he did the future of classical music. When Beethoven arrived in Vienna in 1792, under the auspices of Count Waldstein, the piano was seen almost exclusively as a graceful, singing instrument, and the style of playing—a perfectly even tone and a light, tickling touch, with bent fingers skimming close to the keys—had changed little from the clavichord and harpsichord's day. Beethoven, in contrast, bore down relentlessly on the piano and wrung out of it crescendos that some of his audience found downright frightening. One listener likened his playing to a great fountain spewing forth clusters of notes. Another remarked that

he looked "like a wizard, overpowered by the demons whom he himself has called up." Beethoven's crashing attack shook the pianos of the day down to their soundboards. Anton Reicha, a composer and teacher of the time, witnessed one such onslaught: "He [Beethoven] asked me to turn the pages for him. But I was mostly occupied in wrenching the strings of the pianoforte which snapped, while the hammers stuck among the broken strings. Beethoven insisted on finishing the concerto, and so back and forth I leaped, jerking out a string, disentangling a hammer, turning a page, and I worked harder than Beethoven."

Mozart had written music that exactly suited the Stein piano. Beethoven, in contrast, pushed the existing pianos to their limits—and, in the end, far beyond their limits. His first eight sonatas were written interchangeably for the "clavecin or pianoforte," and the first twenty were written within the five-octave compass of the time. But even in these one begins to hear novel effects. There are more and heavier orchestral echoes than in Mozart—broken octaves imitating tremolo strings, ostinatos in the bass mimicking cello and double bass. Dynamic contrasts, especially from the *Waldstein* Sonata on, are far more extreme. There are long crescendos followed by startling stillnesses, frequent sharp accents, harsh dissonances, and great tempests of chords. Nothing like the three mighty C chords of the *Appassionata* Sonata, which usher in the coda of the first movement, had ever been heard before.

One of the first composers to mark down pedaling instructions, Beethoven might also be called the father of the pedal. While the music of Haydn and Mozart requires little pedaling to effect its smooth flow, the pedal is of critical importance in Beethoven's music. By sustaining bass notes throughout entire passages, or blurring together rapidly articulated chords, Beethoven created stunningly sonorous new effects. Czerny, Beethoven's pupil, later reported that Beethoven wanted to create a wash of indistinct, reverberating sound, as if speaking into a cave. The formidable *Hammerklavier* Sonata—storming across the keyboard in the first two movements, sinking into otherworldly dread in the slow fugal movement, sounding by the end more than twenty thousand notes—definitively marked the piano's metamorphosis from a charming chamber instrument into the modern leviathan, capable of standing monumentally alone in the concert hall.

It was during Beethoven's lifetime that piano makers first began to curry favor with famous artists—and court endorsements—by supplying them with free pianos. In 1796 Johann Andreas Streicher, a German maker of renown, sent Beethoven one of his best instruments. Beethoven replied: "There is no doubt that so far as the manner of playing it is concerned, the pianoforte is still the least studied and developed of all instruments; often one thinks that one is merely listening to a harp. And I am delighted, my dear fellow, that you are one of the few who realize and perceive that, provided one can feel the music, one can also make the piano sing." Despite that praise for Streicher, the instrument that proved best for Beethoven was the English Broadwood, by far the most powerful in frame and volume of the day. In 1818 Broadwood sent Beethoven a piano that traveled by boat to Trieste and then, by mule-drawn cart, the 360 miles over the Alps to Vienna. In the end even the Broadwood succumbed. One visitor described the unfortunate instrument: "Beethoven complained of the imperfection of the grand piano, upon which one could not perform forcefully and effectively under present conditions. 'I myself possess a London instrument, which, however, does not live up to my expectations. Come along, it's in the next room, in a most miserable state.' When I opened it, what a sight confronted me! The upper registers were mute and the broken strings in a tangle, like a thorn bush whipped by the storm. . . ."

Still, the Broadwood was only daunted; the Viennese piano was doomed. The first decades of the nineteenth century saw what amounted to a revolution in musical taste. The elegant, silvery sound that had predominated in music from the Middle Ages on began to change in favor of the more rounded, golden sound of the romantic era. A new style of music emerged, based on massive chords and pyrotechnic flourishes; with it came the virtuoso, who powered his attack from the shoulders down, bringing to bear a strength unheard of in

Mozart's day. Meanwhile, the pitch of orchestral instruments was raised a half step in order to make them sound more brilliant. The piano, already overstrained by the rising tension of its strings, was hard-pressed to follow suit. Something, clearly, had to be done to strengthen it. As early as 1808 Broadwood began to add iron bracing bars to the previously all-wood piano. Soon afterward the firm added iron plates to the wooden tuning-pin block at the front of the piano to help hold the pins against the tension of the strings. Sturdy, copper-covered wires began to be used for the bass notes, and the soundboard was thickened to withstand the increasing strain. The Viennese pianos copied the new English methods of bracing, the extended Broadwood keyboard, even the use of foot pedals. But nothing could be done to strengthen the Viennese action; since the hammers were attached directly to the keys, there was no way that the instrument could get the same sort of powerful, deep blow as a Broadwood. The light action that had once been the pride of the Stein proved its downfall.

For a while it seemed that the piano had reached an impasse: if pianists wanted power and volume, they had to put up with a heavy-handed action. Credit for combining strength and suppleness—and, in the process, creating the modern grand—goes primarily to Sébastien Érard, an engineer in Paris and a genius of invention. Érard, né Erhard, had arrived in Paris from Strasbourg when he was sixteen and had quickly alienated the Parisian piano builders by knowing more then they. His mechanical talents were recognized nonetheless; he lived

Facing page: Top, a view of the Chickering piano factory in 1887. Chickering iron-frame pianos were the cream of American instruments in the 1830s and 1840s but later lost out to the Steinway. *Bottom left,* Henry Engelhard Steinway (1797–1871). *Bottom right,* the Steinway piano factory in New York City in the 1850s. An immigrant from the Harz Mountains region of Germany, Steinway founded in 1853 what was to become the most successful piano-making firm in America—and the world. Hector Berlioz praised the Steinway for its "noble sonority," and the fledgling piano won a gold medal at the prestigious Paris Exposition of piano manufacturers in 1867.

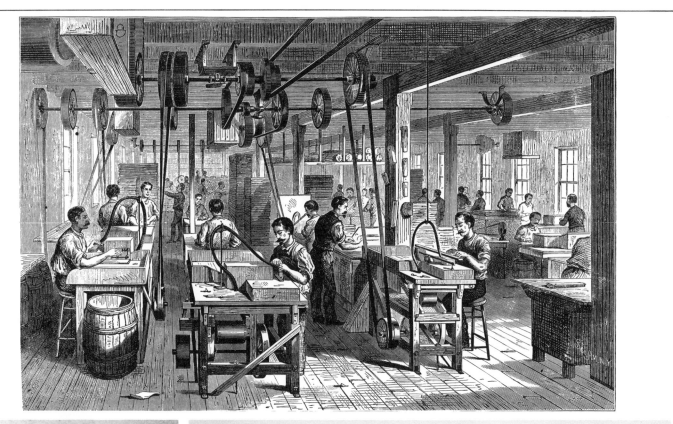

"WEBER"

GRAND, SQUARE AND UPRIGHT

PIANO-FORTES.

THE WEBER PIANO-FORTES have become the *FAVORITE INSTRUMENTS of the ARTISTIC* World, and are endorsed by every Musical Authority as the

BEST PIANO MANUFACTURED.

The special adaptation to the human voice has induced *every celebrated* Singer to use them in *preference* to any other.

The Weber Upright Piano has no Rival!

MME. ARABELLA GODDARD says of it: "I certainly have not seen any instrument in America which approaches them even."

JOHANN STRAUSS, who *purchased* one for his Music Room in Vienna, says: "I assure you (MR. WEBER) I have never yet seen any Pianos which equal yours, and how so small an instrument can contain a perfect Orchestra surprises me."

The sale of the WEBER PIANO-FORTE has increased in four years 368 per cent., as per Internal Revenue returns, while the other leading Piano-Forte Houses have increased but 20 to 25 per cent.

PRICES AS REASONABLE AS CONSISTENT WITH THOROUGHNESS OF WORKMANSHIP.

WAREROOMS.

FIFTH AVENUE, corner of West Sixteenth Street, New York.

MANUFACTORY—121, 123, 125, 127 Seventh Avenue, and 147, 149, 151, 153, 155, 157, 159, 161, 163, 165 West 17th St.

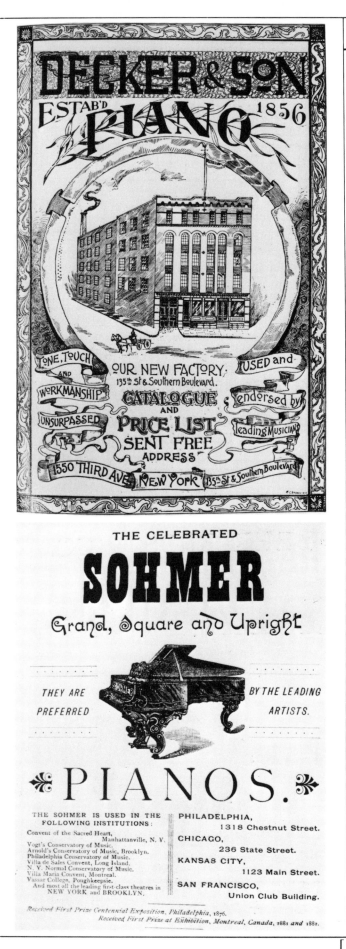

for a time at the château of his patroness, the Duchesse de Villeroi, and while there built her an exquisite harpsichord. With that credential behind him, he opened his own business in the rue Bourbon, survived the efforts of French makers to put him out of business (Louis XVI granted him protection and what amounted to a royal seal of approval), and along the way invented the modern double-action orchestral harp.

Érard's greatest invention came after the French Revolution, which he had weathered in London. Equally familiar with the English and Viennese pianos, he determined to combine the best qualities of both. The so-called double-escapement or repetition action that he invented—which is universally used, in varying forms, today—retained the powerful English action but added a set of small levers and springs that kept the hammer from automatically rebounding all the way to its original position after each blow. As long as the finger depressed the key, the hammer remained suspended in the air just below the string. Thus, if a note were repeated rapidly, the hammer would jump back almost instantly. (On a good modern piano, a note can be repeated six times per second, compared with a far slower frequency on the earlier pianos.) Érard's invention all but transfigured the art of virtuoso playing. "This quicker action of the hammer seems to me so important that I prophesy a new era in the manufacture of pianos," wrote the virtuoso Ignaz Moscheles after playing on Érard's perfected mechanism.

In the early nineteenth century, Paris's musical star ascended rapidly; displaced aristocrats converged on Paris during the years of revolution and unrest in Europe, and those eager for artistic patronage, including Chopin and Liszt, followed them. Thanks to Érard's genius, the fortunes of the French pianos rose as well. The Érard and Pleyel pianos, both incorporating the repetition action,

---

On these and the following pages are examples of nineteenth-century advertisements for American upright, square, and grand pianos. By the 1860s, piano making had become big business; the era of the hard sell, and of tinny-sounding, cheap pianos, had arrived.

dominated the stages of Europe during the early virtuoso period. In mid-century a new wave of German pianos, including several of the great names of today, joined them as favored instruments—the Blüthner, the Bechstein, the Bösendorfer. Hans von Bülow, Cosima Wagner's first husband, inaugurated the first Bechstein piano at a festive concert in 1856, where he played a Liszt sonata. The Bösendorfer could claim an even more impressive public debut. At one recital in Vienna, Liszt, that legendary destroyer of pianos, was forced to perform on first one instrument and then another as each gave out in turn. Finally, in desperation, he turned to the Bösendorfer, an unknown new piano. Its reputation was assured when it finished out the evening intact.

The most spectacular debut of a new piano power, however, was fledgling America's. Until 1788, when a German piano maker named Clement Claus settled in Philadelphia and began to make the popular square model, America did not even have a resident artisan; it imported its pianos, most of them from England. Then, in 1825, a Boston maker named Alpheus Babcock took what amounted to a heretical step: he cast a one-piece iron frame (the sturdy bracing frame that fits over the soundboard and is bolted to the case). This allowed the strings to be stretched to a previously unheard-of tension, and the volume of the piano increased tremendously. The tradition-bound Europeans had always been suspicious of adding iron to pianos, since they felt it might somehow interfere with the tone. The Americans, whose vast continent, with its extremes of high and low temperature, required extraordinarily durable instruments, had no such qualms, and the triumph of the new iron-frame pianos proved them right. In 1867 the flourishing Chickering company, which had been founded in Boston in the 1820s, won a coveted gold medal at the annual Paris Exposition of piano makers for its iron-

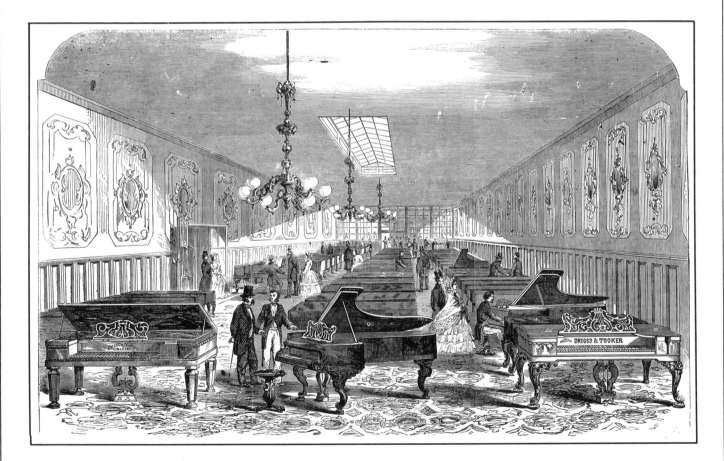

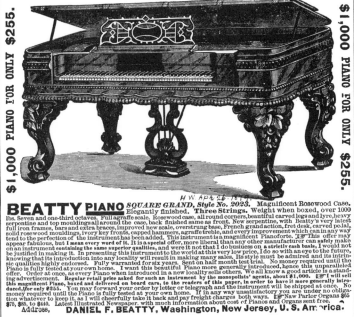

ENLIGHTENMENT'S GIFT TO THE AGE OF ROMANCE

frame grand—the first such victory against the long-entrenched European makers. Liszt, presented not long afterward with one of the new high-tension Chickerings, called it "lordly."

The Steinway piano, the next great American piano, surpassed even the Chickering's success. Heinrich Steinweg, the founder of the famous American piano-making dynasty, was the son of a forester in Braunschweig, in the Harz Mountains region of Germany. He began his career as a cabinetmaker and then switched to making instruments, exhibiting his first piano at the State Fair in Brunswick in 1839. When the February Revolution in Paris stirred up unrest in Austria and Germany in 1848, the piano business went under and Steinweg, with four of his five sons, set out for America. There the family—rechristened Steinway—worked for several years in established piano businesses before opening their own firm in 1853. For the first three years the Steinways produced only unpretentious square pianos. (Until 1850 there was hardly a grand piano to be found in America; among other things, the squares were far less expensive and fit better into the covered wagons that carried settlers to the West.) But the Steinway was no ordinary square. For the first time it combined the one-piece iron frame with a technique known as cross-stringing—a way of fanning the bass strings over the treble strings, originally invented by a Parisian piano maker named Henri Pape, which produced richer overtones and which also used a greater proportion of the soundboard. Recognition of the Steinway sound came swiftly. In 1855 the piano jury at the American Trade Fair in New York had all but decided on the winner when one judge happened to open a nondescript instrument bearing the unfamiliar label of "Steinway." The sound of the first few notes was so superb that the rest of the jury came running, and the prize was won. That early victory was followed by a gold medal at the same Paris Exposition at which the Chickering triumphed.

With the Steinway the ideal piano of the romantics had arrived—round and ringing in tone, huge in volume, all but indestructible in body, with a cloud of soft overtones surrounding each struck string. Hector Berlioz praised the Steinway's "noble sonority," and Rossini was said to have described it, in the exaggerated style of the day, as "a nightingale cooing in a thunderstorm." The Steinways gradually strengthened their piano still further. They built up the tension of the strings from the twenty-one tons of an Érard to the thirty tons that are standard today. (An early fortepiano, by comparison, could stand only two tons of pressure.) They covered the hammers with much heavier felt and adjusted the action to provide the strongest possible blow. It was clear to all concerned that the Steinway was the sound of the future. The German piano makers rapidly converted to the iron frame and overstringing of the "American plan," as it was called; British and French makers, unable to change their manufacturing methods as quickly, followed as soon as they practically could. By the 1870s the Steinway had surpassed the older Chickering in America, turning out some two thousand pianos annually. After acquiring a sister plant in Hamburg, it also began to challenge the hold of the reigning Bechstein and Blüthner pianos in European concert halls. The age of the Steinway had arrived.

So had the age of industrialization. By far the most striking development in piano making during the second half of the nineteenth century, and the first decades of the twentieth, was simply the industry's growth. In the 1770s or 1780s a piano maker might produce 19 or 20 instruments a year. But in 1827 Pleyel employed 30 men and produced some 100 instruments a year; by 1855 the firm had grown to 400 men and an annual output of 1,500 pianos. The English makers, first to use the steam engine in the mass production of the piano, churned out about 23,000 pianos in 1850. Just prior to World War I, at the peak of the piano's production and popularity as home entertainment, European and American makers were manufacturing a prodigious 600,000 pianos a year.

Like everything else about the industrial age, the piano's progress would prove both good and bad. Fine craftsmanship vanished; by the middle of the

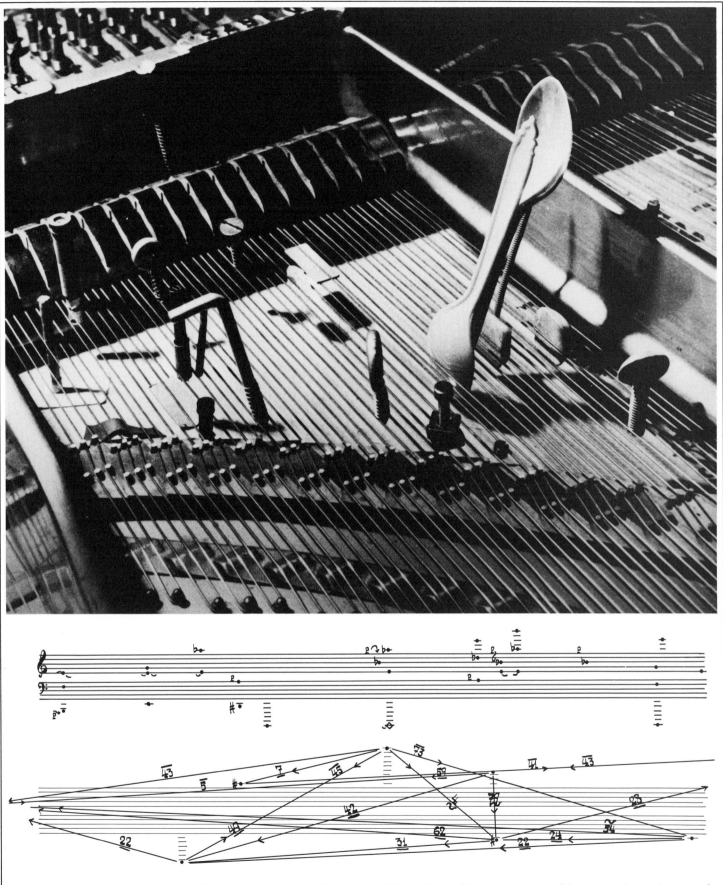

Inside view of a "prepared piano" by composer John Cage, in which various objects are inserted between the strings; and a passage from Cage's Concert for Piano and Orchestra.

The modern grand, made sufficient to stand monumentally alone.

nineteenth century piano parts were made separately by specialist manufacturers and then assembled into a whole, creating a cheaper but far less well-made instrument. The 1860s saw the emergence of truly cheap pianos. Only a tiny percentage of the pianos made annually were expensive—and high-quality—grands. Instead, crude, tinny-sounding uprights and squares proliferated. (Cumbersome, antiquated square pianos, which had long since disappeared in Europe, continued on in America until 1903, when the Society of American Piano Manufacturers, eager for new sales, built a fifty-foot-high pyramid of square pianos at their Atlantic City convention and set fire to it.) By the twentieth century most piano makers had become merely manufacturers, and good sound had widely become secondary to good sales.

There comes a point in the development of every instrument when, perfect or not, it stops. Most modern orchestral instruments have remained basically unchanged since the late nineteenth century. In the case of the piano, the modern instrument is far more powerful than its predecessors: the fortissimo of Liszt's day is barely equal to a mezzo forte today. In other respects the concert grand of today differs little from the grand of the 1870s. There have been efforts to create a quarter-tone piano, or a piano with a semicircular keyboard (making it far easier to reach the extreme treble and bass). Paul von Jankó, a Hungarian nobleman, even devised a reordered keyboard, without black or "accidental" keys, on which the twelve major scales could be played using only two different fingerings. None of these caught on in the face of standardization.

Far from wanting change, most modern pianists fight it.

As any music critic knows, predicting the future, whether it be of a composition or of an instrument, is a foolhardy business. There is, for example, the classic premature obituary written in 1925 by Walter J. Turner, the music critic of the London *New Statesman*. Titled "The Passing of the Pianoforte," the article predicted that the piano would be featured at a concert in 1975 as "the antiquarian pièce de résistance—as extinct as the viol and harpsichord." That year has come and gone; the piano remains. Certainly it belongs most to the romantics; the elegiac beauty of Chopin and the mesmerizing fire of Liszt are a priceless legacy. But the piano, without itself changing, has proved remarkably adaptable to changing musical tastes—and to the genius of individual composers. In the last century Debussy turned it into a thing of blurry, evanescent beauty, in part by using the pedal in new and dramatic ways. ("You forgot that the piano had hammers when Debussy played," his publisher, Monsieur Durand, once said.) Bartók, Prokofiev, and Stravinsky turned the piano into an instrument as strident as the new century: "The piano is only a percussive instrument," Stravinsky said. Henry Cowell attacked it with fist and forearm to produce his explosive tone clusters, and John Cage, that most irreverent of modern composers, mocked its sonority by inserting foreign objects into its strings and renaming it the "prepared piano." What next for the piano may be a valid question, but perhaps a more appropriate one is: What more may reasonably be expected of it?

Magnificent, if rather overwrought, this nineteenth-century Bösendorfer was a birthday gift from Napoleon III to his Empress Eugenie.

III

ANTHONY LIVERSIDGE

Of Wood and Iron Wrought

The Making of a Bösendorfer

❧

One of the purest joys of life is to stumble upon something wonderful whose existence is unknown to you. I remember vividly one clear summer day in the early 1970s during a visit to Amsterdam when, too long away from my elderly but resonant upright in New York, I began to crave a piano to play. On an impulse I walked into a local conservatory and, as a stranger, begged the favor of an hour with one of their pianos. Perhaps because it was vacation and most of the students were away, I was graciously admitted to an upstairs room. There, dark against the bright light from tall, arched windows, stood four beautiful keyboards: two fine, ornate harpsichords and two huge black grand pianos, shiny as mirrors. Sitting down at the piano by the window, I gazed for a moment at a rose garden below, where a few young people were sitting on wrought-iron benches and chatting in a warming sun. Then I began to play a Chopin Nocturne. With the first notes an aural enchantment filled the room, as if the roses below had been transformed into sound. The gratifying effect was not produced by the player, alas, but by the piano.

The live, almost vocal resonance and warmth of its sound, the deep tonal bloom, was like nothing I had ever heard before. The feel and responsiveness of the action, moreover, were completely generous. There seemed to be no barrier between the music and the sound. I looked down to the gold script stenciled on the face board and read then, for the first time, the name Bösendorfer.

Ignorance of the name and the piano was not, at the time, entirely shameful. Among cognoscenti the Bösendorfer had been renowned for more than 150 years, but the firm had suffered the ravages of two world wars and the Great Depression and in the early 1970s was almost as obscure in Europe as in the United States. Bösendorfer had, however, been recently acquired by the largest U.S. piano manufacturer, Kimball & Company, with the express intent of giving it a rightful place in the market for world-class concert pianos. For the purposes of publicity, the Bösendorfer had two natural assets: size and expense. The price of the Imperial Concert Grand in 1980 was $55,000—nearly twice the cost of the Steinway concert grand (though Steinway

pianos were not discounted and Bösendorfers some-times were). It was also—and is at this writing—the only concert grand of its stature regularly made in the world: nine feet six inches long, with a key-board stretching nine keys below those of all other pianos, to a growling C below bottom C. Not many musical compositions actually use those notes (Bar-tók's Second Piano Concerto is among the few), but the larger sounding board and the sympathetic vi-bration of the lowest strings lend the Imperial an undeniable richness of tone. (The Bösendorfer nine-foot and seven-foot-four-inch grands have four extra bass keys, the lowest of which is F below bottom C. The smaller grands have standard-size keyboards.) Quite apart from its musical merits, however, the Bösendorfer drew attention particu-larly in the United States simply because it was big and expensive—and because, as it appeared with increasing frequency on American concert stages, it seemed a promising interloper on territory once the nearly exclusive preserve of Steinway & Sons. *Time*, inevitably, called the Bösendorfer "the Car-tier of keyboards," and one *New York Times* critic was so taken with the instrument that he all but ignored the program that was played on it. The rivalry between Bösendorfer and Steinway was more fabricated than real, but the Bösendorfer nevertheless was soon as widely known in New York as in Vienna, where the instruments are made.

None of that would have occurred, of course, had the Bösendorfer been a less than worthy peer of Steinway. As it happened, its emergence coin-cided with some changes in the manufacture of Steinways in the United States with which many Steinway artists were distinctly unhappy: specifi-cally, a change from ivory to plastic key coverings and from felt to Teflon bushings. Plastic does not absorb sweat as well as ivory and therefore tends to become slippery during performances. Teflon bushings are said to cause squeaks and rattles after use. Yet the Hamburg Steinway continued to use ivory keys and felt bushings, and in this competi-tion the Bösendorfer survived on its own merits. Some pianists complained that it was the less pow-erful instrument, and their point of view was un-derstandable: the Steinway sound is utterly coher-ent, solid as a tank even during crashing fortissimos; the Bösendorfer is more vulnerable to the technique of the pianist, resolutely refusing, for example, to disguise pummeling. In response to complaints about weakness in the treble, the firm redesigned the top three octaves to enhance their clarity, but the midrange and bass of the Bösendorfer remained less blatantly muscular than the Steinway's. Some pianists and critics concluded that the Bösendorfer was probably best suited to chamber music; its transparent sonority clearly blended superbly with strings and held the separateness of polyphonic voices with unusual clarity. Finally, however, the debate as to which piano is better was quite beside the point: both the Steinway and the Bösendorfer pianos are of the highest quality, and they are dis-tinctly different from each other.

The Bösendorfer is very much a creature of its place and time of birth; its light, feminine quality is inherited directly from the Viennese fortepiano. (The comparison of Bösendorfer and Steinway seems strikingly reminiscent of the eighteenth-cen-tury rivalry between the Viennese and British pi-anos; perhaps, indeed, it is more than simply co-incidental that Bösendorfer's ascendancy comes during a vogue for playing Mozart, Haydn, and

Facing page: Top, Ludwig Bösendorfer, son of the foun-der, plays for the Hapsburg emperor, Kaiser Franz Josef I (in uniform). Overlooking the stiffly posed scene is a portrait of Anton Rubinstein, a Bösendorfer patron and founder of the St. Petersburg Conservatory. Ludwig traveled with Liszt and Rubinstein on tours and filled the long hours on trains with his pianist patrons by playing cards. Ludwig tried to ease the trials of touring for his artists by ordering a private railway car with music rooms and sleeping chambers, but his plan was thwarted by officials of the Austrian railroad. *Bottom*, Liszt playing a Bösendorfer for the Emperor Franz Josef I and, seated next to him, Crown Prince Rudolf. Build-ing a piano to withstand the fury of Liszt's playing was a great feat in the Vienna of 1828, and thus Ignaz Bösendorfer won his laurels. One difficulty was that Viennese pianos had a lighter action than the English models of the period.

A winter view of the wood yard at the Wiener Neustadt factory. It can take up to seven years before this lumber is deemed sufficiently dry to be brought in at the first step of the piano's construction. Spruce predominates here, most of it from a cool, dry region of Bavaria where the annual rings grow close together, creating a wood whose density enhances the transmission of sound.

even Beethoven on the fortepiano.) The Bösendorfer firm was founded in 1828 by a cabinetmaker's son, Ignaz Bösendorfer, who had been apprenticed at the age of nineteen to Joseph Brodmann, one of the leading fortepiano makers in Austria. By then Vienna had been a capital of the music world for more than sixty years. The seat of the Hapsburgs and the political and commercial capital of the Holy Roman Empire, it was full of noble families who competed with one another in their patronage of music. For piano makers it was therefore a paradise of commercial opportunity, but a crowded one whose prizes went only to those who somehow emerged from the throng. Ignaz Bösendorfer did so shrewdly and directly: he approached Liszt, then a virile prodigy in need of a piano that could withstand his storming performances. As the story goes, Liszt had just broken strings on three different pianos, including one made by the reputable Conrad Graf, when Bösendorfer presented himself and his instrument.

The piano survived Liszt's playing, Ignaz was appointed piano maker to the emperor, and his piano went on to win first prizes and gold medals at the Vienna Industrial Exhibitions of 1839 and 1845. By the time he died in 1859, Bösendorfer was established as the premier (and virtually the only surviving) Viennese piano maker of repute.

His son Ludwig proved to be a worthy heir, equally alert to opportunity, and the company prospered. Orders from nobility and royalty at home and abroad were soon being filled from a new factory in Vienna begun by Ignaz and completed after his death. Ten years before Ludwig died, however, having no suitable heir who could take over the business, he sold the company to a banking family, the Hutterstrassers. Without much effort on their part, the business thrived. By the beginning of the First World War, Bösendorfer was producing 434 pianos a year. But the war nearly halved production, and in the twenties the invention of more readily stimulating pastimes—the radio, the phonograph, movies, and nightclubs—decimated the piano industry around the world. The onset of the Great Depression added injury to insult, and in 1933, while doggedly maintaining every standard of quality, the firm completed only 40 instruments. The Second World War brought Bösendorfer's production virtually to a standstill—and wiped out Blüthner and Bechstein as well. In 1944 Allied bombing blew apart the Bösendorfer lumberyard, the factory was later wrecked by artillery, and at the end of the war many of its technicians fled from the occupying Russian soldiers, who camped in the showrooms, splintering pianos to feed open fires on the parquet floors. (Steinway was the only quality piano factory in Europe left even partially standing in 1945, and it is largely on this good luck that its current predominance in Europe is founded.)

Facing page: The woodworking department of the Wiener Neustadt plant. Here the raw wood is cut up into various sizes and shapes, planed and sanded, and then assembled into the piano's basic parts. On the wall, like model railway yards, are assembling patterns, which hold smaller components in position while a larger part is being glued together. In the foreground are keyboard pieces for the outer case.

In each of the first two years of peace Bösendorfer gamely managed somehow to build 11 instruments. The number climbed slowly thereafter, and by the mid-1960s Bösendorfer was assembling about 100 grands a year. (Steinway of Hamburg, in contrast, was producing 1,700 grands a year, its New York partner about 2,000.) Bösendorfer was financially weak by that time besides, and the Hutterstrassers were not enterprising. It was at this juncture that Kimball took over.

Quite naturally, given the relative size of the two companies, there were fears that the factory would be streamlined and automated, and that craftsmanship would succumb to cost accounting. At this writing, those fears have not been realized. Kimball had itself been bought in the late fifties by the Jasper Corporation, a wood-products firm run by the Habig family of Indiana. The Habigs, whose ancestry is Austrian, purchased Bösendorfer precisely for its tradition, and they apparently gave a free hand to the firm's managing director in Vienna, Dr. Roland Radler, who had been with the company since 1961 and had felt himself hamstrung by the inertia of the previous owners. From the time Kimball assumed ownership to 1980, Bösendorfer's work force grew to 250 men and women, and the number of pianos that left the factory each year rose to 750.

And still in 1980 Bösendorfer proudly called itself "the slowest piano makers in the world," citing a total building time of sixty-two weeks (more than five years if the seasoning of the wood is included). The Kimball grand, by contrast, was allotted fourteen weeks' assembly time. For much of its time the Bösendorfer's component parts simply sit quietly, sorting out internal problems like a butterfly

Facing page: Top, plates stacked in an open shelter, like a cast-iron wave about to break. They rest for some six months, allowing the internal stresses set up at the foundry as the iron cooled to be slowly resolved. Workers check for interior flaws by tapping and noting any telltale sounds. Exposure to rain would rust the plates, but direct exposure to the extremes of weather aids their seasoning. *Bottom,* plates being sanded. A penetrating scream and the sharp smell of burning metal fill the air as rotary sanders smooth the blemishes from the raw iron surface.

A craftsman fitting the wooden pin block to the raw iron plate. He finds gaps by probing between the two surfaces with a wafer-thin blade, then planes down the wood until the fit is tight. The precise matching of the pin block and plate rules out the danger of unequal stress on the pin block and resultant cracks. Since all iron plates have their own idiosyncratic shape, matching components to a specific one makes each piano individual in character.

in chrysalis. The promotional literature of 1981 waxed lyrical on this subject: "We are building not just an industrial product but a musical instrument which is something living. Living things need a rest now and then in the course of growing, to help settle childhood problems."

In its basic design, the Bösendorfer is of course like every other grand piano. Its circumference, the inner rim, is made of thick planking braced by horizontal struts. On this platformlike structure rests the soundboard, a slightly convex thin wooden diaphragm which resonates in sympathy with the strings and greatly magnifies the volume of sound

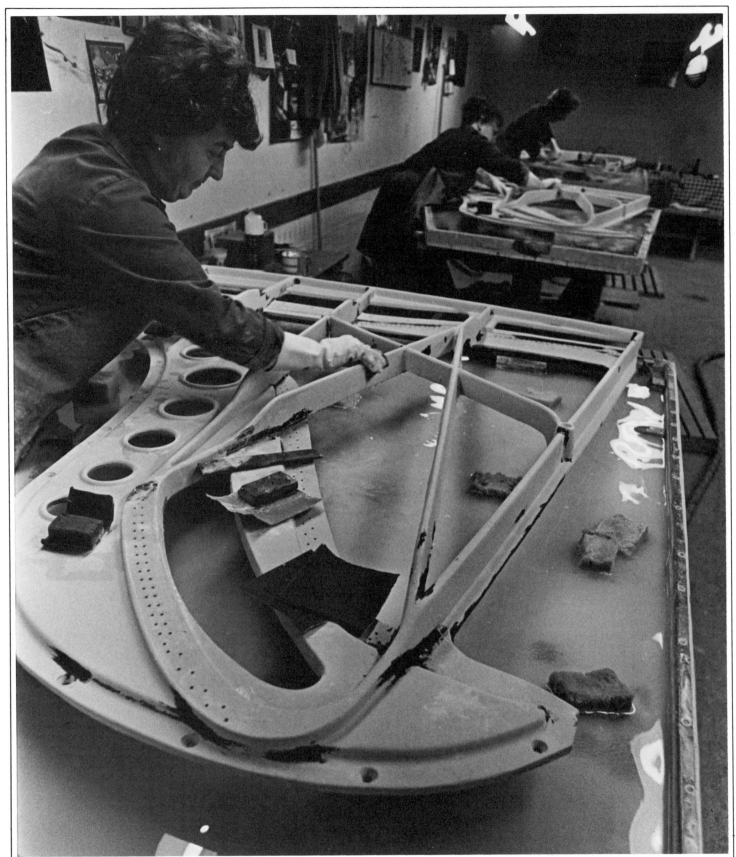

Bösendorfer goes to extraordinary lengths to enhance the surface of the iron plate to no musical purpose whatsoever. First, the iron is sprayed with yellow polyester resin, then it is laboriously rubbed smooth by hand (*above*). The spraying and sanding processes are repeated, and the plates are finally coated with four layers of lacquer. The rich golden-brown finish which is reflected on the inside of the lids of the finished pianos instantly identifies the maker.

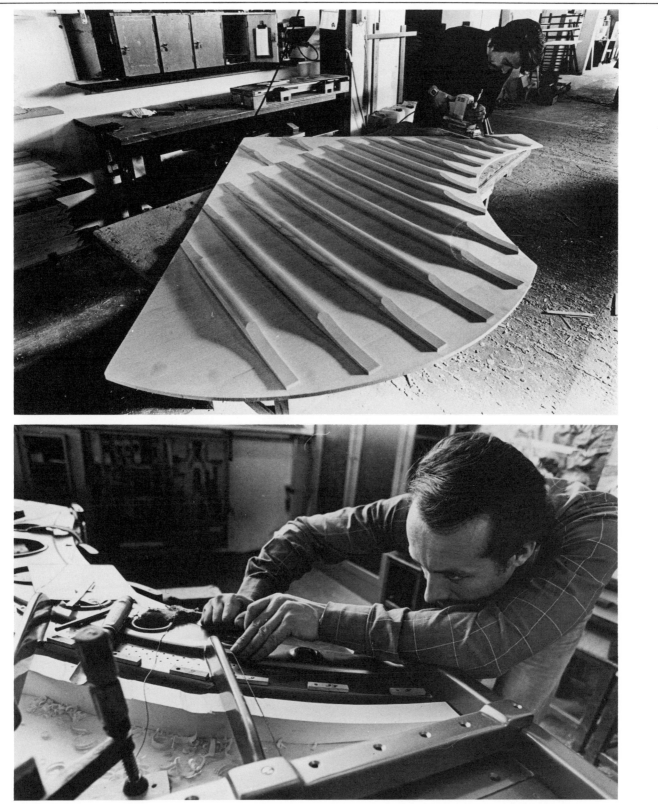

Top, the underside of a solid spruce soundboard, crossed with ribs of solid spruce to improve the conductivity of the board across the grain. *Bottom*, a workman checking the bridges, slim beams of spruce that snake across the top surface of the soundboard. When the piano is assembled, the strings will bear down on these pieces, so that when a note is struck, the energy will be transmitted to the soundboard. The downward pressure of the strings modifies the convexity of the soundboard, so the top surface of the bridges must be gauged precisely to ensure that the curvature of the board is ideal—not too bowed and not too flat. To accomplish this, the craftsman runs a string from the pin block over the bridges at numerous check points.

they produce. Bolted over the soundboard is the harp-shaped iron casting called the plate (frame in Europe). At the plate's back end the strings are attached to fixed hitch pins. At the front end they are wound around tuning pins, which are driven into the wooden pin block fitted to the plate. The whole is then wrapped in an outer casing, and a playing mechanism—keyboard, action, dampers—is inserted into the body. When a key is pressed, the movement is transmitted through the action to the hammer, which strikes the string and rebounds. Since the damper is lifted off the string at the same time, the string trembles rapidly, and the vibration is picked up by the bridges, two S-shaped bars that cross the soundboard and across which the strings are stretched. The soundboard resonates and the piano sounds its full tone.

Even in some particulars the difference between the Bösendorfer and other pianos is not great. Their actions, for example, though made to their specifications, are made by Renner of Germany, the firm that supplies Steinway actions as well. The damper and *sostenuto* pedal mechanisms diverge from others in that they are designed to be more accessible for purposes of adjustment. But that and the care taken by Bösendorfer technicians in their regulation are the Bösendorfer's only significant differences. Where Bösendorfer has distinguished itself is in the construction of the piano's body, that great wing-shaped sandwich of wood topped with iron and

Facing page: Top left, a workman planing the bridges. When the wood has been gouged out at the check points on the bridges, the interstices are planed away until the top surfaces are level. *Top right,* the setting of the bridge pins. *Bottom,* the construction of the inner rim and its bracing struts. In the Bösendorfer the components of the inner rim are made of solid spruce (except for its top layer, which is beech, a wood hard enough in which to secure the screws that hold down the soundboard). Solid spruce is used instead of laminations in the inner rim—and the outer case as well—so that the entire body of the piano will resonate in sympathy with the strings, not merely the soundboard. Unlike the side of a Steinway, which, when rapped with a knuckle, gives a dull knock like a tabletop, the side of a Bösendorfer rings hollow, like the back of a great, thick-sided cello.

rimmed in solid spruce which gives the instrument its characteristic singing tone.

A tour of the factory at Wiener Neustadt, about fifteen kilometers from Vienna, begins in the lumberyard, where sawed lengths of tree trunk lie in neat stacks the size and shape of small barns. There is beech, maple, and other wood, but the slim conifer trunks of spruce predominate. Bösendorfer constructs as much as possible of its piano from this elastic, resonant wood, which is the preferred variety for all piano soundboards. Most of Bösendorfer's spruce comes from a chilly, arid, and mountainous region of Bavaria near the Czech border, where the sap rises slowly and the annual rings grow close together; the wood's density enhances its transmission of sound. In the yard each plank in the pile is separated from its neighbor above and below by struts so that the clean Austrian wind can blow freely through, helping to cure the wood. Bösendorfer allows four to seven years for the curing, depending on the condition of the wood when it arrives.

This quiet outdoor space is a monument to the Bösendorfer philosophy of piano building: the willingness to take as much time as necessary—perhaps more. The company could perfectly well use, at some point, the shortcut now almost universal in piano making, the electric oven or drying kiln. But it prefers tradition and nature. Inside the factory, after the wood has been sawed, planed, and sanded into various shapes and sizes for individual parts, it rests for another year or longer in a drying room, until its internal humidity reaches four percent. No one knows if this measured pace and natural method result in any tonal enhancement of the finished piano, but it is central to the philosophy and identity of the firm.

The wood yard entrance to the factory leads into the woodworking department, where one is surrounded by tidy piles of wood pieces, clean machinery painted red and green, and white ceilings—an atmosphere of strict order that contrasts sharply with the chaos of most piano factories.

In the woodworking department the noisy

Top left, the solid spruce outer rim of the pia[...]
Bösendorfer, whose case rings when tappe[...]
the outer rim is wrapped about the piano[...]
carried out: on the far right, the planing of t[...]
around the frame.

with grooves to make it flexible enough to wrap around the inner rim. Making the outer rim of solid wood is unique to the : laminated cases of other pianos give a dull knock. *Bottom left*, a worker fills in the triangular gaps left by the grooves when erior frame. *Above*, a view of the floor in the Wiener Neustadt factory where the three most basic assembly operations are ndboard bridges to fix the bearing; in the rear left, the construction of the inner rim; in the foreground, the outer rim in place

shrieks and whines of saws, planes, and sanders fill the air. There the raw wood, after its blemishes and cracks are sorted out, is cut into various dimensions. After the pieces have fully dried, they will be fashioned into legs, pedal hangers, rims, lids, and other parts. Among the most important is the pin block, whose top surface is made up of three thick layers of maple glued together with their grains crisscrossed to make a firmer bed for the tuning pins. The maple is backed by numerous laminations of beech, a wood hard enough to resist warping under the terrific pull of the tuned strings.

Next door, in a roofed, open-ended shelter, the gray, glistening cast-iron plates lie like silver stingrays stacked against each other. They are settling—resolving the internal tensions set up at the foundry as the molten iron cooled in the mold. Stresses that conflict sharply enough to cause a structural flaw are detected by a man who taps the plates like a railway wheel checker, listening for signs of trouble in the ringing. After five or six months' rest, the plates are taken into the sanding department. There shrilly screaming hand-held rotary drills send out comet tails of red-gold sparks as the rust and roughness are removed from the plate surface. Holes are drilled, then, for the plate hitch pins, the hand-guided, bench-mounted drills carving up iron shavings like gray butter.

Nowhere else do plates receive the royal treatment accorded to Bösendorfer's. After being sprayed with a yellow polyester cement, they are taken to a room where they are set above large water trays and laboriously rubbed smooth by the gloved hands of women who work in a silence broken only by radio music, the scratches of the sanding, and the slop of the water shivering below the plates. After the second spraying and hand sanding, the smooth plate is coated with red nitro lacquer overlaid with two coats of bronze paint and one of clear lacquer. The cold iron now boasts a delightful silk-smooth surface glowing with warm autumnal color. The appeal is purely aesthetic; the surface work makes no difference at all in the piano's tone.

Wood and iron meet for the first time when the pin block is fitted to the plate. The careful matching of this wooden piece to the plate epitomizes one

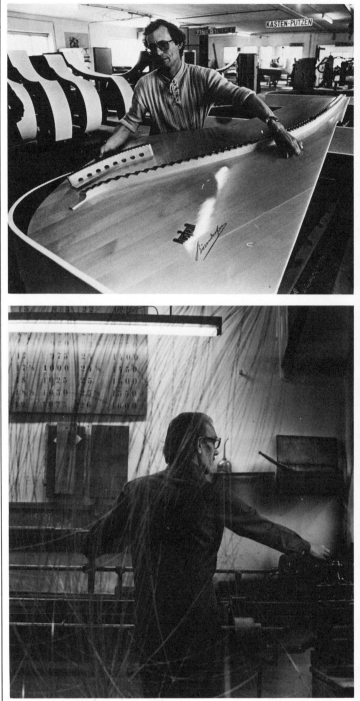

Top, a finished soundboard being placed into its piano. *Above*, bass and mid-range copper-wound strings being fashioned at an ancient but serviceable belt-driven lathe. The machine stretches the steel core wire from left to right. The operator hammers flat one end of a copper wire, wraps it around the steel string, and switches on the lathe. The copper, fed through finger and thumb, spirals down the steel until it reaches the point where the string should end. The lathe is stopped and the copper end hammered flat and tied. *Right*, the stringing of the piano. When this job is done, the sounding portion of the instrument is complete. All that remains to be done is the insertion of the keyboard, the action, and the damper assembly, the regulation of the action, and final finishing of the case in the Vienna workshop.

practically significant effect of the Bösendorfer method: it recognizes the individuality of each iron plate. Throughout the factory, every piece of every piano down to the smallest two-inch propstick dowel has a number written on it, identifying the particular plate to which it belongs. The fitting of the pin block to its plate is accomplished by a craftsman with a wafer-thin blade with which he probes the interstice, marking any gaps with a pencil and then hand-planing the wood until there is no room at all for the blade. Because the fit is tighter than in any mass-produced instrument, the block will be more stable in the piano, where it is subjected to the great, constant pull of the strings. Unlike other pianos, the Bösendorfer pin block is open, not covered by the plate—a feature that allows the tuning pins to be driven more deeply into the wood. Since the pins are thus more firmly held and bend less with the pull of the strings, tuning is easier and more durable.

The fitting of the soundboard to the plate is crucial to the tone of the instrument. The soundboard is made up of vertically grained planks of spruce, about a hand's breadth across, glued together in a sheet. Sound travels rapidly along wood grain, slowly across it. Ribs of solid spruce are fastened beneath the soundboard across the grain so that it resonates fully in both directions. The whole is pressed together and glued in a large vertical press, which holds the soundboard against the curved ribs. When set, it emerges with a convex silhouette or "crown." The two snakelike bridges are then glued and pressed in place on its surface. (Bösendorfer uses solid maple bridges, rather than laminated ones, to enhance their conductivity.)

When the plate is on top of the soundboard in the piano casing, the strings, once they are tuned taut, press down on the bridges of the soundboard. This "down-bearing" should reduce the convexity

---

The action assembly room of the Wiener Neustadt factory, where the pianos are taken once their sounding parts are completely assembled and installed. Here the damper mechanism, keys, and hammer assembly are inserted and given a first rough regulation.

of the soundboard by just the right amount: too little and the board will be flabby and weak-toned; too much and it will be stiff and hard-toned. To achieve the precisely proper bearing, the bridges are hand-planed at Bösendorfer. (Mass manufacturers design and build the several parts to specifications and adjust the bearing by moving the plate. This risks minute errors in the bearing and very large differences in the tonal quality of the piano.) With the plate on top of the soundboard, a thread is run from the hitch pin to the pin block at thirty checkpoints on the bridges, mimicking the piano string that will eventually be installed. Then the bridge is planed with a razor-thin chisel until the height is ideal.

The sounding parts, still separate but already fitted to one another, are ready at this point to be put into the body of the piano, which is built in another part of the factory. Its construction, which is unique to Bösendorfer, has a great deal to do with the piano's special sound.

The inner rim and the supporting beams that crisscross the bottom of the piano are built entirely of top-grade spruce, except for a beech top surface to take the screws that hold down the soundboard and plate. More important, the outer rim, which forms the entire side casing of the piano and is composed in most of laminations, is made at Bösendorfer of solid white soundboard spruce, veneered on its faces with four millimeters of mahogany. The thick plank is bent by cutting deep grooves in its flank, which compress together as the

Once the damper mechanism is installed, the piano is worked over by an automatic playing machine, a noisy contraption set off in a narrow, two-story room. The machine is no virtuoso; it moves all the keys at once in a regular, steam-engine-like series of thumps. The playing is otherwise silent; the hammers have been removed. Three hours of this workout are given to each piano.

Facing page: Top, a worker installs the action assembly. *Bottom,* once the action is on it, the keyboard moves to the table of a technician who, among other things, sands away the hard outer layer of felt on the new hammer heads. As is evident in the top photograph, all white keys on Bösendorfers are faced with a single piece of ivory, without the seam visible in standard two-piece coverings. Only pianos bound for very hot climates are fitted with plastic, since ivory does not keep out humidity and will therefore come unglued. It is precisely the nonporous quality of plastic that makes many pianists detest it as a covering for keys: it does not absorb sweat and thus becomes slippery during performances.

casing is wrapped around the inner rim. The theory is that if the entire body of the piano is a single thickness of spruce, and not merely the soundboard, it will resonate in sympathy with the strings like the body of a guitar or a violin. Unlike the side of a Steinway, which, when rapped with a knuckle, gives a dull knock like a tabletop, the side of a Bösendorfer rings hollow, like the back of a great, thick-sided cello. The effect is to give the piano's tone a peculiar bloom, a rounded, open quality that gives volume without hardness in the bass and midrange and a bell-like quality in the treble. Modern high-fidelity speakers that mix direct and reflected sound offer much the same kind of enhanced aural image.

When the outer rim has set, the structure forms

Facing page: Completely assembled now, except for some unfinished case work, the pianos are taken to the Vienna workshop, where the motions of the action are adjusted to within tolerances of a millimeter or less. The accuracy of this work determines the "feel" and responsiveness of the action. *This page: Top,* a craftsman regulates the backcheck, which catches the hammer on the rebound after it has struck the string. The hammer must be caught precisely twelve millimeters from the string if the action is to be capable of fine repetition. *Bottom,* a technician voices the hammers. The felt is pricked with needles to achieve the desired tone, volume, and evenness of scale. The job requires a keen subjective faculty and the result is individually distinct; Bösendorfer's technicians say they can nearly always tell which of them voiced a particular instrument. The nine extra black bass keys identify this model as an Imperial concert grand.

After final regulation, the piano is lacquered, sanded, and buffed to a brilliant polish. Even though the surface is tough, highly resistant to marring, and easily repaired if spoiled, the finishing is left for last to minimize the risk of damage.

a hollow receptacle into which the soundboard and iron plate can be fitted and screwed down. The piano is then strung. In the Bösendorfer each string is tied to its own hitch pin; in others, the wire is looped around the pin in back and returned to make two strings. Thus if a Bösendorfer string breaks in concert, only one note is spoiled, and the string will probably fly up out of the way instead of being held down to touch other wires and cause a buzz. Another asset of the Bösendorfer string section is a separate pressure (or *capo d'astro*) bar in the treble section of the plate. This is screwed on separately rather than built in as part of the plate as it is in other pianos. This has the effect of insulating the strings from the deadening effect of the plate as the bar serves its function, which is to hold the strings firmly down when they are struck. On the

Bösendorfer the brass agrafes (screws with holes in their flat heads for the strings to pass through) are fitted to the plate by hand to ensure that the string plane is perfectly level and the scale even.

With the strings in place, the sounding part of the piano is complete. The only assembly that remains to be done is the insertion of the keyboard, the action, and the dampers. At this point the raw pianos stand under a notice that reads *"Endcontrolle,"* and there they wait until they are driven into Vienna for final adjustment and finishing.

The plant in Vienna is a fine old pink-brown building with arched windows on a side street. It was a convent when Ludwig Bösendorfer bought it in the last century, and the nuns' bell still hangs high on a wall in the courtyard. The huge trucks from Wiener Neustadt have barely enough room to pass under the gateway arch into the yard. When the pianos are unloaded, they are hauled to the top floor, where the apprentice craftsmen undertake the first of three exacting action regulations. In its journey through this building, the piano will be tuned at least six times and often more.

On the second floor the piano cases are finally given a finish of polyester lacquer. The action and keyboard are removed and the works covered with paper. The body and parts are sprayed and later sanded and buffed to a brilliant high polish. Only final tuning and voicing are to follow, so the danger of marring the mirrorlike surface is minimal. Tuned for the last time, the instrument is complete, ready for the showroom in this building or for shipment to other dealers and waiting customers.

There is something impressive about the Bösendorfer that has nothing whatever to do with its musical merit but pertains rather to the spirit signified by those steps in its construction which have no practical purpose whatever: the laborious rubbing of the plate, for example, and the slow natural curing of the wood. One is struck no more by the physical order of the factory than by its spiritual order: the workers very clearly like their jobs. The fact that visitors come stimulates pride, of course; the Bösendorfer factory has come to rival the Vienna Riding School as a tourist attraction. But there

A lid is given its final buffing to a high polish.

is also a sense of satisfaction among the Bösendorfer workers that can derive only from a proud sense of craftsmanship. Their involvement in their work is consciously encouraged by the company's policy of distributing among them free tickets to concerts—and asking performers who come to the showroom to choose a piano and give a short performance for the apprentices. Piano makers are notorious for being unable to play the instruments they make, but most of the workers at the workshop in Vienna and many in Wiener Neustadt play one or more instruments well. In an age that celebrates quantity more than quality, Bösendorfer represents a salutary adherence to the craft tradition, particularly so since that adherence through wars and depression very nearly brought the firm down. In resisting mechanization and standardization to the extent that it has—and in building each piano so precisely to fit a single iron plate—the firm constructs not only a superb instrument but a thing unique, something that may not be exactly reproduced. It is fitting that the piano that results is so demanding, meting out its rewards in mercilessly direct proportion to the player's merit. Why should its charms, so painstakingly crafted, be easily given away?

I do not mean to imply that Bösendorfer is the only such exemplar of high craftsmanship; it is simply the one at hand. Like the Steinway, the Bechstein, and other great pianos, it gives reassurance that technology cannot match the human hand and eye and that actions taken with purpose, even in the absence of proven practical effect, have meaning. When animated by the fingers of a great player, the Bösendorfer seems hard to separate from the art it serves. But even when it is still it touches the aesthetic sense that quivers in the presence of quality and idealism. If an object produced in a factory can ever be called a work of art, the Bösendorfer is one. And if it is a work of craft and not of art, it is most certainly a thing of beauty.

Franz Mohr, in the Basement at Steinway & Sons in New York.

IV

DOMINIQUE BROWNING

Finding the Sound

Portrait of a Master Technician

One winter night in 1943 the American air force bombed the Hochschule für Musik in Cologne, Germany, where Franz Mohr was a student. Mohr ran from his house and by the time he got there, all the buildings were on fire. As he watched them burn, he heard the music that instruments make when they are dying. Instruments caved in with a wild jangle of sound. Piano strings screeched and snapped. In the concert hall an organ burst into flames. As hot air rushed through the organ's pipes, it began to bellow and wail. The sound of it has haunted Mohr ever since.

Since 1965 Franz Mohr has been the chief concert technician of Steinway & Sons. His job is to keep fine pianos alive. Mohr is one of a populous breed of craftsmen who build and maintain pianos, some in private homes, some in music schools and concert halls. His trade is widely malpracticed and misunderstood, but Mohr is universally regarded by his peers as a master. He presides over a legendary collection of artists' concert grands under the Steinway showroom on West Fifty-seventh Street in Manhattan, known among musicians all over the world simply as the Basement. By the charter of William Steinway in 1865, any artist may borrow a piano to play in concert from the Basement (or from one of its three hundred outlets across the United States) for the cost of the necessary tuning and round-trip carting. In return Steinway usually receives a credit line on the artist's program and in advertisements for the concert. Mohr's regular visitors in the Basement have included virtually every major concert artist—Gilels, Gould, Horowitz, Richter, Rubinstein, and Serkin among them—and many less famous pianists as well. Mohr has estimated that 250 artists avail themselves of this service each year, and each of their pianos—indeed, every one of the concert grands that leave the Steinway factory in Long Island every year—is indebted to his scrutiny.

When Mohr is at the keyboard, it will most likely be resting on a massive oak workbench. His spotlight in the otherwise dimly lit, windowless space is a long fluorescent work light suspended from a ceiling that is covered with plumbing and heating

William Hupfer in the Basement in 1964. Hupfer was chief concert technician when Mohr joined Steinway & Sons in 1963. When Hupfer retired in 1965, Mohr took over.

pipes. Mohr's work is physical, but the artistry of the technician is as mysterious and elusive as sound itself. Though tuning is important, the technician's most critical responsibilities are action regulation (seeing that the moving parts of the piano operate smoothly and precisely) and tone regulation or "voicing." The technician cannot change the character of an instrument, but he is charged in the voicing procedure with developing to the fullest its natural voice, an operation that involves subjective judgments of every instrument's essential character. "We are dealing with materials that are natural,"

THE LIVES OF THE PIANO

Mohr told a visitor to the Basement in 1980. "Wood, felt, metals. There are subtle differences in trees grown in different parts of the country. The age of a piano has a lot to do with its quality; often, a young or new piano is not opened up, the sound is closed. Some pianos are born chamber music instruments. They are pretty, but they never have a big enough sound for a concert hall. Other pianos have a huge voice, which many artists cannot control."

In the Basement on this particular day Mohr was surrounded by about twenty of the sixty grands in his inventory. They were arranged back to back, tails tucked into each other, in two massive rows. Every piano has a serial number printed inside its case, and as Mohr talked, the numbers became names. "Three-twenty-one has a rich, mellow tone, but it's a little weak in the treble section these days," he said. "It has been taking a beating at music festivals all summer. Forty-one has a bright tone and a light action. It is hard to control, though. It tends to run away under the fingers. Three-forty-three is beautiful and quiet, easy to control. A good pianist can coax a range of sounds from it. He can take risks that aren't really risky. Thirty-five is like silk all the way through."

It takes years of training and practice to become a piano technician, and there is no special characteristic that can be singled out as a sign of a great one, unless, as William Hupfer, Mohr's predecessor in the Basement, once said, it is that "you've got to be a little off the beam." Though there is some physical strain in a technician's work, especially in the arm muscles, it is the emotional frustration of learning that takes its toll on many students.

Mohr has insisted that the aspiring technicians who come to the Basement as his assistants learn to give a piano a solid and deep tuning—one that will last through a heavy session of playing—before they learn regulation. (He claims he once tuned a piano that Horowitz played in Chicago before it was shipped to New York City, where it sat for two weeks until it was sent to Boston. There Horowitz played it again before Mohr had a chance to work on it, and the piano was still in tune.) Many professional tuners do not meet Mohr's standards.

He has listened to pianists play instruments that slipped gradually out of tune in the course of a three-hour recital. He has met tuners who can tune uprights but are incapable of working with grands. Mohr believes that when a tuner is trying to reach a certain pitch he must try to get a feel for the way the entire string works, not just listen for the right tone. It took Mohr's assistant of six years, Ron Conners, four months to tune a piano to Mohr's satisfaction. It was tedious work, and Ron complained of headaches that seemed to last for days. Yet the real challenge—and art—is in hearing tone quality. To Mohr the main difficulty in teaching a student how to voice a piano has been in finding words to evoke an instrument's *Spielart*, a German term Mohr hit upon while talking of different pianos with Rubinstein. The word means, roughly, "speaking nature" or "speaking quality." Many people simply cannot grasp that an instrument can have a *Spielart*.

Very few Steinway artists understand—or want to know—exactly what Mohr does to their instruments. "Sound is tremendously mysterious," Mohr told his visitor. "An artist hears musically; I hear technically. I listen to beats, to sets of waves, and must trust my ears and my feelings to judge the character of an instrument." As he spoke, his hands never stopped moving; he ran his fingers over keyboards, and plucked strings, and lifted rows of hammers and let them drop freely, one by one. He was always watching, listening. Artists who have chosen one of his pianos sometimes try to articulate a vague suspicion that something might be wrong with its tone. (Often the problem is simply that the piano needs a good tuning.) Or they try to describe a sound they hear in their mind's ear, expecting that Mohr will make the piano match that sound. But mainly they trust Mohr's judgment, and he takes that trust to heart. "When an artist is unhappy, I am heartbroken, even if I cannot understand what it is that bothers him. I suffer if he does."

One morning Mohr came into the Basement and noticed on his workbench a message scrawled on a white index card with green felt-tip marker: "Dear

Franz, The Hamburgs are beautiful. I like No. 328 especially, but the voicing in the treble notes is uneven. With warm regards, Sir Clifford Curzon." The British pianist, in the United States at the start of a concert tour, had added a little drawing to indicate the range of notes on the German-built Steinway—from E-flat above middle C to the E two octaves above—which he thought needed voicing.

It is not unusual for Mohr to find such a message; they are left frequently by those he calls "my nocturnal artists," the ones who insist on being let in by the Steinway security guard to select their pianos in the dead of night when the Basement is deserted. Richter, Claudio Arrau, Rudolf Serkin,

Sir Clifford Curzon, a British concert pianist, a consummate tone colorist—and one of Mohr's most outspokenly grateful clients. He always makes his U.S. tours with a Steinway from the Basement collection.

and Van Cliburn are among the pianists who rarely come to the Basement in the daytime, and Mohr respects their need for solitude. "If there is a cat in the room with me," Curzon once told him, "I am conscious of it. I am playing for it."

Knowing that Curzon enjoyed playing a Hamburg Steinway when he toured Europe, Mohr had opened the two new Hamburg concert grands that Steinway had recently purchased before he left work the night of Curzon's visit. Now he asked one of his assistants to roll 328 to his work area under the lamp. Mohr put on the old white lab coat he always wears while working and emptied the contents of his black tool bag, no bigger than a man's shaving kit, onto the workbench. He had a very different idea from Curzon's of how much work 328 would need before it was truly presentable.

Mohr was born in 1927 in Düren, Germany. His parents loved music, and Franz and his two brothers often entertained each other, forming guitar, piano, accordion, and violin ensembles. At the Hochschule für Musik in Cologne, he studied violin and oboe as well as theory and composition. Then, shortly after the Hochschule was bombed, Mohr was drafted into military service. His older brother, who had gone into the army some months before, had been declared missing; the Mohrs eventually learned that he had been taken prisoner in Russia and killed. Franz hated military life and spent a few months in misery until he got a few days of leave in November of 1944. The reunion with his parents and younger brother lasted one day. On the next, American fighter planes wiped out the town of Düren. More than twenty-two thousand people, ninety-eight percent of the population, were killed in twenty minutes. Franz escaped with his parents, but his younger brother was buried in the rubble that had been their house. "I remember looking back to our town from surrounding hills. It was a sight I will never forget. It is carved into my heart as long as I live. All the fires of the burning city joined together in one big funnel. In the blackness of this funnel we could see the explosion of bombs." Franz deserted the military and went into hiding in the German countryside.

Above, Mohr as a teenager, when he hoped for a career as a violinist. *Above right*, building a piano in 1948 at Ibach, a piano-manufacturing company in Wuppertal. *Right*, with his parents in 1955 at their home in Düren, Germany.

The bombing of Düren was devastating to Franz; for years he felt nothing but hate for the Germans who had started the war, for the Americans who had killed one brother, and for the Russians who had killed the other. Franz could find no consolation in the religious beliefs that had been instilled in him as a child by his strict Roman Catholic parents, and, unable to reconcile the existence of God with the horrors of the war he had witnessed, he rejected God.

In time he enrolled in the Nordwest Deutsche Musikakademie in Detmold to continue his education and began to play guitar in a Dixieland band with friends. The group played for American soldiers at drunken barracks parties where the soldiers amused themselves by throwing live grenades out the windows while the frightened musicians hid behind an upright piano. "My life was wild in those days, but I was never scared enough to quit," Mohr says. "All of Germany was starving at the time. But the band had everything we wanted—food, girls, money, black-market cigarettes, even a car. One evening, while we were waiting at a barracks to perform, our manager got up very quietly, went out to the backyard, and put a bullet through his head. I never found out why. But he had been the one who seemed to have it all figured out, who knew how to survive. He was showing us how to do it. His suicide made me think hard about what I was doing."

When he was eighteen Mohr dropped out of the Dixieland band and went back to his parents' home. He continued his studies in music until chronic pain in his wrist made it clear that a concert career as a violinist would be impossible. Finally Mohr left music school and went to work at Ibach, a large piano-manufacturing company in Wuppertal. The training was comprehensive and rigorous. Mohr worked directly under a master craftsman stringing pianos, putting in dampers, building actions and installing them, tuning, and regulating. He was at Ibach for nearly six years, and his skill and devotion to the work steadily increased. He discovered that he loved working with his hands, and when he sat down to play a piano, he took great satisfaction in knowing so intimately what was going on inside.

During this time Mohr returned to church with his parents; he could not help but think about the faith he had lost. One night he had a vision that convinced him that he could find his faith again; as a consequence he decided to join the Baptist Church. Ecstatic, Mohr told his family of his religious awakening. His parents were shocked. His father, declaring that he had lost his third and only remaining son, asked him to leave the house. Mohr went to the industrial city of Essen, and in 1952 he was baptized there. In 1954 he married a woman he had met in Essen, who shared his faith. Their first son was born within the year.

For almost ten years, Mohr commuted from Essen to work at the Düsseldorf branch of Steinway's extensive dealership network; he was a tuner, technician, concert manager, and troubleshooter for Steinway in western Germany. In 1962 he saw a notice placed by a New York City Baptist church in his local church bulletin that offered aid to would-be émigrés. Franz responded, and to his amazement the pastor wrote back immediately to tell him that Steinway & Sons in New York was looking for a tuner and that an apartment had been set aside for the family. By September the Mohrs were in New York City. "When I decided to come to America, I had every paper I'd ever received—certificates of piano-building apprenticeships, diplomas from schools—translated into English, at great personal expense. I even had them sealed by a notary. When I got to Steinway in New York, I tried to show my precious papers to the vice-president who had hired me. 'Put them away, Franz,' he said. 'You start at the beginning like everyone else.' I was so upset that William Hupfer, who was Steinway's chief concert technician at the time, took pity on me and looked them over. And then

---

Facing page: Top, pulling the key bed into his lap, Mohr checks the movement of the hammers; using a screwdriver (*bottom left*), he adjusts the lateral position of each hammershank at its base to ensure that every hammer will come straight up and strike the piano strings squarely; later he works on the repetition section of the action, adjusting the balancier with a regulating tool (*bottom right*) so that every note can be repeated with ease and velocity.

I started at the beginning." After two years of working as a tuner and regulator in the retail division, however, Mohr was transferred to the Basement. When Hupfer retired in 1965 at the age of sixty-nine, Mohr took his place.

The transition to concert work in America was smooth; Mohr had worked with many of Steinway's artists during their European tours, and they gave him a warm reception in New York. Mohr worried only about meeting Rubinstein, who had refused to play in Germany. (Rubinstein later told Mohr that there were only two places in the entire world he would not play: the Himalayas, because they were too high, and Germany, because it was too low.) To Mohr's relief and pleasure, Rubinstein welcomed him warmly to America in German.

Mohr turned his attention to Curzon's piano, 328, which his assistants had rolled over to his workbench. Like all Hamburg Steinways, 328 had a polyester finish that made it very shiny. TV crews hate pianos like 328 because they reflect light so vividly. And, like all Hamburgs, it would be difficult to care for. The finish bruises easily and, when it does, it looks awful. The wood in the Hamburg comes from Africa. It is dried at a lower temperature than the wood in American-made Steinways and therefore cannot withstand the severe temperature and humidity changes of the American climate. The sounding board cracks easily, and the piano does not hold a tuning very long. Yet Mohr had lobbied intensely to get the Hamburgs to New York, arguing that the European artists who were accustomed to them should be able to use them during their U.S. tours. Number 328 was indeed impressive: when the piano's tail was up, the brass plate inside cast a warm, rich reflection onto the shiny black lid. Under Mohr's bright lamp, the entire piano seemed to glow.

Mohr began by regulating 328's action. Each technician has his own ritual for this procedure (which is always done before the voicing), but the basic techniques of giving a keyboard consistency are universal. Mohr removed the key blocks and, as though he were pulling out a drawer, slid the key bed into his lap and hoisted it onto his workbench. He lifted off the brass carriage that supports the action—the action hanger—and set it aside. Next he took off the key stop rail, a narrow wooden bar across the keys that helps to keep them aligned. The keys, made from one block of wood, seemed to want to heal their eighty-seven long wounds. "This is fresh wood," Franz explained, "and as it expands, things get tight." He could hardly budge each key from side to side. Lifting each one off its guide pin, he loosened the felt bushing lining each hole with key-easing pliers. When he finished, he jiggled each key to make sure it moved freely on its pin. Next he checked 328's "hammer traveling" to ensure that each hammer came straight up to strike the strings squarely. He began with the hammer-

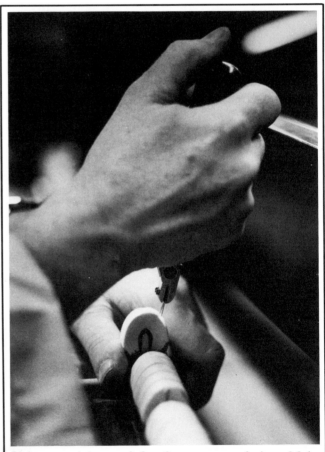

Using a voicing tool for fine tone regulation, Mohr wedges the needles into the dense felt of the hammer to loosen its fibers and make it give a warmer, mellower sound.

shanks, sliding a ruler under the shanks and lifting them in groups of about twenty. Those that slid left or right instead of rising straight up were marked with chalk. Then, having loosened the screw at the base of each wayward shank, he slipped in corrective paper—a thin sliver of wet adhesive tape—and glued it to the hammer rail. That done, he turned his attention to the vertical line of the hammers themselves. Some of the hammers were cocked at odd angles; Mohr corrected each one by heating the underside of the shank with a small alcohol lamp and bending the hammer into place.

Mohr slipped the action into and out of the case many times, making minuscule but critical adjust-

ments. With the action in, he went over the screws (called let-off regulating screws) that regulate the height at which the fly kicks off the knuckle. Then, with the action out, he adjusted the drop screws at the end of the hammershank flanges that regulate how far the hammer drops away from the strings before it strikes. Then he smoothed out the horizon of the hammer line, raising or lowering each hammer by turning its capstan screw. To ensure rapid, smooth repetition, he bent the repetition springs slightly where necessary, then aligned the balancier, the fly, and the knuckle. These adjustments threw some hammers out of line. They were heated and brought back. The backchecks at the end of each key had to be studied and adjusted so that they

With gentle strokes of a sand file, Mohr rubs some loose felt from a hammer that is making a muted sound.

To make sure that the hammer's fall is stopped at the correct height, Mohr adjusts the position of the fly to the knuckle.

would catch the heels of the falling hammer as high as possible to allow good repetition. Mohr slid the action back into the case to see how the hammers hit the strings. He held each hammer against its strings and plucked each string with his fingernail. Every one should have been muffled by the hammer; some were not, indicating uneven hammer tops. These were given a few light strokes of his sand file.

Because 328 was new, there were fewer problems with the action than there would be once the piano had been played for several months. Still, Mohr believes that every piano leaves the factory a few days too soon; he takes nothing for granted about an instrument's condition. "You see, each piano has its own problems, and each problem requires a different amount of attention. We could never be

paid piecework in my department, as they are beginning to do at the Steinway factory. It bothers me when some artists do not give me the time I need to do my work. I cannot perform five-minute miracles. Thirty, maybe." So far, the regulation of 328's action had taken almost four hours.

Curzon's piano was now ready for voicing. The shape and density of the hammers, particularly of the felt that touches the strings, are critical to tone quality. When a hammer is not properly shaped, it cannot bring the strings to the full potential of vibration: if the area of felt that touches the strings is too large, the resulting sound will be dead, unfocused; if the hammer is too pointed—if the amount that hits the strings is too small—the sound will be tinny. Hammers are misshapen by use. Because 328 was new, no shaping was necessary. But

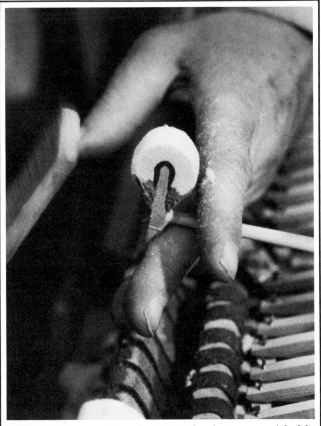

Mohr rarely touches the top of a hammer with his sand file; a hammer lasts longer if the felt on its tip is preserved.

also because it was new, its hammers needed softening. With the keyboard in place, Franz worked his way up the keyboard note by note, being careful to apply the same pressure to each key. He made a small chalk mark on each key that sounded too loud. The piano had many more rough spots than Curzon had noticed, and they were not confined to the range he had outlined. When Franz had covered the keys, he pulled the action forward into his lap. From his workbench he took a voicing tool—three fine needles mounted in a five-inch wooden handle. The voicing tool separates and loosens the interlocking wool fibers to produce a warmer, mellower sound. Mohr worked the needles into each hammer that he had singled out. The new felt was so dense he had trouble getting the needles in. When he had rubbed out every chalk mark, he replaced the action

and worked through the keys once again. This time he decided that some of the notes were too muted. He marked those, slid the action into his lap, and went to work with a sand stick. If a note is too soft, it means the hammer is not dense enough. One way to correct this is to file some of the looser felt off the outside of the hammer. Mohr gently rubbed off felt, using quick strokes up each side, or shoulder, of the hammer. He rarely touched the top, because a hammer lasts longer if the felt on its tip is preserved. It takes years to develop a feel for how much pressure and how many strokes to apply to a hammer when filing; a novice can easily ruin a set of hammers within fifteen minutes.

Voicing a piano to bring out a certain tone quality is the sort of fine tuning a technician can do after shaping a hammer. It does not change the basic character of an instrument, and some artists, much to Mohr's exasperation, refuse to understand that. Horowitz, having chosen number 41 for a concert recording of the Rachmaninoff Third, asked Mohr to give it a more brilliant voice. He was afraid he would not be heard over the orchestra—a fear many musicians have when they play with accompaniment. As Mohr began to file down the hammers, Horowitz kept insisting that he take off more and more. "I protested all the way, and told him his piano would sound like tin cans. Well, Horowitz got the sound he wanted, but it was the sound of tin cans, and I had to throw away the hammers after his performance. No one else would have used them."

Because Curzon likes a mellow piano, Mohr concentrated on bringing the tone down. The Hamburg had what he called "a typically European sound" anyway; it did not have the depth and richness of most American Steinways. "The sound seems to come from the surface of the piano, somehow," he explained. "It is clear; it simply isn't that powerful. But whether you like that or not is a matter of taste. And program. Debussy would sound excellent on number three-twenty-eight, and so would Mozart, which is what Sir Clifford will play. Now if I were playing Beethoven . . ." He broke off and walked to number 460. "A glorious piano. Or four-twelve, Serkin's piano. It is new,

FINDING THE SOUND

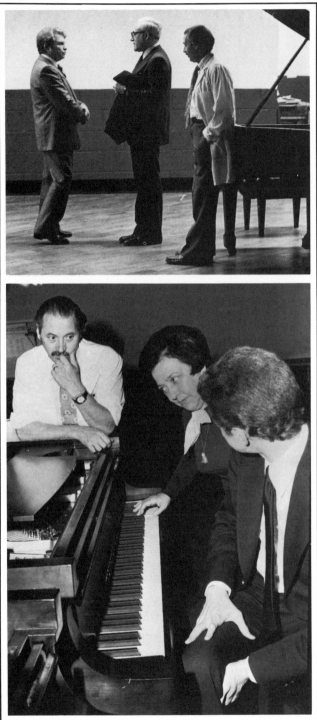

Top, Emil Gilels (*left*) consults Mohr and a Steinway executive on his choice of a piano for a New York concert. *Bottom*, Van Cliburn makes a rare daytime visit to the Basement to choose a piano with help from Mohr and Alicia De Larrocha.

and the tuning hasn't settled in yet as the strings are still stretching, but that is the perfect piano for Rudi." He finished his work on 328 by checking the key level and the aftertouch, then made sure that the lyre was secure and the trap work was operating smoothly. The entire job had taken about six hours.

Mohr would probably be happier if more of the artists he has served so well cared more about understanding his work. One of the few who does is Alfred Brendel, who has often stayed by Mohr's side as his chosen instrument is voiced. But many pianists treat even master technicians like Mohr as handymen. One of Mohr's favorite stories is about the time Horowitz's wife persuaded him not to sit in the wings but to join her in her box for a performance by Horowitz in Chicago's Orchestra Hall. "I had prepared the piano carefully; this was Horowitz's first appearance in many years and he was extremely tense. He performed the first number, a Haydn sonata, I think. I was electrified, on the edge of my seat. No one affects me the way Horowitz does. His performance was brilliant; the piano was fine. He walked offstage as is his custom after the first number, but then he did not come back. The audience grew restless, and I became very uneasy. Suddenly, the door to the box burst open, and a stagehand called me downstairs. It seemed to take forever to get there, and I saw my entire career, Steinway, America, wash down the drain. When I got to the stage, Horowitz turned to me with an air of desperation. 'Where have you been? I cannot play again; the piano stool is much too high!' Horowitz indicated something less than a quarter of an inch with his fingers. I had to go onstage and adjust the seat, and of course the audience, expecting Horowitz, began to applaud. Naturally, I took a polite bow. What else could I do? I was mortified." Mohr's job demands the statesmanship of a diplomat. "It is not always pleasant, but I remind myself that it is a tremendous privilege to work with these artists."

A man who cannot afford a Steinway of his own (even an upright cost in 1980 upwards of $4,400), Mohr must also deal with the discomfort he feels when called upon to attend the high-social events that are part of any pianist's concert schedule. He remembers with particular vividness the time Van Cliburn insisted on his presence at a white-tie reception following a performance he had given at the White House during the Ford administration. Mohr rushed out to rent an appropriate outfit, but late that afternoon discovered that the white tie was missing. Ever resourceful, Mohr bought three handkerchiefs and a sewing kit from a local drugstore and made himself a tie. "It was way too big—I miscalculated somehow—and I felt ridiculous, but Cliburn was delighted with it and made everyone admire my creation." With the passing of years, Mohr has become more amused than embarrassed by such incidents, and if he harbors any anger or frustration he does not show it. "I love my work. I am happy to be doing what I am doing. That is more than many people can say."

His patience is inspired in part by sympathy for the psychic stress he perceives in his eccentric clients. He recalls how furious some of them became when Steinway stopped using ivory to cover the keys. (Since the new plastic key covers do not absorb sweat, the keys become slippery.) With the exception of Rosalyn Tureck, who has been known to clean her keys on stage and still feel that they are dirty, most artists are desperate to find ways to keep the surface of the keys sticky. Mohr once made the mistake of cleaning Rubinstein's keyboard before a performance; his emergency recoup—covering the keys with hair spray—struck Rubinstein as a work of genius, and he carried a can of Elnett Satin from then on. Eugene Istomin had resorted to filing down his keyboard with sandpaper and then rubbing dirt into it. But when he heard about Rubinstein's hair-spray technique, he added a fine mist of lacquer to his recipe. Mohr puts up with it all, though sometimes he is scandalized.

"These people seem to need some peace," he said with a sigh as he opened the lid of 328, which Curzon would be coming in to play that night. "If music were a substitute for God, they might not be tormented all the time. Music is a wonderful thing, and I couldn't live without it. But it will

Mohr, at the keyboard, with his three young assistants (from left, Dan Jessie, Ron Connors, and Jim Cordice), who will leave him eventually to head the concert departments of other companies or to start their own businesses. Most master technicians hold the secrets of their craft closely, but Mohr is generous with his time and wisdom.

never give me the peace my faith brings me."

Mohr's efforts with 328 did not go unappreciated. The little white card Sir Clifford Curzon left for him the next morning said: "Dear Franz, No. 328 is the final choice for all the Philharmonic concerts. You have done miracles with it and Mozart will always be indebted to you." Mohr smiled wryly as he read this message and pushed some graying strands of hair out of his face. "Miracles, he calls it. I just did a little bit more than he expected." Nonetheless he was pleased. Three-twenty-eight was ready for the road.

Mohr gazed fondly at the instrument, then looked out over the others standing in the half-light of the Basement. A rare silence settled over the room. Mohr sat down at 328, wiped off the keys with the corner of his lab coat, smiled contentedly, and played a few measures of Schubert's "Rosamunde," momentarily lost in a dream.

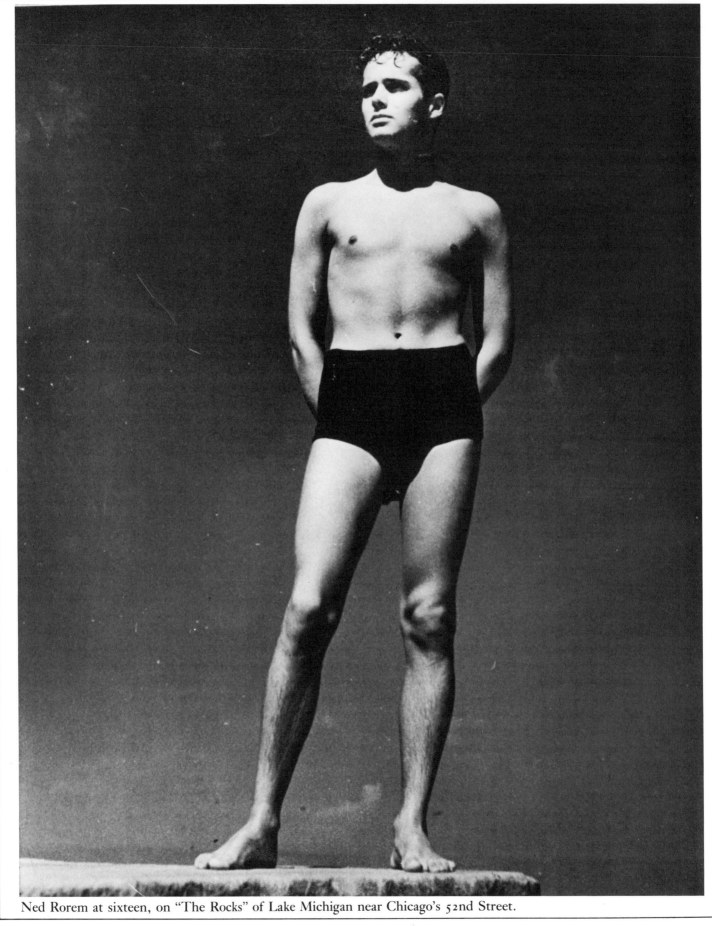

Ned Rorem at sixteen, on "The Rocks" of Lake Michigan near Chicago's 52nd Street.

Beyond Playing

A Composer's Life with the Piano

I am my ideal pianist.

Quick, an explanation.

If I'd rather hear myself play than anyone else, it's not that I'm better than anyone else (there is no "better than"); it's that my fancy fills in missed notes, my inner ear camouflages mere sloppiness. I play just well enough for perfection, whereas virtuosos play too well for perfection. Most great pianists perform the same repertoire. They can't all be right. But I am right for me. Perhaps the gambit should read: The only pianist for my idealized performance is myself.

I have never needed to lament, "If only my parents had forced me to practice!"

In 1972, when I was forty-eight, I wrote in my diary on April 30: "Margaret Bonds is dead. So closes the miniature dynasty of female piano teachers who taught me all I knew by the time I was fifteen. Nuta Rothschild, Belle Tannenbaum, Margaret Bonds, two Jews and a Negro, all dead. In this day or any other it's scarcely revolutionary for a pupil to have a woman tutor. But for a white child to have a black music teacher was not standard practice in Chicago during the 1930s, and is there a reason not to be proud of it? (Margaret was only ten years older than I.)"

In 1975, while working on a "memoir" for Maurice Ravel's centenary, which occurred March 7, I made this aside: "Needing tangible references I removed from an old storage box, labeled *Ravel: Piano*, dozens of crumbling Durand editions procured in high-school days. Keyboard facility then was a curse; wanting quick results I acquired early the skill of fakery, and never practiced. Today my hands recall like yesterday how I counterfeited fingerings. I still play the music in *the same wrong way*. Would it have been so painful to have learned it right? (Recurring dream. Jailors tell me: Sight-read this unknown Ravel scherzo an augmented fourth higher than written, without an error, and you will go free. Miss one note and you are burned alive. . . . But who is the judge?)"

In 1978, on the sixtieth anniversary of Debussy's death, I talked with a friend and later noted: "JH takes exception to the remarks on Debussy, refuting my claim that melody, like sex and food, is actual experience, enjoyable in the present as it unfolds.

JH contends that *harmony* is Now; that melody depends on what has happened while harmony is what is going to happen. Well, both reflections—they are reflections, not assertions—hold water. *Reflets dans l'eau.*"

Six years after Debussy died in Paris, I was born in Indiana, where my father was teaching accounting at Earlham College. At the age of eight months I moved to Chicago, taking the elders with me. My parents, then financially lower middle class (on a professor's salary), were culturally highbrow, and as liberal citizens they were already what they remain today: well-read left-of-center Quaker converts. Mother (Gladys Miller), whose younger brother had been killed at Belleau Wood in 1918, bore that trauma by joining the Society of Friends and becoming a "militant pacifist." Father (Rufus Rorem), the first in his enclave of Norwegian farmers to be elected to Phi Beta Kappa, was fomenting the notions on medical economy—once maligned as socialized medicine—that would evolve into Blue Cross.

Although not specifically musical, our parents "exposed" my sister, Rosemary, and me to concerts, mainly high-class piano recitals.

I recall the hoary sight and sound of that archetypical genius, Paderewski, furrowing his brow 'neath a snowy mane and curving an impudicus o'er his own Minuet in G. (Paderewski's heart—his pickled heart—reposes in a Brooklyn bank vault, deposited there by patriotic Poles after he died in New York in 1941, a relic of the man not only as musician, but as first premier of the newly created Polish nation in 1919.)

I recall the giant specter of Rachmaninoff, his salt-and-pepper crew cut set off by a military tux, hovering over his inevitable Prelude in C-sharp Minor which he deigned to offer as *bis* after a gorgeous version—and my first hearing—of Beethoven's opus 31 no. 3. I was not yet aware of Rachmaninoff as final embodiment of the nineteenth-century virtuoso wherein pianist and composer were one, the composer being not only his own best interpreter but a finished performer of other men's music as well. Nor was I aware of

Rachmaninoff's self-destructive youth by which I would later justify the poignance of my own.

I recall the businesslike stance of Josef Hofmann, acolyte of the legendary Anton Rubinstein, seated at his forty-five-inch Steinway keyboard specially built to accommodate his little hands. Hofmann too was a sometime composer (pseudonym: Michel Dvorsky) and a sometime carouser who in 1926 became for twelve years the director of the Curtis Institute, among whose students I would later be listed and on whose faculty I would eventually preach.

Was it not meet that, on reaching the age of reason, the artistically disposed son of intelligent parents should commence formal training in music?

All piano teachers are women, and they are all called Mrs., the noun—or is it an adjective?—of the safely mated or widowed. There exists no such breed as the male music instructor for beginners, men having more solemn concerns.

Such misconceptions are no less prevalent today than in 1930 when, at age seven, I began to "take piano" from the first of seven women who would represent Art in my early life. Mrs. Pickens, who lived two blocks away on Chicago's Kenwood Avenue, wore purple and served tea brewed from senna leaves after each lesson. With her guidance I quickly mastered "Cherry Blossoms," all on the black keys, and another more complicated number named "Mealtime at the Zoo" in which I *crossed hands*. Soon I graduated to Mrs. Hendry, befriended by my parents at Friends' Meeting. At her students' recital on Blackstone Avenue I played, badly, the Brahms A-flat Waltz, after which I felt undeserving of the hot chocolate and oatmeal cookies served to the assembled families. To this day I'm queasy about eating if I've not worked well, and I still nurse a vague guilt—increasingly vague, thank God—about taking money for the exhaustingly agreeable task of composing music.

After Mrs. Hendry came Aunt Agnes—Mrs. Thompson—who was considered the musician of our clan. (Her daughter Kathleen became first violist of the Toledo Symphony, married the first flutist, and their son Ross Harbaugh is the Cello of the New World Quartet.) But Aunt Agnes lasted for only an Oberlin summertime. In the autumn I began "taking" with Mrs. Davis, spouse of a paternal colleague, and in the spring came the luminous Mrs. Rothschild.

Now, none of those women, before Mrs. Rothschild, provided a sense of need. I may have been learning piano, but I was not learning music. Nuta Rothschild was the Russian wife of art historian Edward Rothschild, and like many a sensitive university wife she had time on her hands. Our first meeting opened the gates of heaven. This was no lesson but a recital. She played Debussy's "L'Isle joyeuse" and "Golliwogg's Cake Walk," and during those minutes I realized for the first time that here was what music is supposed to be. I *didn't* realize that this "modern stuff" repelled your average Music Lover, for it was an awakening sound that immediately, as we Quakers say, spoke to my condition, a condition nurtured by Mrs. Rothschild, who began to immerse me in impressionism. With Perry O'Neil, our grammar school's official genius (he had a scholarship and was elsewhere a pupil of Rudolph Ganz), I would go Saturdays to the record booths of Lyon & Healey's and listen and listen and listen. Debussy led us forward to Ravel and Stravinsky, not backward to Brahms and Verdi, and I was unquestioningly at home with the garish roulades of *Scarbo* and the so-called percussion pianos of *Les Noces* before I'd ever heard a Chopin Nocturne. (I say "so-called percussion" because Stravinsky, like Copland after him, is said to have fostered a new approach to the piano. In fact, Mozart and Beethoven and Liszt and Mussorgsky all treated the piano as the percussion instrument that it is. The difference between the keyboard writing of Stravinsky and, say, Rachmaninoff is not that Stravinsky treats the piano as a percussion instrument, but that with his leaner harmonies and dearth of pedal, he treats it more *percussively.* Both composed percussion music. A piano is always a piano until physically modified, as by John Cage's "preparations," when it becomes a new instrument, but still percussion.) Such scores and disks as we could not afford with our allowances we stole. I devoured Romola Nijinsky's dubious portrait of her husband

Claude Achille Debussy (1862–1918), who, with Ravel, Poulenc, and Messiaen, was one of his country's four greatest composers. He signed himself "Claude de France" and was as cataclysmic a force in French art as Schoenberg was in German art. Debussy's piano works, as inherently tonal as Schoenberg's are not, do depict new perspectives despite their generally foursquare formats.

and Lockspeiser's biography of Debussy, which remains, alas, with its mean, inexpert biases, astonishingly the only extant book on the subject. I had half learned all of Debussy's piano repertoire when Mrs. Rothschild, upon the death of her young husband, left Chicago forever.

Like every other child I hated scales. As soon as I was able to get around the keys, I became more intrigued by improvisation than by practice. I spent whole days pounding our baby grand Starck, making up pieces but not writing them down (except for the titles: "Tragic Bubbles on the Ruby Lagoon," "Corpse in the Meadow," "A Streamlined Carol"). Most parents do not have a preadolescent son who prefers Scriabin to softball, nor does every

Josef Hofmann—he of the small hands—in 1927, surrounded by future virtuosos at the Curtis Institute: from left, Shura Cherkassky, Lucie Stern, Martha de Blassis, Joseph Levine, and composer Jeanne Behrend.

son assume that his classmates rush home after school, as he does, to listen to Delius.

"How do you plan to make a living?" asked Father, on learning I wanted to be a composer when I grew up. Apparently I replied, "What difference does it make, if I can't be a composer?" That answer was so un-American as to impress Father, who, although a breadwinner, was also a not-so-sublimated baritone. To his eternal credit he agreed then and there to be supportive of the family freak. He has never been a stage mother, but Father nonetheless believed in work. It was time for a real teacher.

The Julius Rosenwald Fund in Chicago was not only the backbone of the Committee on the Cost of Medical Care of which Father was coordinator, but sponsor for Negro fellowships in the arts and sciences. Among the beneficiaries in those days were Katherine Dunham, W. E. B. Du Bois, Marian Anderson, Howard Swanson, Margaret Bonds. The last-named at twenty-two was a middle western "personality," having played Carpenter's *Concertino* with the Chicago Symphony under the composer's direction, and being herself a composer of mainly spiritual arrangements and of original songs

Left, Ignace Jan Paderewski (1860–1941), the most famous pianist who ever lived. His name was known to the man on the street, and his frizzy-haired dishabille, like that of Einstein and Stokowski, was synonymous in the layman's ken with Genius. *Right*, Sergei Rachmaninoff (1873–1943), who more than any other musician of the twentieth century was publicly a pianist and composer in equal proportions—the last of a breed that began with Beethoven and all but ended with Chopin.

in collaboration with Langston Hughes. It was Margaret Bonds—*Miss* Bonds—who was to be my next piano teacher.

Every Saturday morning I boarded the streetcar for her house on South Wabash. At our first lesson she played me some ear openers, "The White Peacock" by Griffes and Carpenter's "American Tango." Had I ever heard American music before? Fired by my enthusiasm, she assigned the pieces on the spot, with no talk of scale-and-trill practice.

Margaret Bonds played with the authority of a professional, an authority I'd never heard in a living room, an authority stemming from the fact that she herself was a composer and thus approached all music from the inside out, an authority that was contagious. She dusted off the notion that music is solely for home use. She also showed me how to notate my ramblings ("Just look at how other composers put it on the paper"), hoisting the ephemeral into the concrete: once his piece is on the page, a composer is responsible for it, for it can then be reinterpreted by others, elating or embarrassing its maker.

The first piece I wrote down, "The Glass Cloud,"

Myself in Yellowstone Park, summer of 1935.

was influenced by Margaret's other prize pupil, Gerald Cook. Gerald was a pop pianist and serious creator who would soon spend a term with Nadia Boulanger. In the years to come his identity with Margaret would shift from student to colleague as their two-piano team, Bonds and Cook, became a glamorous enterprise at Cerutti's in New York and at Spivy's Roof. After Margaret went her separate way to marriage, motherhood, documentation of Negro song, and opera writing, Gerald turned into the greatest living accompanist of the blues, working first with the lamented Libby Holman, then (and as of 1981) with Alberta Hunter. (Accompanists dislike that word and call themselves pianists. Once I identified song as "a lyric poem of moderate length set to music for single voice with piano." If

the definition holds for everything from "Der Doppelgänger" to "Le Bestiare," with my own songs thrown in—and I don't write "accompaniments," I write integrated piano parts as important as the vocal—it must be expanded for the blues, which by its nature is never repeated the same way. Then what is Gerald Cook? A contradiction in terms, a composer of improvisations, a jazz accompanist who repeats himself literally, and whose repetitions become art? Hear the disks with Holman and Hunter: how, beneath their subjectively raw but subtle and moaningly spoken incantations, he weaves an icy, classical, velvet, inexorable web to encase and soothe forever the open wound.)

Did I outgrow Margaret Bonds? Why were lessons discontinued? If there was an objection to a seeming glib jazziness *chez elle*, Margaret thought of herself as classical and deep. (Conversely, I feel as influenced by prewar jazz as by "serious" music. Not the tune itself but Billie Holiday's *way* with a tune taught me to knead a vocal phrase, just as Count Basie's piano playing still shapes my piano composing.) In any case Margaret and I lost track of each other until we had all moved east during the war. Then we remained close friends until she died.

In 1980 I went back to Chicago—to accompany a vocal recital, as it happens. Not one old friend remains in the city that was once my world. The weird thing was how little had changed; there was a new cast of actors in the same old decor. Or almost the same. Nothing, nothing was left of the brief block of one-story artists' studios just east of the I.C. tracks on 57th Street. That was once Hyde Park's Montmartre. Rolf Beman, Georg Redlich,

Facing page: Top, Margaret Bonds, one of my first true teachers—who did not distinguish between so-called classical and pop, only between good and bad—with her prize pupil, Gerald Cook. In the early 1940s they were a two-piano team. When they disbanded, Gerald became what he remains today—the sought-after accompanist of female *monstres sacrés*, notably Libby Holman and Alberta Hunter. *Bottom*, N.R. musing at the new Steinway, at 5617 Dorchester Avenue in Chicago. The year was 1941 or 1942, when I was at Northwestern.

My beloved parents, Clarence Rufus Rorem and Gladys Miller Rorem, whose support I will always joyfully acknowledge. This snapshot, taken at Lake Michigan, dates from around 1940.

Gertrude Abercrombie—how many vanished painters, brought to the fore by the WPA, were toiling and giggling and drinking and dying within a Bohemia that casually bisected the university milieu of my parents! Charlie Biesel was the cross-point. At one of his parties early in 1938 Mother and Father met and liked Belle Tannenbaum, who became my next piano teacher.

Belle was a big-time local virtuoso and free-lance professor, bitter rival of Molly Margolies, who was Ganz's tenured assistant and scapegoat. She immediately tried to discourage my French disposition in favor of the more "honest" repertoire of Haydn. Coincidentally, I got special dispensation twice weekly from gym to attend harmony classes in the Loop with an expert, Leo Sowerby, another

stickler for basic training. Belle was maybe fifty years old, four feet eleven inches tall, plump, with spindly calves, platinum hair, a huge bosom and tight black dresses, a coarsely amicable social style, and the keyboard technique of Horowitz. I adored her. Thanks to Belle, we cashed in the old Starck and invested in a new Steinway "B." I can still see us that afternoon in Lyon & Healey's vast storeroom crowded with instruments like winged horses, Belle testing the mahogany lids with her tiny fists, kicking at the brittle wooden legs which she likened to her own "piano legs" (though aren't true piano legs those foot-thick cylinders found on earlier models?), sitting now at this keyboard, now at that, each time easily playing—as though opening a faucet of nectar—the infinitely melancholy Prelude in G by Rachmaninoff.

Under Belle Tannenbaum's tutelage I memorized the first movement of Grieg's Piano Concerto, which, on June 21, 1940, I performed, in my white graduation suit, with the American Concert Orchestra, a subsidiary of the WPA's marvelous Illinois Symphony, with one William Fantozzi, conductor. That is the only time in my life I have played with an orchestra.

Also that month, at the age of sixteen, despite low grades, I emerged from U-High (in the white suit), and the following autumn I entered Northwestern University's School of Music, despite the same low grades, on my creative potential.

All through high school, and indeed through grammar school, it had been Perry O'Neil, not I, who was the star pianist; I was known at best as a "dreamer." To be a composition major now seemed eerily official. I remember less about the lessons with tiny Dr. Alfred Nolte (a former protégé of Richard Strauss), however, than about lessons in my "minor" with Harold Van Horne, my first male piano teacher and the impulse for my first intense piano practicing. Suddenly I dwelled in a competitive world of pianists better than I, who practiced nine hours a day on the standard classics. That none of these wunderkinds were obsessed with, or even really knew the music of, Debussy and Stravinsky was no less bemusing than my ignorance of

Schumann and Mendelssohn. The target of my new concentration was not cheering crowds but repertorial lore. In two years at Northwestern I learned all thirty-two Beethoven sonatas and the entire keyboard catalog of Bach and Chopin. Today I have a wider range than most pianists because I never bogged down in perfecting any one piece. (Oh, I *did* give a pretty accurate rendition of Ravel's Concerto in "solo class," with Van Horne at the second piano.) Indeed, it's shocking how *few* pieces most successful pianists have in their fingers; after a point in their careers they're stuck with a few recitals, a few concertos, and have no more time, or, seemingly, curiosity, to revive more warhorses, let alone to learn contemporary works. But by the same token my appreciation—my "whistling knowledge"—of basic symphonic and operatic chestnuts is surely narrower than your average Music Lover's. And if once I lusted after the French aesthetic, and later tried to keep up on the output of my fellow creators, today as a composer I'm less and less interested in the music of other people. As a pianist I'm more and more interested in the hours I spend alone with the Bach Inventions, which I first enjoyed with Harold Van Horne. He was a quiet, charming, black-haired, thin, bespectacled family man whose robust pianism belied his outward passivity. He committed suicide in 1959.

I spent 1943 at the Curtis Institute in Philadelphia on a scholarship with Rosario Scalero, whom I despised. The study of composition, to bear fruit, must be done solely with a successful practitioner, one who has himself learned from hearing his music frequently rendered by the best executants. True, Scalero had in the 1920s been an exemplary professor for Barber and Menotti, but they were younger then than I was now, and I had ideas of my own. That old Scalero should proscribe original work, and prescribe only counterpoint and more counterpoint (which I'd already had to excess at Northwestern), meant that he, like Nolte, had failed. For the record, my "secondary" piano teacher was Freda Pastor. What I retained from Curtis was not the wisdom of a dusty maestro but the still vital friendship of young pianists, notably

Eugene Istomin and Shirley Gabis Rhoads; also the rich flock of wartime *jeunesse*: Gary Graffman, Seymour Lipkin, Jacob Latiener, Theodore Lettvin.

Nineteen forty-four brought me to the magic of the Empire City against the better judgment of my parents, who stopped my allowance. I have never regretted the crucial step from Scalero's security to the adventure of Virgil Thomson. The first year in New York I acted as Virgil's copyist in exchange for twenty dollars a week and orchestration lessons, learning more about the real world of music in that short time than in all my twenty years. Through his friend E. Robert Schmitz, Virgil found me yet another piano instructor. The intelligent Betty Crawford imparted the Schmitz "method"—"natural" hand position, thumbs on black keys, and so on—which, for better or worse, I'm still stuck with. One thing leads to another. Betty, with whom I gave the first public hearing of my Four-Hand Piano Sonata (in the Statler Hotel at a regional meeting of Blue Cross, thanks to Father), got me a job as accompanist for Martha Graham's classes. Martha thus became my first official employer, for whom I drew out Social Security number 091-22-5307 and earned two dollars an hour.

In 1945 I was back in school, this time at Juilliard, urged by Father, always the academician, who felt it more honorable to have a degree and pooh-pooh it than not to have a degree and pooh-pooh it. The name of my "secondary" piano teacher at Juilliard I've forgotten, but I played better than she, and she was the last I've ever had.

Father maintains that when I was four I stood at the piano one fine day and to everyone's surprise played, lentissimo but without missing a beat, "My Country 'Tis of Thee" in C. Obviously I was imitating some grown-up. Since then, most of what I've learned about piano playing has come from emulating peers. The same goes for composition: I've gleaned less from formal lessons than from piracy. (Charlie Chaplin, on being complimented for his singing voice, answered: "But I don't sing at all. That was an imitation of Caruso.")

Do I play in public these days? Not as often as I'd like. When I do, it's always as accompanist to

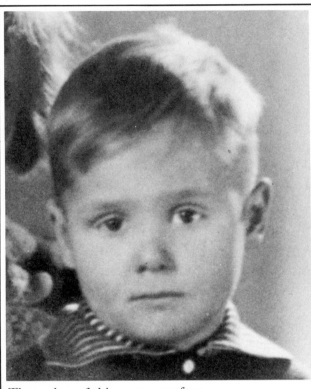

The author of this essay, age four.

my own songs, and to those of French masters. Not that my solo works are necessarily too hard for me, but most of them were conceived for other hands with different shapes and more experience.

The five most urgent pianists from my generation (urgent because they've cared enough about my music to play it) are Eugene Istomin, a Serkin pupil, who once, while attempting a vibrato on ivory as though it were catgut, said he'd learned as much from Heifetz as from any pianist, and who, in his record of my *War Scenes* with Donald Gramm, proved again that the greatest "accompanists" come from the ranks of great soloists; Leon Fleisher, a Schnabel pupil, who offered the 1950 premieres in Paris of my Second Sonata and *Barcarolles* (Shirley Gabis Rhoads gave the first *Moroccan* performance of these) and whose record of the *Barcarolles* is a moral in how underplaying can break the heart; the late Julius Katchen, pupil of Yves Nat, to whom I owe the existence of my Second Concerto and of the exemplary record of the Second Sonata, and

who belied the small-repertoire syndrome of virtuosos by having in his fingers, at a day's notice, any one of thirty recital programs and thirty concertos and by learning new ones all the time; Jerome Lowenthal (younger than the rest, but a pupil of their colleague William Kapell), whose blinding disk of my Third Concerto shows his seniors that intellect and fire are the same thing and whose vision of my chamber works exceeds what composers find (so rarely) merely satisfying.

Who is the fifth pianist? She is a secret.

❧

A hundred and fifty years ago composer and performer—hitherto, often as not, the same person—began, for whatever reason, gradually but inexorably to turn their backs on each other so that they now face in opposite directions. That situation is unique to music, the other arts having kept pace with the moment. Books reviewed in this morning's *Times* were published this year; movies showing around town are by definition contemporary; most choreography today is by living persons; and most galleries exhibit living painters. As for theater, "legitimate" and otherwise, it is so regularly the work of active playwrights that when a drama of O'Neill's comes along, we speak of a revival. But we do not speak of a Beethoven revival where Beethoven is the rule. Music is the sole art that still hovers over the fading past.

Nineteenth-century repertoire, which dominates our orchestras, looms even more darkly over small instrumental ensembles and piano soloists. Ninety percent of the works of ninety percent of their programs are a century old, whereas the Bartók quartets and Prokofiev sonatas generally proffered as token modernisms are from fifty to seventy years old. American music is almost nowhere played, even by serious young American virtuosos whose equivalents in the pop world, whatever their worth, quiver with the pulse of the times. That this active malady should forever come as news—bad news—to the pedantically powerful peddlers of musical flesh who presume to know what audiences want is degrading to living composers, in whom it has formed a deep wound.

The wound was temporarily salved for me in the summer of 1980 in Santa Fe, New Mexico, where, during an exceptional fortnight, I was a "public guest" of the Chamber Music Festival. Old and new works of mine were maximally rehearsed and glitteringly dispatched by first-rate general practitioners, as distinct from first-rate modern music specialists so often met in academe. I was also displayed, for better or worse, as pianist and speechifier, and surely got as good as I gave. With a kind of morose joy I discovered that general practitioners, no less than the general public, when they think of composers at all, still think of them as in the grave.

My *Santa Fe Songs* for baritone and piano quartet were premiered at the festival. One stipulation by the commissioners of this piece was that I myself act as pianist in the first performances. During an open discussion rehearsal for the nonpaying public I announced that although I am vastly experienced in hearing my music performed and in performing myself as accompanist to singers, I have never

Virgil Thomson, myself, the late William Flanagan, and soprano Phyllis Curtin rehearsing at Virgil's, in front of a painting by Leonid Berman, for a recital of American vocal music to be performed in Carnegie Recital Hall on November 16, 1959.

Left, Julius Katchen and N.R., in 1952, discussing my Second Piano Sonata, which Katchen would play at the Théâtre des Champs-Elysées, then in New York's Town Hall, prior to recording it for London FFRR. Julius was uncommonly versatile in both technique and repertoire. Like all other pianists, he liked to dine expensively and to collect *objets d'art*. The plaster hand that seems to extend from his left ear is a sculpture by his then protégé, François Jèze. *Bottom left*, Eugene Istomin, the pianist who has most influenced me. If I play fairly well, it's less from a knack for the keys than from a knack for mime: I imitate Eugene. When we were all teenagers at Curtis, it was Eugene (three years my junior) I most attended. His approach to the piano, in both speech and action, was terse, cultured, yet sensuous and unforgettable. *Below*, Leon Fleisher, who was the youngest—and perhaps the most intellectually tactile—of that triumvirate of keyboard stars (Gary Graffman and Eugene were the others) who rose in the mid-forties. I feel honored that he debuted in Europe playing my music. Today Leon conducts more than he plays, his right hand having been capriciously incapacitated for some years.

Jerome Lowenthal does the undoable—makes ivory vibrate, so that a note, struck only once, will melt from an ice cube into a tear. He would seem much of the time to be emulating vocal cords, and according to the composer he is playing—singing—he becomes a radically different person and performer. Except for Emanuel Ax (who premiered my *Eight Etudes* in 1976), Jerry Lowenthal is the only pianist for whom I've composed on commission. Phyllis Curtin, in whose Riverside Drive apartment we are here shown in 1973, is the soprano with whom I have most recitalized and whom I continually cite as a golden proof that beauty and brains, in art as in life, are not mutually exclusive.

played with a chamber group. (Whispers of disbelief from the audience.) Turning to my string-playing colleagues, Ani Kavafian, Heiichiro Ohyama, and Timothy Eddy, all vastly experienced themselves, I asked if any of them had ever performed—not coached, but actually played—with a composer. Silence. (More whispers of disbelief.)

In retrospect I realize that the unusual inclusion of a live composer at the open rehearsal had seemed, both to the artists and to the listeners, so uncoercively logical that I was momentarily regarded less

as a talking dog than as a functioning member of the musical community. That such a community in America should be an exception and not a rule is outrageous. That for the Santa Fe Chamber Music Festival it should now be a rule and not an exception suggests that, gradually, performer and composer may be turning around to face each other again.

In 1945, when I moved into my first apartment alone (one large room on West 12th Street for twenty dollars a month), Virgil Thomson lent me an antique upright. That piano, like an elderly foster child, had been kicking around among his friends for years. Five feet high and embellished with a pair of triple-pronged candelabra jutting from the music board, it filled my room. Everything functioned except the E key a thirteenth below middle C, which did not exist. In 1949, before leaving for Paris, I gave the piano (to Virgil's annoyance) to the Salvation Army. During the intervening years all my music was composed in reference to—or, as choreographers say, was made on— this instrument, a series of pre–opus ones that had nothing in common except a notable lack of low E's. (Coincidentally, my current piano, a mellow Baldwin bought from Earl Wild twelve years ago, is faulty on the same low E.)

Which brings up the question composers hear most often: "Do you compose at the piano?" They react uneasily, since a method is less important than its outcome.

Some composers always use the piano, some use it part-time, some never. Music being *the* intangible art because it is heard and not seen, the composer's workshop is more intriguing to the layman than that of other artists; and there is a vague notion abroad that something is wrong with a musician who composes at the piano, even if the composition is *for* the piano. The notion results from the image of Hollywood Beethovens ambling through fields with the muse and penning inspirations on the spot as full-blown overtures. Yes, music did use to be simpler; harmonic relations were heard by the inner ear without need to confirm them at the keyboard. But today's knottier sonorities are not dictated by the muse alone. If Britten claimed that the discipline of avoiding a piano sharpens the fancy and precludes superficial solutions to profound conundrums, Stravinsky claimed that it is unmusical to write *away* from the keyboard, for music deals with sound and composers ought always to be in touch with *la matière sonore.*

Now musical composition, though always dealing with sound, does not deal with sound primarily but with the cohesion of ideas eventually expressed through the language of sound. Ideas can occur today in fields as they did yesterday; the difference is that as they seldom occur fully formed, their ultimate usefulness might not be ascertained until they are remodeled at the piano. Which does not mean that a composer rambles over the keys hoping to hit the Lost Chord. It means that once an idea is found, immersion in the sonic element will indicate the natural "tone" of the idea by subjecting the tone to the artifice of form.

Music designed to be played on a piano is certainly more effective when contrived for what that instrument can do. All masters of virtuoso keyboard writing, from Scarlatti through Chopin to Rachmaninoff and Ravel, "realized" their material in keyboard contact. Can you imagine the source of Liszt's glittering fountains as being mere silence?

These aperçus apply to the so-called creative act, not to orchestration (to the second-most-asked question "Do you do your own orchestration?" the only answer is: Who else would be more qualified?). Orchestration at the piano makes no sense since it requires extraneous choices of color. Unlike composition, orchestration is a craft that anyone can learn.

It does not follow that to compose "tellingly" for an instrument one must know how to play it; and if composing for a group of instruments there is even less reason since no one can play them all at one time. A musical author is trained in orchestral theory—the physics of sound as pertaining to relationships of balance, weight, and hue of various solo or choirs of instruments. He is also trained to write characteristically for individual instruments according to their possible range, their happiest tessitura within this range, their shading potential and dynamic restriction. No one has time to master wholly each instrument and still to compose, and half-mastery inhibits.

Nor does a composer who is a proficient performer necessarily write best for his instrument. Facility in performing, hence in writing gratefully for an instrument, may induce casualness about

Facing page: N.R. accompanying William Parker in the small, exquisite Guadalupe Church of Santa Fe in July of 1980. The piece is *War Scenes*, the only music of mine that purports to make a political gesture.

An "open rehearsal" of my brand-new piece, *The Santa Fe Songs*, scored for baritone, violin, viola, cello, and piano. (From left, Ani Kavafian, Heiichiro Ohyama, the composer, Timothy Eddy, and William Parker.)

structure. Meanwhile, a composer who does not play a given instrument might happen upon usages that would not have occurred to the specialist. Hindemith, a violist who never composed at the piano, wrote keyboard works that don't sound hard, though they don't always "feel right" under the hand. Accidents of instrumental dialect are like the writings of Conrad and Dinesen and Nabokov, who, because their native tongues lay elsewhere, lent our language a dimension unimaginable to authors raised in English.

Successful composer-singer teams during the past fifty years have been rare and strictly from overseas. Who is there besides Britten and Pears from England, or Poulenc and Bernac from France? Is it more than coincidence that Benjamin Britten and Francis Poulenc were the greatest voice composers of our time and also intensely accomplished pianists? If tenor Peter Pears and baritone Pierre Bernac enjoyed careers distinct from their composer colleagues, still their way with *all* music stemmed from constant truck with those active inventors rather than with "mere" accompanists or, indeed, with mere great pianists. The two *équipes* performed naturally the works of the *maîtres*; and Pears and Bernac each have written the last word on how to interpret, respectively, Britten and Poulenc. (Did Bernac and Poulenc ever perform Britten, I wonder? Did Britten and Pears ever perform Poulenc?) Yet the whole spectrum was fair game for each pair,

Facing page: What is a piano sonata? Beethoven composed thirty-two of them, thereby providing thirty-two separate definitions, none of which jibes with Haydn's definition (if he had one), much less with Scarlatti's. Here sits the master, pondering the problem.

the mode of execution in Schubert and Debussy and Purcell and Fauré fermenting through the decades into flawless unities.

No American equivalents. Samuel Barber and Leontyne Price were an item for gala moments, mainly at premieres of cycles by Barber for Price. But when they went on the roster of Columbia Artists Management as a duo for sale, they had no bids. (Nor were there buyers for Donald Gramm and myself on the same roster ten years later.) *Americans do not know what a composer is.* If they can raise the money for a prima donna, they're not about to waste it on a crank piano player who demands equal billing.

In 1926 Eugene Goossens conducted the first performance in Britain of *Les Noces*. Stravinsky's score is, of course, notable for its four pianos, manned on that historic occasion by four composers: Georges Auric, Francis Poulenc, Vladimir Dukelsky, and Vittorio Rieti. I phoned Rieti for his recollection of how it went. "It was a publicity stunt, a bad performance. We had done it pretty well in

---

Facing page: Top left, Maurice Ravel (1875–1937). Despite his up-to-date harmonies, he composed piano pieces in the glittery nineteenth-century manner of Liszt (*pace* Glenn Gould, who contends that "Liszt had no idea of how to write for the piano"). Indeed, it could be argued that Ravel stretched the virtuoso viewpoint to the splitting point; no one has convincingly composed that way since. Ravel himself was a lackluster and inexact executant. Fortunately, his interpreters were marvels like Ricardo Viñes, Marguérite Long, and Jacques Février. *Bottom*, Aaron Copland. Precisely because the Ravelian path had come to an end, Copland needed an opposite approach to piano writing. Like Stravinsky, he exploited the instrument's so-called percussive aspects, and in his three huge works for solo piano, the *Variations* (1932), the Sonata (1943), and the *Fantasy* (1957), he gave the world a brand-new sound. Copland himself plays admirably, his touch tailor-made for his own pieces, never lush, often crass, always direct and telling. *Top right*, Virgil Thomson, a less persuasive pianist than Copland, if accuracy is the standard, who tends to betray his own best music. Like many other composers, however, he sometimes sheds new light on old notes just because he's not inhibited by his lack of proficiency. I've never heard Mozart more interestingly rendered than by Virgil on his good days.

Paris the week before with Marcelle Meyer instead of Dukelsky on piano three. When Dukelsky joined us in London, it turned out he'd been practicing piano two, which was my part, but he wasn't quick enough to switch parts, so I took over piano three, which I hadn't rehearsed, and he played piano two. The ensemble was shaky, but got better in Belgium when we did it in concert without the ballet. I later played it in Spain with three other composers—Count Chigi, I think, and Nino Rota, and I forget who else."

The piano is Auric's instrument, but he's not a soloist. Poulenc was a soloist, but not an ensemble player. Dukelsky played piano but was not a pianist. Rieti is a pianist in private (he says) but has stage fright. As for the spectacular Marcelle Meyer, she was not a composer but a composer's servant who, like Ricardo Viñes, Jacques Février, Marguérite Long, Wittgenstein, Gieseking, even Arthur Rubinstein—and how many others?—specialized in new music during those old golden days. (Have we their parallels? William Masselos, perhaps? Paul Jacobs? Anyone else?) No doubt Madame Meyer singlehandedly—or eighthandedly—held the piece together in Paris. Yet one ponders how bad or how revealing the London version actually sounded. Did Stravinsky like it? Years later he himself conducted a recording with four American composers as his pianists: Copland, Barber, Sessions, and Foss. Whatever is lost in the disparity of egos is perhaps regained by a sense of homage.

For two hundred years the instrument known as the pianoforte has evolved according to the composer's needs, not the pianist's. If today composer and pianist are generally separate concepts, the "pianism" of a given piece results from the composer's, not the pianist's, ingenuity. No evidence remains of that first notorious *Noces*, but we do possess mementos of still earlier masters. Before he died in 1915, Alexander Scriabin recorded himself (that is, his own music) with hair-raising precision. "When Scriabin played his Fifth Sonata," wrote Prokofiev, "every note soared. With Rachmaninoff all the notes lay on the ground."

Maurice Ravel, on the other hand, played poorly. Photographs of Ravel's studio display Moreau-like exotica, checkerboard tiling, nonfunctional globes supported by twisting brass snakes, accouterments of the sort Napoleon rifled during his Egyptian campaign and which remained *à la mode* until after the First World War when style turned sparse and "modernistic." Ravel's piano music bridged the period. *Gaspard de la nuit* alone, with its burning sprays and waves of flame, exhibits every shimmering convention of the improvisatory past, yet is "modern" in its economy, with not one note too many. His Tiffany-like structures being compact as marble, it comes as a surprise to hear Ravel's own mushy executions, left hand forever anticipating right hand in the hiccupy manner of, say, Paderewski's *Moonlight* Sonata.

If Ravel's piano music closed the door on nineteenth-century France by funneling all of Liszt into the smallest possible space (as Schoenberg funneled Wagner into a somewhat larger space), Debussy, fourteen years Ravel's senior, opened a door onto the twentieth century with his once-ambiguous harmonies and so-called fragmented forms. Even if composers had the last word on how they should be heard, Debussy's own surviving interpretations are too blurred for much use. On a recording made in 1902 with Mary Garden he sounds merely remote, and "D'un cahier d'esquisses" is most memorable for wrong notes. Nevertheless, Debussy clearly played his own pieces straighter than Ravel played his. Misty music to sound misty must be played without mist, whereas pristine music to make its point must be played pristinely.

If these "impressionists" seemed to sabotage their own music, the explanation lies partly in fashion (possibly all nineteenth-century music was played half as fast and half as rigidly), partly in the player-piano rolls from which their performances are extrapolated. But what of a living master like Messiaen whose performance refutes his notation? A two-piano recital with his wife, the expert Yvonne Loriod, is like one by Beauty and the Beast, so oblivious is his account and so accurate is hers of the intricate rhythmic patterns engraved on the page. And I have seen Virgil Thomson raise his hands over the keyboard and let them fall with great authority on all the wrong notes. These men

Francis Poulenc (1899–1963). He played his own music better than it will ever be played again. More than a mere professional, he had the secret (as great performers do) of extracting from his instrument sounds we never knew were there. More discreet than truffles, more opulent than teeming butterscotch, he dazzled as a soloist, and he was the dreamed-of accompanist, especially of baritone Pierre Bernac (above, with Poulenc). The two of them recorded Poulenc's complete vocal works several times and also gave recitals featuring the works of Debussy, Schubert, and others.

are not out to undermine themselves; they are playing what they heard while composing. Their music is on the paper, not in the performance, and although they have a right to play it as they wish, no professional would think of imitating them.

Still, one always learns from a composer at the piano, especially when he is playing someone else's music. He is less maniacal than "real" pianists about the technique of trills, and about historical truth (which is never true and never historical). Hence

Benjamin Britten (1913–1976), at left. Britten too was an accomplished and subtle pianist, performing (and conducting) the works of many composers besides himself. With tenor Peter Pears (*above*, with Britten), he formed a team that for decades was as distinguished as the Poulenc-Bernac *équipe* across the Channel.

he gets to the quick more quickly—speaks, so to speak, with colleagues long gone. Virgil's version of Mozart's K. 330 is a primer in human relationships; the ineluctable *vocality* in Mozart's piano pieces comes immediately to the fore.

If sometimes composers' bloopers exude more authority than "real" pianists' accuracy, while "real" pianists play subtler accompaniments than professional accompanists, nothing is more rewarding than a composer who is also a real pianist accom-

panying other composers' songs. Listen to the disks of Jennie Tourel "supported" by Leonard Bernstein, and savor the sense of the song's skeleton. Bernstein is deferential without being cowed, acting the piano's role with a composer's knowledge, not with the soft-pedal furtiveness of an illegal alien.

A composer is often pestered with "Come on, play us your symphony," and when he explains that his

symphony was not conceived for the piano, and that anyway he doesn't recall how it goes, there's a bemused reply: "You wrote it, so you of all people should know it." But on completing one piece he leaves it to begin another. It is his interpreter's job to master the problems, memorize the notes. Composition and execution, though not mutually exclusive, do not go hand in hand. Some fine composers do not play any instrument competently. The true virtuoso-composer really has two professions: he must sit down and *learn* his own music as he learns anyone else's, by practicing.

The piano is the least expressive of all musical instruments, and the most popular.

Insofar as expressivity is measured in ratio to the human voice (that vibrating primal force and ulti-

---

Facing page: Top, Samuel Barber with Leontyne Price. Barber was one of the rare composers with a listenable singing voice. His piano playing was adept, if not so authoritative as Poulenc's or Britten's. Still, that was probably not why his joint concerts with Leontyne Price had few buyers; it was rather that America is less concerned than Europe with composers as facts of musical life. *Bottom left*, N.R. with Shirley Rhoads, one of my friends since Curtis days. Although she is an affecting pianist, her career has nonetheless been more private than public, and she is the confidante of some of the grandest performers of our day. She is also a distinguished teacher. Here we were in Paris in 1950, at 53 rue de la Harpe, looking through my new *Barcarolles*, which she would play—using the name Xénia Gabis—in June of that year at the Salle Gaveau. *Bottom right*, composer Georges Auric with me. He and his wife, the painter Nora Auric, were my next-door neighbors for a decade when I spent summers (sometimes springs and falls) in Hyères at the home of Marie Laure de Noailles. Auric today is best known for his evocative music for Jean Cocteau's movies, although his catalog contains everything from ballets for Diaghilev to a two-piano partita for Fizdale and Gold. Georges was a pretty good pianist and an expert sight reader, but he didn't perform professionally except on one recording—now a collector's item—on which he plays Satie's *Suites* for four hands, rollickingly, with Poulenc. Did Cocteau know anything technically about music? Georges claims that Cocteau could pick out anything with one finger, provided it was in F major.

mate criterion), the piano, by way of all media, whether bowed, blown, or banged, is as far from a soprano as you can get. Even a kettledrum with its intrinsic quiver resembles a singer. (I discount the nonpitched percussion, which, though probably as old as, and surely the original supporter of, organized chant, is today mainly decorative.)

Insofar as its popularity rests on the potential for being complete unto itself, the piano is second to no contraption, even the guitar. More than any other single instrument, it contains means for rich harmony, counterpoint, rhythmic variety, and color complexity. Only the violin supersedes it in melody, though it lacks the piano's dynamic range. The piano is the most useful of instruments because it can *counterfeit* expressivity, thanks in part to its pedal facilities, and because it can emit any number of notes up to eighty-eight at one time. That is why composers work it as a tool, and why of all solo vehicles it has the widest first-class literature.

Nevertheless, America today, unlike Europe of yesterday, is a land of specialists in music as in all else.

Composers who are also pianists? At random, a few: Leon Kirchner, Robert Helps, David Del Tredici, Charles Wuorinen, Lukas Foss. All play their own music dazzlingly, as well as that of other contemporaries. I can think of but one—Lee Hoiby—who feels compelled to specialize, as Rachmaninoff did, in standard fare.

Pianists who are also composers? At random, fewer: Glenn Gould, William Bolcom, Leo Smit, Noel Lee, each no less serious than their predecessors Busoni, Schnabel, Casadesus, Steuermann.

Francis Thorne has worked as a barroom pianist, like Erik Satie of yore. Other composers, other instruments. David Diamond has worked as a violinist; David Amram as a french horn player; Barbara Kolb as a clarinetist; Daniel Pinkham as an organist; Lou Harrison as a sitarist, not to mention tack pianist and player of any number of Korean instruments including jade flute; Conlon Nancarrow as confectioner of etudes for piano rolls to be inserted into the old-fashioned player piano, etudes too elaborate for living hands; Harry Partch and

Lucia Dlugoszewski as players on instruments of their own manufacture, instruments never before seen on earth.

But your average American composer—if there is such a thing—gets along as a normal pianist and even accompanies his songs if called upon. George Perle and Miriam Gideon, Jack Beeson and Hugo Weisgall, do not as public pianists betray the products of their private selves. At the same time they do not have the souls of hams, the extrovert-intro-

vert flamboyant reticence of a Gershwin, who, it could be argued, was at once the most "modern" musician of his era and the last of a race of full-time composer-pianists.

A note on notation. Unlike the painter's action which produces an absolute product, transcription of musical ideas from mind to paper is only approximate, which is why there are as many interpretations of a given work as there are interpreters;

Facing page, top: What is a more touching scene than a composer paying homage to another by performing his music? Here *four* composers prepare to man the four pianos required by Stravinsky's *Les Noces,* under the composer's conductorship in Town Hall in December of 1959. From left, Samuel Barber, Stravinsky, Lukas Foss, Aaron Copland, and Roger Sessions. *Bottom,* Jean Cocteau at the piano, ca. 1953. His famous long fingers conveniently reposing on an F-major configuration, he rejoins the notorious *enfants terribles* known as Les Six, thirty years after the fact. From left, they are Darius Milhaud—a good pianist who played his own concertos; Georges Auric—a capable pianist; Arthur Honegger—my teacher during a Fulbright year in 1951, but I don't know how he played; Germaine Tailleferre—an excellent pianist who, for a time, formed a team with baritone Bernard Lefort, now director of the Paris Opéra; Francis Poulenc—a great pianist; Louis Durey—I think he played viola. *Above,* Lenny Bernstein in 1958, flanked by Lukas Foss (a composer who plays Bach on the piano almost as well as Rosalyn Tureck, and that is well) and by the incomparable Jennie Tourel. Jennie was the most satisfyingly wise mezzo soprano of her time (she died in 1973); her programs with Lenny reached the altitude of paradise.

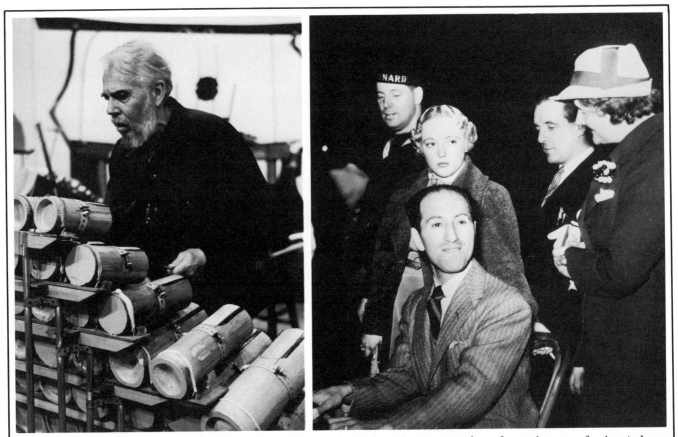

Left, Harry Partch, whose sounds, drawn from his own inventions (a vast gamelan of nonpiano confections), have been ever wondrous to hear. Once, after a performance of *The Bewitched* during which the stage had been quite littered with a score of malleted instruments for several hours, painter Maurice Grosser remarked simply: "Seated one day at the marimba." *Right*, George Gershwin, the American introvert-extrovert composer-pianist *par excellence* until he died, entertaining in 1937.

why composers themselves, even the most accomplished, veer from the text; and why, according to trends, pieces are played faster or slower or more strictly or freely. The simpler the music, the harder it is to notate; there is more variance in playing Haydn than in Schoenberg. Metronome marks don't help much, except in practicing. The only precise tempo indication is *presto possibile*. The vaguest is *con moto*. Meanwhile the Mona Lisa smiles unchanging through the centuries.

Long ago Lou Harrison picked up some money working on a jazz book for author Rudi Blesh. Lou's job was to notate for posterity the rags of Jelly Roll Morton by listening to old records and writing down what he heard. Since Jelly Roll never played the same piece the same way, Lou wrote down only the passing version captured on disk. Now jazz, as everyone knows, is rhythmically rigid, its nature emerging from—being defined by—how much freedom a soloist (or a right hand) dares, while still jibing with the measure (or with the left hand). Lou's transcriptions of this music, so easy to listen to, looked as elaborate as Stockhausen's and would have been impossible to play except by piano roll, never by Jelly Roll.

In 1948 I was interviewed by Alfred Kinsey (and so, later, were my parents; when he could, Kinsey liked to keep it in the family). He was plotting a book on the sexuality of the artist. After the interview we had an off-the-record chat about other musicians, in particular and as a breed. I offered my considered opinion about the penchants of male as opposed to female pianists, concert tenors as opposed to operatic baritones and as distinct from pop singers of both sexes, solo string players versus orchestral string players, drummers and harpists versus choristers and organists. But I could absolutely not formalize about the sexual makeup of composers. Now, thirty years later, I still cannot. The sexuality of performers, however, remains fairly predictable if not identical to what it was in the old days. Kinsey never completed the book. But just as his treatise on the human male should have specified the human *American* male, so his new book should have been named *The Sexual Life of the American Artist*. I was to discover that just as genus *Homo* was sexually another species abroad than at home, so genus *Musicalis* followed other patterns in Europe (where, for example, organists are mainly heterosexual). The sexual life of human pianists— are there other kinds?—is varied enough to inspire another essay.

The ugly turn beautiful while playing the piano, the drab become desirable, as though lit by a halo or hit by Cupid's arrow. But only momentarily. When they stop, they revert. The beauty, the carnality oozing from an artist at work, is due to concentration on something not himself. The concentration is the one refuge from ego, from the mask, from the hurly-burly, and is never visible on the face of a mere audience, which displays the stupor of ecstasy or of boredom. Not that geniuses in their daily lives are selfless. Heaven forbid that they be loving and sweet like everyone else! But the *act* of genius is selfless. And so is the act of interpreting

I had been living in Europe for almost three years when Man Ray and his wife, Juliet, returned to Paris in 1953. That year Man took a series of pictures of me in his studio on the rue Férou. Plastic artists were then thought to be ignorant of music, especially those in the surrealist party of which Man was a founder— which, indeed, was categorically against music. Yet music as a *visual* art intrigued them. Thus Man invited me to scratch some notes on the photographic plate. The tune, from a waltz I wrote called "Tout beau mon coeur," I dedicated to the Rays.

genius, which ironically is more often found with amateurs in the parlor than with virtuosos in the concert hall.

Among the greatest of the jazz dancers, the Nicholas Brothers were featured in such movies as *Kid Millions* (with Eddie Cantor, 1934) and *The Pirate* (with Gene Kelly and Judy Garland, 1948). They and other such dancers—Cole and Atkins, Buck and Bubbles, Bill Robinson—had an inestimable influence on the music of their time and place.

Song and Dance

The American Way of Pianism

I am a composer who plays the piano. There is a distinction between this and a "real" pianist. At least when I was a boy this was true. Thirty or so years ago real pianists played nothing but Rachmaninoff concertos (I suppose there is nothing wrong with Rachmaninoff concertos, but I shudder to think of having to play them, day in, day out, with different orchestras, as a regular occupation). Well, this is not quite fair. Real pianists also played recitals that invariably went like this: first you played a Bach prelude and fugue, as fast as possible; then you did a Beethoven sonata; then came intermission; then came the entire Chopin *Préludes* or something else huge by Chopin; then something showy by Liszt; encores (usually unidentified); and that was that. When I was little I showed aptitude in both piano and composition, but even then the life of a concert pianist struck me as unutterably boring because of the imposed repertoire. Things have loosened up somewhat; now the Bach fugue can be played more slowly. And, among American pianists, one of the unidentified encores will probably be a rag by Scott Joplin.

I have something to do with the latter phenomenon. Around 1967, in a conversation with Norman Lloyd at the Rockefeller Foundation, I came upon his name. Joplin had written an opera in ragtime, Norman said. Who was Scott Joplin? "Well, he wrote the 'Maple Leaf Rag.'" Now came the job of finding the opera, unobtainable through the Library of Congress, Lincoln Center, or any of the usual sources; a copy of *Treemonisha* came to light through Rudi Blesh, who wrote the classic *They All Played Ragtime*, still the best book on the subject, and I was hooked. *Treemonisha* is not really a ragtime opera, by the way, containing only two or three numbers in that vein; but Joplin's piano music *is* really ragtime, and of a sort that would appeal to a classically trained musician. The musical details are of a refinement not found in barrelhouse or honky-tonk ragtime. There is an underlying earnestness in many of the Joplin rags that would allay the suspicions of any serious critic. Best of all, the notes aren't hard, and playing a Joplin rag as an encore is a socially acceptable bow to American music in a program usually distinguished by its absence. I suppose that my brief career (as well as Joshua Rifkin's) as an advocate of Joplin rags in piano concerts had something to do with giving Joplin enough cachet that real pianists could include him in their concerts among the "Islameys," the "Isles joyeuses," the "Trianas," and all the other traditional "enders," and it's probably a good thing.

I wish I could say that the *way* Joplin is played by most real pianists pleased me more. One of the few times I ever judged anything was when I was on the panel at the Sedalia, Missouri, Scott Joplin Festival about ten years ago and we heard about fifty pianists slog through rags of all sorts. One

contestant, obviously a very talented real pianist, favored us with her rendition of Joplin's "Gladiolus." Every falling phrase sighed; every cadence was lingered upon lovingly; every chromatic note was rubatoed; and, worst of all, every measure was in a different tempo. When she didn't win, she cornered me: "What was wrong with my playing?" You just don't play Joplin like that, I said. The tempo must be strict. You should be able to dance to it. "But those beautiful sighing phrases in 'Gladiolus'! They just *cry* for a rubato!" I was about ready to cry if anybody was going to: No, no, no! You don't do that to poor Joplin. It's all wrong: I

Left, a cover of "The Banjo" from the mid-nineteenth century, when art was raised to a kind of madness. *Right*, a portrait of the piece's equally busy composer, Louis-Moreau Gottschalk, a pianist, world traveler, and tireless womanizer.

know it is. The Joplin style, and the basic American piano style, is something else again. You won't learn it from your real piano teacher. For example, your real piano teacher taught you when you were little to stop tapping your foot when you play. The first thing Eubie Blake taught me to do was to tap my foot again when I played to keep from rushing; it works, by the way, and it's a good step toward leaving the real-pianist world and moving toward the world of Joplin, James Scott, Joe Lamb, James P. Johnson, Luckey Roberts, Art Tatum, Earl Hines, Teddy Wilson, and all those wonderful two-handed rag, stride, and jazz pianists who make up the basic text of the American piano oeuvre.

Even "The Banjo," by Louis-Moreau Gottschalk, to go back a bit, benefits from the use of the foot. It must not vary one iota from the opening tempo, which by the way doesn't have to go as fast as most people play it (that way you can accommodate those two-hand lateral leaps around page three that stop everybody); in fact, "The Banjo" sounds faster if you take it a little more four-to-the-bar than two-to-the-bar, and when you have to take the stretto at the end as fast as possible, it gives you the feeling that accordionist Dick Contino on the Horace Heidt show did at the end of "Lady of Spain": all

The Franz Kline I knew, who was part of the community of artists, poets, and composers in New York around 1960, was a most striking abstract expressionist, with a vigorous black-and-white style that was much imitated. In this earlier work, *Hot Jazz* (1940), he painted the connection between dancing and song: the music is almost visible in the movement.

SONG AND DANCE

Charles Luckeyeth (Luckey) Roberts was, with James P. Johnson and a few others, a major representative of the Harlem stride style of piano. When George Gershwin was a young song plugger at Remick's, Luckey became one of his mentors. Luckey's hit song "Moonlight Cocktail" was one of the mainstays of the 1930s. In his later years Luckey was a sought-after society pianist.

the real vaudeville excitement will be there, and the audience will go out of its mind. It will stomp and hoot and whistle and shout and clap, and you will know that that is how "The Banjo" is supposed to go.

The other thing to remember in "The Banjo" is to keep your right foot *off the pedal* as much as possible, except maybe when it's needed to help those famous leaps and similar places. First of all, it sounds more like a banjo that way. Also, it struts like the old Juba dancers did. And you get all those rhythmic variations you don't otherwise. Most real pianists use far too much pedal anyway, to my thinking, and particularly when they get to American music (and in this I include the Charles Ives piano sonatas, except where he says to use lots, and then they don't use enough). There is a practical reason for their using so much damper pedal: it gives you more volume (not for nothing is it often called the loud pedal), and in big halls more volume is needed. No matter. I still think that "The Banjo" with too much pedal sounds (because so much of it is in the bottom third of the piano) more like "The Tuba." Banjos make an awful lot of noise for their size. Try doing the same thing with the piano—make all the volume you can without the pedal—and you will get more of a banjo effect. George Gershwin, whose piano music positively *must* be played with these precepts in mind, wrote about it very well himself in his preface to *George Gershwin's Song-book* (1932), which includes his own piano transcriptions of some of his most famous songs: "To play American popular music most effectively one must guard against the natural tendency to make too frequent use of the sustaining pedal. Our study of the great romantic composers has trained us in the method of the *legato*, whereas our popular music asks for *staccato* effects, for almost a stencilled style. The rhythms of American popular music are more or less brittle; they should be made to snap, and at times to cackle. [Did he mean "crackle," as in "snap, crackle, and pop"?] The more sharply the music is played, the more effective it sounds.

"Most pianists with a classical training fail lamentably in the playing of our ragtime or jazz be-cause they use the pedaling of Chopin when interpreting the blues of Handy. The romantic touch is very good in a sentimental ballad, but in a tune of strict rhythm it is somewhat out of place."

There! He said it, and I'm glad. It is a pleasure to appeal to the authority of the greatest of all American popular composers. *That* for your drooping "Gladiolus," Miss Real Pianist!

Most American piano music has something to do with dancing. In fact, it could be argued that most keyboard music, period, has to do with dance of one sort or another, but ours involves itself with *dancing* more than it does with the Dance. Dancing means people going to hear a jazz band and dancing to it, as they used to do to Ellington as readily as to Glenn Miller. All the great jazz pianists played

At our informal Monday evening jazz ensembles at the Five Spot in the early 1960s, Larry Rivers (*above*) was featured on saxophone and I was relieved at the piano by Freddie Redd. Our idea was to make jazz that people could dance to again.

for dancing at one time or another in their lives, and they would have lost their jobs if they hadn't picked danceable tempos and kept their time. Sometime in the fifties jazz took on a serious listenership. In many ways that was a good thing, for listener and player alike, being able to hear and be heard easily without fighting the din of foot scraping and drunken conversation in dance halls. But there was one big drawback: jazz concerts became solemn, profound, burdened with Meaning. Little jazz clubs, like the old Five Spot and Jazz Workshop, became churchly, silent shrines, with intense audiences hanging on every note, bodies doubled up in painful concentration. Thelonious Monk, who comes directly out of the great two-handed tradition of James P. Johnson, became amused, I think, by the newly prayerful attitude of his Five Spot audience, and I remember one evening with long silences. *Ptt*, he played on the piano with his index finger; a gasp of appreciation. A pause. *Ptt*. Another gasp. This must have gone on for half an hour, with the audience in respectful ecstasy; Count Basie without the rest of the band was what it sounded like. (This was about 1961, and a bunch of us decided that we wanted jazz you could dance to again. So Larry Rivers, who had played in bands and still played decent saxophone, took over the Five Spot on Monday nights. I sometimes sat in at the piano; Freddie Redd, after playing in Jack Gelber's *The Connection* up at the Living Theater, would come down and take over, and I'd go out front and dance.) I'm not saying that I am against playing too fast or too slowly for dancing, or that I would always play as if I had a full dance floor when playing in concert. I *am* saying that it's important never to lose the connection between jazz and dancing, and by extension jazz-influenced music and dancing. Even if the listener cannot dance to your playing, he/she should be able to *imagine* dancing, and I think this is even true with the Chopin mazurkas and waltzes. The key word here is *imagine*, and this allows you to use considerable rubato, tempo changes, and so on, and never break the thread. To an extent this is true of Joplin rags too. "Gladiolus," for example, is a singing rag, not jazzy like "Magnetic" or barrelhouse like the "Ma-

ple Leaf." So how hard have I the right to come down on poor Miss Real Pianist for wanting to play hob with the note values on those beautiful arching lines? Piano music is related to singing as well as to dancing. This also obviously transcends American music historically: the opening melody of, say, the Chopin E-flat Nocturne is straight out of Italian opera, and to play it as if you didn't know that is to miss the point entirely. Here is where a new and real problem comes in: *The piano is the instrument of illusion.* What I mean by this (and it is the central problem of orchestrating piano music) is that a good piano, with a good pianist, can make the listener *think* of a vocal or instrumental line by shading and careful rubato of the melody, when in point of fact all we are really hearing is a series of thumps—our minds provide the illusion. A composer writing for the piano writes a line that will provide this illusion (and allusion also, if you wish—when you orchestrate that piano line, you replace the allusion to, say, a clarinet with the real clarinet, and often it doesn't work). How hard should the interpreter try

Facing page: Top left, Ferdinand La Menthe, "Jelly Roll Morton" (1885–1941), a composer and pianist who modestly claimed to have invented jazz. Whether or not this is true (and it isn't totally false), Morton's influence is enormous. He had a wonderfully direct style all his own, uncluttered and funky, but he was—as is well documented in his Library of Congress recordings—perfectly able to reproduce the styles of a wide range of other players. *Top right*, James P. Johnson (1894–1955), considered the "father of the stride piano" and an accomplished composer. His show *Runnin' Wild*, following on Sissle and Blake's *Shuffle Along*, continued the short but merry spate of 1920s black musicals. He composed the famous "Charleston," "If I Could Be with You," "Old Fashioned Love," and other hits, but also many wonderful stride pieces. (Stride is a more elaborate form of ragtime, characterized by a wider space between the off- and on-beats in the left hand. Thus the bass notes become a sort of target practice, and rare was the stride master who hit them all. James P. hit a fair average.) Johnson studied piano with Leopold Godowsky, who, along with straightening out his fingering, was perhaps an inspiration to Johnson to extend the use of the keyboard in his own compositions. *Bottom*, the "Three Maniacs of Rhythm"—Ford, Harris, and Jones—with the Earl Hines Orchestra at the Club El Grotto.

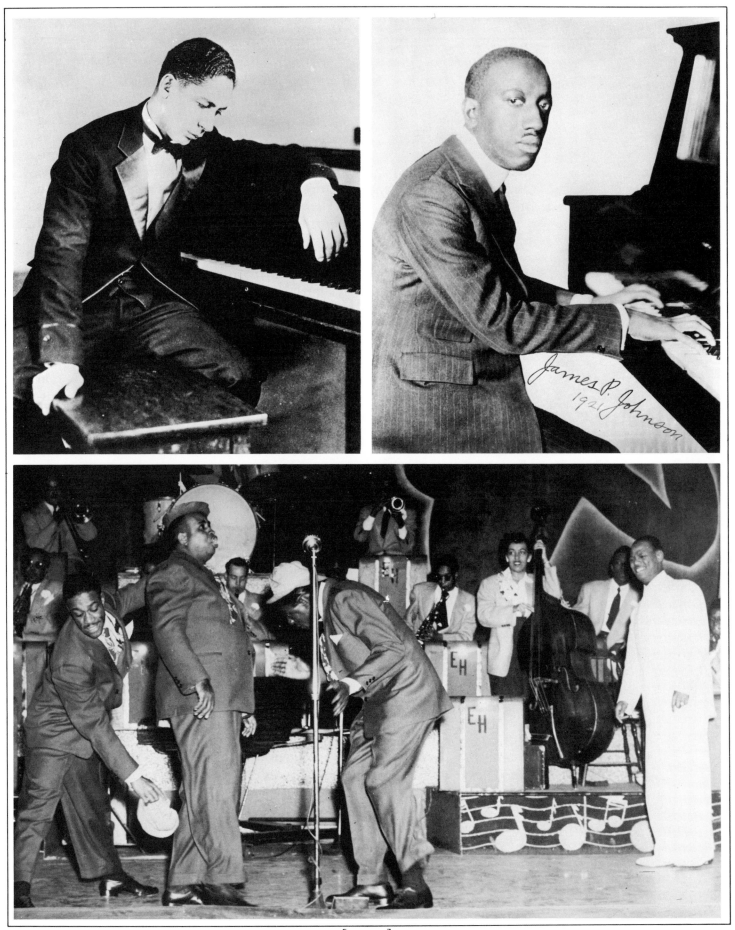

to intensify that illusion in playing the piece? What about "Gladiolus"?

Here we get into the central distinction between American and European piano music, namely, the kind of piano most of the literature was written for and the sort of audience the pianist worked with. The piano grew from Cristofori's 1709 prototype to the modern instrument in almost exactly one hundred years; Érard's piano action, which Chopin espoused out of the plethora of experiments surrounding his time, was invented around 1820 and is essentially the same action we use today. A large part of important European piano literature, however, was written before Érard, including most of the Beethoven sonatas and all of Haydn and Mozart, and the farther back the historian goes in piano literature, the more the music seems and feels like harpsichord music. The big difference between the harpsichord and fortepiano was that the latter could play loud and soft, but it did not approach the volume of the modern piano. Moreover, the pedal of the turn of the eighteenth century did not begin to sustain as long as the modern one. Thus many differentiations in the singing line had to be somewhat exaggerated on the early piano in order to create the illusion of continuity, very much as they must be on a harpsichord. There were big harpsichords that could fill large halls in Bach's day (builders are now beginning to learn to make similar ones), and there were also pianos that could make a lot of noise a bit later. But it was only with Alpheus Babcock's piano "harps" that it was suddenly possible to increase the tension on the piano strings sufficiently to produce a prodigious sound. Pianists could fill larger halls, make much more money, and go for grand-opera effects. With bigger audiences came popularization and thus an entirely different attitude toward the piano. Where your eighteenth-century button manufacturer would play easy piano pieces on his cembalo or fortepiano (or have his marriageable daughter learn how), his (or her) nineteenth-century counterpart could play rumbly battle music, bird-call fantasias, easy operatic paraphrases, and the like with a good deal more noise and panache. Pianists could now become lions to their audiences, romantic heroes who battled with orchestras to uniformly triumphant conclusions (a far cry from Mozart's elegant dialogues with the orchestra in his own concertos).

All this was, however, mostly a European phenomenon, even though an American piano manufacturer had made it possible. (In this respect Gottschalk is as much and as little an American as the painter James McNeill Whistler. Both could pull a "savage American" act whenever it was socially titillating, in the same way Ernest Hemingway and the composer George Antheil were able to in Paris a century later, but they were all really highly cultured internationalists. This is probably why I have always felt Gottschalk's "American" music to be self-consciously nationalistic. In "The Banjo" or "La Bamboula" Gottschalk used the idioms in the same way he used South American rhythms in his habañeras, but a piece like "The Union," which combines American national anthems one on top of another in a flashy climax, always seemed to me a pandering to his audiences here. I don't think he meant it.) More common to the American musical scene would be home amateur pianists, playing on the much simpler square piano, accompanying songs and hymns. In fact it can be argued that, whereas European musical life in general centered more and more on the concert hall, American musical life never really followed suit, not even today. Of course we have concert halls and big, efficient

---

Facing page: These two pictures say a great deal about American versus European pianism. As far as I know, Horowitz's interest in Americana stops with his (quite stunning) arrangement of Sousa's "The Stars and Stripes Forever" for what sounds like six hands, though in fact he performed and recorded it with only two. When I was little I was taken to a Horowitz recital in Seattle; it was truly terrifying. The picture of Noble Sissle and Eubie Blake (*bottom*) was taken in the mid-1920s, when the pair was sailing to England to participate in one of the Charles Cochran revues. Eubie's style is an ironic and humorous conversation among the parlor piano styles of his youth; he reminds me of Poulenc in his ability to do a style and cock a wink at it at the same moment (a prime example is his version of the *Tannhäuser* "Pilgrim's Chorus," first seriously stated, then done in bawdy-house stride as the ride-out).

symphony orchestras just like Europe. But to Europe that was their culture, and to us it was, and still is, Culture, in the same way that there is a distinction between dancing and the Dance.

Concert music, then, will always seem a little less natural to us than it does to Europeans; we will love it, but we will find ourselves listening to it with our ears dressed in their Sunday best. I am not talking about a black-and-white difference between Europe and ourselves; I am talking mainly about a difference in tendency which obtains to this day. Europe is full of amateur musicians; America is full of concert pianists who can be called (in my snide way) real pianists. Of course. But if the basic piano music of Europe is Beethoven, Mozart, Chopin, Schumann, ours is Joplin, Gershwin, and Johnson, and even if those gentlemen sound better on a nice concert grand, that wasn't always what they got to play in real life. A piano in our hemisphere in the eighteenth or early nineteenth century was more of a rarity than it would be at the end of the nineteenth century—this much is certain—and by the time nearly every American home seemed to have a piano, it was usually a square piano (which was wearing out and would be replaced), a new upright piano, or, a few years later, a spinet. And the fact of the matter is that the Liszt E-flat Major Concerto sounds silly on an upright, whereas Joplin's "Gladiolus" sounds just fine.

In like fashion the tradition of rubato in melody, which derived from the harpsichord literature of the middle to late eighteenth century (see Carl

Philipp Emanuel Bach, whom Haydn regarded as the chief influence on his own music) and was passed on to the fortepiano literature, very likely never got a strong foothold in the United States. A graphic illustration of this probability is provided by leafing through an edition of Benjamin Carr's *Musical Journal*, published in Boston at the turn of the century. Carr was a composer, but mostly an entrepreneur in things musical, and his *Journal* was a subscription publication of music gotten together for local amateurs. The selections Carr made for his *Journal* ought to reflect, supposedly, the breadth of musical tastes his subscribers had, and the most revelatory juxtaposition I can remember was between an aria from Mozart's *La Clemenza di Tito* and a simple piano arrangement of "Pop Goes the Weasel" on the next page. I don't guarantee that the same subscriber who battled through the Mozart would go on to the next selection, but very possibly he or she did. In any event the interface of the two types of music is something of a shock even today. Think of yourself playing through the two one after another for the first time, at a point in history when you weren't barraged by radio and records and had to provide your own music, and the sudden cultural dislocation is even greater. The *Tito* is a struggle; the "Weasel" is a little dessert for all the hard work, and it goes by in a breeze. And the mental space between the two selections is right at the balance point in the American musical consciousness. All of our music is somewhere left or right of center on that musical seesaw, and some of it is squarely in the middle, teetering precariously all the same, because the seesaw never comes to rest. If our subscriber plays *Tito* in Boston with as much expressive rubato as he might have in Europe, he probably would feel more than a little uneasy—as if he might be falling off a seesaw. Especially with "Pop Goes the Weasel" staring at him from the next page.

What I've tried to locate is the American musical mentality as it applies not only to playing Joplin's "Gladiolus," but by extension to playing American piano music in general, different as it all is from type to type, composer to composer. The same mentality pervades the American compositional

I had the great honor to share a bill with Earl "Fatha" Hines (*facing page*, in his youth) at the Whitney Museum in New York, where John Wilson characterized me as the "big rumpled man" (which Eubie Blake's wife, Marion, calls me to this day). He was, I suspect, in his sixties, wearing a beautiful russet toupee, a powder-blue jacket, and a painted pipe—and he wiped the floor with all of us, including Eubie, Max Morath, and Willie "The Lion" Smith. (That was Willie's last public appearance. He mesmerized everyone with his exaggeratedly slow movements, asked someone to light his cigar, played a slow Debussyan piece he had written, and slowly exited.) Earl Hines, forsaking the foundation bass of his stride forebears, plays most of the time as if with two right hands.

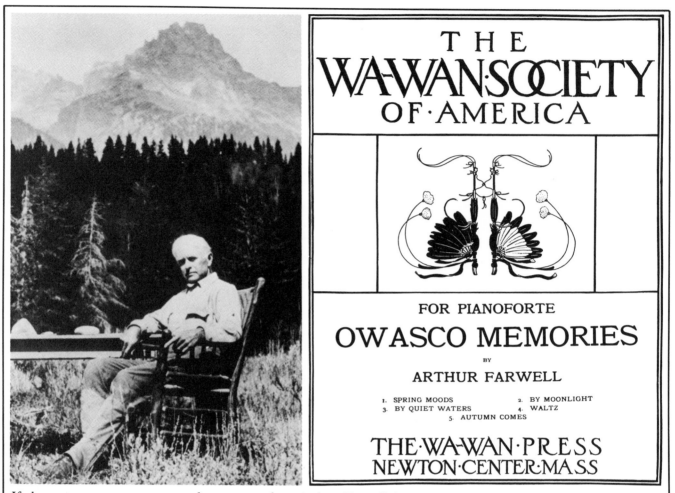

THE
WA·WAN·SOCIETY
OF · AMERICA

FOR PIANOFORTE
OWASCO MEMORIES
BY
ARTHUR FARWELL

1. SPRING MOODS   2. BY MOONLIGHT
3. BY QUIET WATERS   4. WALTZ
5. AUTUMN COMES

THE · WA-WAN · PRESS
NEWTON · CENTER · MASS

If there was ever a more moral composer than Arthur Farwell (1872–1952), I do not know of him. Farwell championed his own Wa-Wan Press, which he established in 1901 for the use not only of himself but of other composers bent on building on our Native American folk music. The Wa-Wan repertoire consisted largely of adaptations of Indian themes—which, when subjected to our equal-temperament piano tuning, sound (to my ears) just wrong—and compositions based on black melodies.

act. Our music still recalls its sources from across the oceans; maybe it won't after a few more centuries, in the way that Huns and Picts and Angles and Normans and Visigoths would become submerged in the culture of the countries they conquered and helped found—except in that when we came here, the culture we found put up remarkably little resistance over four centuries, considering the total. Toward the end of the nineteenth century, after most of the Indian wars were over and the Indian culture was disappearing, the American intellectual community began to be more interested

in it. (This fascination with things Native American resulted in the remarkable Edward S. Curtis series of photographs of Indian life. It also resulted in a large body of salon music, orchestral pieces, songs, and at least one opera—Victor Herbert's *Natoma*—purportedly in an Indian idiom and about Indians. The Wa-Wan Press, elegantly published in several volumes in the 1900s, included much music of this sort by Arthur Farwell, Charles Wakefield Cadman, and others; to my ears, much of it seems excessively high-minded, sentimentalized, and a bit bogus, but there is no telling how our rapidly changing tastes

Above, Edward MacDowell (1861–1908), who wrote "To a Wild Rose." He was one of an elite band of aspiring American composers who got to study in Europe and who could use German markings in their music with impunity. He studied briefly at the Paris Conservatory, but he moved in 1878 to Frankfurt, where he studied with one of the big composing honchos of the time, Joachim Raff (who may be best remembered for his orchestration of Liszt's *Les Préludes*). MacDowell came back to the United States when he was twenty-six—and brought with him a Jamesian diffidence toward his European models that shows up in his musical details. *Above right*, an illustration of Anton Dvořák, whose article in the February 1895 *Harper's* caused a furor among American musicians, revealing as it did his preference for the black musical idiom over that of the American Indian. *Right*, one of Constantin Alajálov's marvelous, though racist, illustrations for *George Gershwin's Song-book* of 1932.

With the American prairie becalmed at the end of the Indian wars, the American intellectual community took a new interest in the dying culture of its landscape, and Baldwin capitalized on the trend in 1900 with a pastoral piano.

might regard it in a few years, in the same way as we are now reviewing American painting of the same period.) When Anton Dvořák came to the United States and confronted the musical community here, he begged to differ; the most fruitful style would be derived from Negro melodies, he felt, not Indian ceremonial music. (There is a vaguely Negro-spiritual quality in, say, the second movement of his *New World* Symphony and parts of the *American* Quartet; but Dvořák rightly set all those pentatonic black-key melodies in a European, or Czech, framework, which was more natural to him.) The uproar against Dvořák's statement was ubiquitous and intense; how could anyone take the music coming out of honky-tonks and whorehouses seriously? Unlike the Indian evocations of Farwell and Edward MacDowell, it wasn't noble and it wasn't nice. Ragtime was not what you wanted your marriageable daughter to play; prospective suitors might get the wrong idea (and you'd never get rid of them). I'm not going to bore all of us with a discussion of reprehensible American puritanism, or of how terribly racist we all are. Parents of nearly any culture become puritanical when it comes to the fate of their own children, and the real threat of black music wasn't that it was from blacks—it was that ragtime was so appealingly anarchic. All this proves is that we are not influenced by what is said to be good for us, but by things we really like. (As William Saroyan told me, "Art is what is irresistible.") Try as we might to deal artistically with the American Indian heritage as part of the national psyche, the fact is that we have largely failed. The rest of us Americans all came here; whether we came here in first class or piled like cordwood in the hold is less important than the fact that we all *came here*—and within living memory often as not. (We will only integrate with Indian music if *we* include *them* in our modern national culture at some point; isn't this ironic, because *we* were the arrivistes, the interlopers? By rights *theirs* should have been the dominant culture.)

Dvořák's pronouncement has turned out to be true; in fact, American music is simply *not* American music without black influence. There are exceptions—I suppose William Billings is one—but

By the time of the Monk (*above*), jazz concerts were solemn, burdened with Meaning. I think he was amused, but the new jazz was heard in Europe—and used by European composers more than ours.

I'm afraid that time may very well be unkind to a large body of music written by serious-minded professors of composition, *à la page* with the latest European developments but unwilling to admit their own background, musically polyglot and unruly as it is (which is why they shy away from it, as any sensible person would).

It might be argued that the "serious" composers of Europe have been more able to draw from American sources than our own have. Ravel's G Major Concerto draws heavily on Gershwin; Milhaud's *La Création du monde* is inspired by American jazz; Satie wrote a parody of an Irving Berlin tune to use in his ballet *Parade*; and Stravinsky was reportedly impelled by the look—only the look—of a page of printed American ragtime to write his *Piano Rag-Music*, the rag in *L'Histoire du soldat*, and other ragtime-flavored pieces. Perhaps the best source of American attempts to return the compliment can

Scott Joplin, one of the saddest of all composers, and "Gladiolus," one of the most beautiful of all rags.

be found in the jazz piano tradition—Stravinsky's percussiveness in Thelonious Monk, Chopin's suavity in Keith Jarrett, Liszt's orchestral piano style in Art Tatum; I've rarely found it in our written music.

The landmark American composers are those who have found ways of integrating the different faces of our messy culture. There aren't very many of them. Even with the best intentions (Aaron Copland, Virgil Thomson, Roy Harris), the conscious effort to *sound* American has sometimes led to iffy results, usually a sort of artificial populism that may not have been meant to sound condescending but comes out that way. Copland and company reveled in Americana from the twenties through the forties, after which such music was considered out of style.

Perhaps efforts by such composers as Frederic Rzewski, William Albright (particularly in his rags), and myself could be considered a revival of that self-conscious Americanism, except that—I hope—there is a difference in the recent work: instead of amplifications and variations on hymn tunes, square-dance rhythms, and the like, some recent music shows a real desire to invent an independently American melody and musical diction, woven on a deeper level into the musical fabric. Scott Joplin stands out as the very first to pull the strands together into an artistic whole. There will be a chorus of protest: what about Gottschalk? He used American idioms. But that's just it: he *used* them, as he used everything else in his travels. He was a musical foreign correspondent. Joplin found the common properties and *fused* them, in such a way that it is impossible to take them apart or find the seams.

The facts of Joplin's life, such as are known, are too widely documented to need recounting here. (A dozen years ago this was not true—how times change!) All the more amazing, then, that Joplin—the "itinerant pianist" (in his publisher John Stark's words) who somehow cobbled together a musical education—should have been the one to write the opening phrase of "Gladiolus" with its Italo-Viennese chromaticism (look at the first full measure all by itself—it could have been part of a Schubert *Moment Musical*) sliding so naturally (in the next measure) into a blue note, followed by a syncopation:

Right at the measure line, the European meets the black American, but there is not the slightest stylistic jog or bump as the music flows. It's like those passages in Mozart where the music moves naturally from Italian opera to learned fugal style and ends, in the same phrase, with a German contredanse. After you've heard it and can look at the score, you can see where the styles begin and end, but your ear doesn't detect them the first time, and your brain amalgamates all the styles into one perfect whole. It is an enormous accomplishment, one that I have tried many times as a composer and often failed in—and a necessary accomplishment too, for this is the sort of stylistic marriage that begets many healthy children. I don't know if Charles Ives, Joplin's exact contemporary, or George Gershwin knew the piece. I don't think it matters. The fact that somebody in America made it happen put something in our national collective unconscious (I really believe in such "mystical" things) and made it easier for the rest of us.

Now, maybe, it becomes a little clearer why I got so mad at Miss Real Pianist's playing of this,

One of the youngest and brashest of song pluggers, George Gershwin would become a published composer in 1916 with "Rialto Ripples" (later to become Ernie Kovacs's theme song). His talent would frighten the well-behaved composers of his generation; he fearlessly fused the world around him with the Highest, and that wasn't done.

Composers and musicians of all persuasions, these men (*above*, seated from left, Leon Kirchner, Aaron Copland, Israel Citkowitz, David Diamond, Elliot Carter; standing, Gerhard Samuel, Donald Fuller, Arthur Berger, Jerome Moross) are united by classical training and a distinctly American stamp. *Left*, Charles Ives's Uncle Isaac and Aunt Emily ride by the house where that greatest of all American composers had been born not long before, in 1874. Ives developed a style that captures the nuances of this untrammeled and nutty culture of ours—and in doing that did more. In being so much of this place, he wrote music with universal meaning. In being so much of an age (in the sense that Varèse put it, meaning he was not *before* his time—all others were behind theirs), he became for all time.

one of Joplin's greatest rags: she gave all her interpretative weight to the first measure and not enough to the second. Syncopation depends on our knowing where the beat is; otherwise the throwing off has no meaning. To distort the opening half of the phrase in European fashion, as if it were Schubert or Chopin being played by a nineteenth-century pianist, could very well confuse the listener as to where "one" was. The blue note then loses all its blueness, the syncopation (which is integral to the blue note) loses its force, and we are left with an ordinary salon piece.

Similarly, a pianist who takes the second measure as the stylistic cue and decides that "Gladiolus" is nothing but a study in syncopation will miss something. The trouble with available documents on how to play ragtime is that most of them give a false idea of what it sounded like. What right have I to say that: "Vass you dere, Sharlie?" Only in that what we have, for the most part, are popular-style piano rolls and popular-style recordings. I emphasize *popular-style* because neither process tried for too much detail in pedaling, phrasing, or dynamics. The Duo-Art and Welte-Mignon rolls were reserved for people like Debussy, Mahler, Percy Grainger, and Saint-Saëns to record on; these contain all the refinements that make a difference. The popular recordings were usually not carefully monitored by a recording engineer who, while following a score, could widen or narrow the space between the record grooves as changes in loudness or softness came up (if he didn't do this, the needle would jump out of the groove when the record was played); the usual solution was to put a compressor on the recording apparatus, which flattened out the dynamic peaks. A pianist who takes the rolls and recordings of popular artists as primary sources and doesn't know that the compressor ironed out the players' accents, or that pedaling and other nuances simply didn't show up on the cheaply cut rolls,

usually ends up with dynamically flat, clattery, machinelike performances. Pianists of this sort, often heard in pizza parlors and the like, represent the other extreme in how not to play Joplin or Johnson or Gershwin. The truth lies, as I hope is apparent, somewhere in the middle. Johnson and Gershwin made many rolls and recordings, and they can be of help if you remember the limitations of the medium I mentioned. Joplin made a few rolls in 1916, the year before he died; there are those who doubt that he actually made them, but I wonder why anyone would fake them in just that way, because what you hear is rhythmically inchoate and uncontrolled—by 1916 Joplin's paresis was advanced to the state that his motor control was adversely affected, and these documents can only be described as heartbreaking. In the forties, however, S. Brunson Campbell, one of Joplin's few white pupils, made several recordings. He was by then an old man and he hadn't played Joplin for almost thirty years, but, despite the stops and starts and similar human failings, they are the best idea we have of what Joplin's playing may have been like—at once rhythmically solid and intensely lyrical, as "intoxicating" as the master had felt "what is scurrilously called ragtime" to be in its heart and mind.

I feel that if the pianist can learn to play Joplin rags with the right style and grace, that person can go on to play anything from Gottschalk to the Copland Piano Variations, from the Ives sonatas to the Gershwin Preludes and beyond, with the right insight. I am not a nationalistic composer or pianist or musician. By accident of birth, however, I am American, and for much of my life I have been fascinated by what that means. One can't be bound by it, but one ignores it at one's peril, for then the musician is fated to be nothing but a dispossessed European. Only by understanding it and accepting it can one transcend being American to make music that is truly universal.

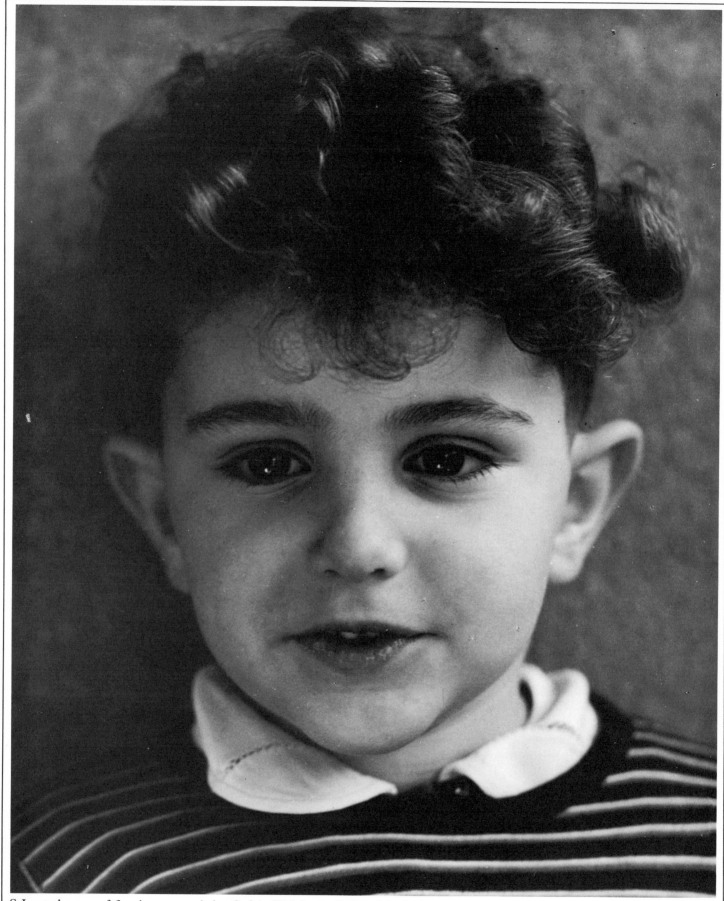

S.L. at the age of five in a portrait by Cedric Wright, a distinguished photographer and one of my early musical boosters.

VII

SAMUEL LIPMAN

The Ordeal of Growth

Confessions of a Former Prodigy

❦

Let others remember their growing up by houses, schools, and friends; I remember mine by piano teachers. For twenty-five of the first twenty-eight years of my life I was locked in an intimate relationship with one or another of these masters of the keyboard, all of whom were insatiable, finding in my progress and future both their present welfare and some faint, absurd hope of immortality.

So ubiquitous were these demanding creatures in my life that even before I encountered my first real teacher, I had already had two others. It was all begun, of course, by my mother. When I was three, she decided—I think because I cried when I heard the piano—that I was talented. So she started me out, using what knowledge and love of music she had gained during her own studies in Canada before World War I. In a few months she felt the need to pass me on to the neighborhood teacher in the little town where we lived, but she too was inadequate to what my mother thought of my talent. In this way, without my doing anything about it, I was propelled, not yet four, into the pedagogical big time.

This great world of music appeared in my life in the person of Lev Shorr, a man at once artistically distinguished, endlessly complicated, and more than a little mad. He was the most notable piano teacher of the second quarter of this century in San Francisco, and that is not faint praise. Those years were a golden age of music in northern California. Ernest Bloch, Darius Milhaud, and Roger Sessions were among the composers in residence for extended periods during that time; Pierre Monteux conducted the San Francisco Symphony Orchestra from 1936 to 1952; and Gaetano Merola at the same time established the San Francisco Opera as second in the United States only to the Metropolitan. The local musical press, led by Alfred Frankenstein and Alexander Fried, was serious, dignified, sophisticated, and responsible—qualities in short supply across the country in recent years.

During this period the Bay Area produced a dazzling number of brilliant young musicians. The most famous have been Isaac Stern, Leon Fleisher, and the Menuhins—Yehudi, Hephzibah, and Yaltah. Like my parents, the forebears of these talents

came from the sturdy stock of Russian Jews yearning to breathe free; like my parents, it was their fortune to find in San Francisco an aristocracy of German Jews, including such august names as Ehrman, Heller, Hellman, and Zellerbach, for whom the support of culture was the road to heaven.

Lev Shorr fit into this sophisticated milieu perfectly. He was a Jew, born in Russia in the late 1890s. He had studied at the St. Petersburg Conservatory with Annette Essipoff, a brilliant pianist and a teacher of great renown. Her thirteen-year marriage to the almost mythical Theodor Leschetizky, the chief piano teacher at the turn of the century, linked her to the greatest tradition in the history of the piano: Leschetizky had studied with Czerny, and Czerny had studied with Beethoven himself. But in her own right Essipoff had been an important part of the Russian pianistic world of the early twentieth century, a world distinguished by the playing of such young virtuosos as Rachmaninoff, Scriabin, and Prokofiev.

As a pianist Lev Shorr was intensely musical in an emotionally pronounced way, physically tense, and intellectually limited. He played as he felt—impulsively, sensitively, and capriciously. The great virtuoso music of Liszt and Chopin was technically beyond him; similarly out of his reach, but for musical reasons, were the more profound utterances of such giants as Mozart and Beethoven. But in the most direct and songful romantic styles—including much chamber music, which he played with his wife, the violinist Frances Wiener—he was a moving and dedicated player.

Facing page: Top, an early performance photo, also taken by Cedric Wright. The audience at this junior musicale was composed of students at the high-minded, progressive elementary school I attended for several years. *Bottom left*, Lev Shorr, standing over me in an uncharacteristically restrained mood. The occasion for this picture session in 1945 was my second San Francisco recital. The sunken knuckles of my hands provide visible evidence of the physical tension constantly underlying my approach to the keyboard. *Bottom right*, my parents and me. I must have been about four. My parents' appearance and bearing document for me, in a most poignant way, just how possible it was in the 1930s for the proud to achieve respectability even when mired in poverty.

His teaching displayed virtues and defects seemingly transferred directly from his playing. He was as careful in his choice of repertoire for me as he was for himself. He mixed the simpler Mozart, more reflective Chopin, and less complex Bach with piquant contemporary music—Bartók, Shostakovich, Prokofiev, and Villa-Lobos—written in surprisingly large quantities for pianists of limited technical proficiency. What I couldn't reach (I had, even for my age, tiny hands) he altered or eliminated in an always ingenious fashion. What he didn't play well, I didn't even attempt. What he knew, however, he could teach. It was not until much later that I realized that the technique he had not himself mastered he had also neglected to give me.

Shorr was, like a true disciple of Sigmund Freud (of whom I am sure he had never heard), a believer in infantile pianism—the idea that the most significant pianistic impressions are the earliest. He had much experience and success in teaching children; both Menuhin sisters and Leon Fleisher had been his students. It was clear that to catch talent young was his dream; to shape it in his own image was his professed goal. Starting with him when I did, long before my feet could come near reaching the pedals, I fit perfectly into his scheme. Because I was quick at playing by ear and imitating complex motions, I needed little articulated explanation—explanation that in any case he could really give only by demonstration. I quickly soaked up what he had to teach, good and bad alike. The good was musical. The bad, in part because of Shorr's insistence that I lift my fingers as high as possible in rapid passages, was technical. The result was that I played well only as long as the music didn't move very fast.

But both the musical and the technical aspects of my lessons with Shorr were overwhelmed by their emotional atmosphere. By turns the climate swung from love to rage, from hyperparental indulgence to excoriation, even to intimations of physical violence.

In the course of my twice-weekly two-hour lessons, little causes could have momentous effects. An apprehensive sigh from my mother—who, as

A picture with Shorr dating from 1943, when I was preparing for my upcoming San Francisco debut.

was typical in the case of child prodigies, was always present when I was being taught—would bring down on her a torrent of abuse. If I chose the wrong clothes to wear to a concert or lesson, Shorr was capable of taking it as an act of betrayal. If I commended another teacher or his student—or even praised a touring musician—he would rail at me and my ingratitude.

Mostly, however, it was my own failings that caused trouble. At the heart of these failings was one that no amount of effort or goodwill on my part could cure: my hands always were, and have always remained, too small. It was not simply a matter of my not being able to reach an occasional chord or octave; these problems Shorr could fix in a trice. Finally, though, virtuoso piano music de-

mands speed, agility, power, endurance, relaxation—all natural expressions of a hand that covers many keys at once. If Shorr had not himself played so tensely, my insufficient hands might have been trained to substitute to some extent quickness for reach. This wasn't to be, and I was invariably blamed both for how I played and for how much of the most immediately affecting part of the keyboard literature was thereby closed off.

Worse still, all this railing against fate spilled over into blame for my supposed lack of preparation. I didn't like to practice, and what organized work I did took place only under what might euphemistically be called supervised conditions. Because Shorr quite correctly pressed me at all times to learn new pieces, my performances of those that

Lev Shorr's musical and pianistic progenitors: Annette Essipoff (*top left*), Theodor Leschetizky (*top right*), Carl Czerny (*bottom left*), and the immortal Beethoven. Shorr studied with Essipoff, who was married to Leschetizky, who in turn had studied with Czerny, Beethoven's most famous and influential pupil. Czerny was not only a brilliant pianist and authoritative performer of Beethoven's piano music but also—and more important for the history of piano playing—a prolific writer of technical exercises. These exercises, widely used today, are valuable because they prepare both the ear and the hand for the patterns that regularly occur in classical piano music. Unfortunately, however, their emphasis on dexterity and velocity opened the door to the rigidity and tension that are the inevitable results of attempting to achieve virtuoso effects without the necessary physical preconditions.

had already provided me with sizable audiences and critical successes were subject to marked deterioration. As a result, Shorr never felt he could trust me to put his best foot forward. He was right. Once, when I was not yet in my teens, he summoned me at an hour's notice to play for Mishel Piastro, formerly the concertmaster of the New York Philharmonic and at that time making a fortune by conducting the popular Longines Symphonette. I had been out the whole day on my bicycle, and my playing made a bad impression indeed.

I suppose it could be said that beginning well and ending badly characterized the entire course of my piano studies with Lev Shorr. The two public recitals I gave, first at the age of eight and then at ten, followed by appearances with the San Francisco Symphony under both Pierre Monteux and Rudolph Ganz, were the summits of my career as a prodigy. My last recital appearance as a child, in 1948 when I was thirteen, though performed to a sold-out house, was a critical failure; my attempt to play Beethoven's late Sonata opus 110 seemed a

S.L. on the left of a group of performers at a San Francisco celebration, ca. 1946, of Soviet Woman's and Child's Day (an appearance I made as a result, I suppose, of my teacher's politics). It is reassuring to me now that I was actually positioned stage right.

particular miscalculation. The fall was devastating; a few short years after the bright future of my talent had been the subject of an editorial in the *San Francisco Chronicle*, I had become so tense in playing and so troubled about performance that my career ground to a halt.

The principle of teaching that Lev Shorr used, like so many of his gifted colleagues, was emulation. He did not explain; he did. He deeply wanted me to play the way he played, and the only way he could accomplish this was to play for me. So I grew up knowing how music was supposed to sound but not how or why it was to be played that way. For a gifted child this may seem like enough. But not for long. The child is succeeded by the adult, and youthful mindlessness and boundless confidence are all too soon gone forever.

The directions to copy that came to me in the atmosphere of terror he created also came packaged in an attitude of almost cloying love, which he expressed both verbally and physically. I was an adored object who, if only I were to will it so, could do no wrong. As long as I performed, I was showered with gifts, as pampered as any concubine, as protected as any court treasure. When things soured, however—because of my lack of diligence, my incapacity of nerve, and most of all the very real difficulties that arise when a child is given an adult's work—the storms immediately broke over my head. In punishment for mistakes my hands were ground down into the keys; music was thrown across the room; my habits and personal bearing no less than my talent were reviled. And it was never anyone's fault but mine how I played. The suffering I caused him, he often said, caused the glaucoma that eventually blinded him. The terror, the love—both were expressions of a relationship between puppet and puppeteer. On this point Lev Shorr was explicit. In what could stand as an epitaph for our relationship, several times he said to me: "Other people may think you're wonderful, but you'll always be my Charlie McCarthy."

My parents realized the pain all this was causing me. But their desire to extricate me from it always foundered on their unwillingness to send me to an undistinguished teacher; the agony would be

wasted. Finally in 1948, however, an interesting and brilliant teacher arrived in northern California, and it became possible for me, just turned fourteen and not a moment too early, to leave Shorr.

His successor was in most ways—virtually all of them for the better—the exact opposite of Shorr. Though both he and Shorr were Russian as well as Jewish, Alexander Libermann had come from an assimilated, cultured, and prosperous family rather than the quasi-ghetto life from which Shorr had arisen. While Shorr had seemed puffy and decid-

This picture dates from some time after I left Lev Shorr in 1948. It shows him, his blindness sadly apparent, with his wife, the violinist Frances Wiener. One of my early musical memories is of listening to them play sonatas on a late-Saturday-night radio broadcast around 1940.

One more relic of my 1943 San Francisco debut. Here, as usual in Shorr's studio, my hands betray the tension with which I was working.

edly immune to exercise, Libermann was thin as a rail and an addict of swimming and long walks. While Shorr had the restricted educational background and limited intellectual outlook characteristic of so many musicians, Libermann had received a university education in Russia, where he was trained as a lawyer; he was deeply interested in both history and literature. Even politically they were different; while Shorr was a Communist sympathizer and tended to force his beliefs on others, Libermann was politically both conservative and skeptical, opposed to the Soviet Union and a proud new American.

Most directly significant for my piano playing, of course, were the differences between my old and new mentors as musicians and teachers. Although Libermann had, like Shorr, been educated in Russia (his teacher was Blumenfeld, the teacher of Vladimir Horowitz), the greatest influence on him was the vigorous musical, intellectual, and pianistic personality of the great virtuoso Ferruccio Busoni, as transmitted through the witty, cynical, and inventive mind of Busoni's great disciple Egon Petri. Libermann had studied with Petri in Berlin during the 1920s and subsequently became his assistant for several years prior to Libermann's Hitler-enforced departure for Paris after 1933. Indeed, the very fact of Petri's being at Mills College in Oakland was responsible for Libermann's coming to northern California from France, and thus for my being able to study with him.

From Petri (for whom, at Libermann's urging, I often played) the young Libermann had learned of the vast world of the piano compositions, both popular and often cerebral, of Franz Liszt; of the gigantic Busoni transcriptions of Bach; of the sublime late Beethoven sonatas so alien (with the partial exception of opus 110) to Lev Shorr. Whereas for Shorr performance was all, for Libermann the music came first, not only as feeling but even more as thought. This quintessentially German attitude toward music—and his banishment of the oppressive atmosphere which I had thought natural to music and life to that point—remain in mind as Libermann's most important contributions to my development.

Top, a memento of survival. This snapshot, taken at a party after my second Town Hall (New York) recital in 1956, shows my parents standing on either side of me and Alexander Libermann between them. There is more than one survival here: my father had survived a serious heart attack the previous year, Libermann had survived the Nazis' attentions, and I had survived my childhood. *Bottom*, Libermann at the piano during one of his master classes at Mills College in the mid-1950s. The relaxation apparent in his hand position remains exemplary.

Center, the American pianist and epistler Amy Fay, whose 1880 collection of letters home, *Music Study in Germany*, has become a minor classic. She was a trenchant, even skeptical judge of the teachers she encountered. Of her work with Theodor Kullak (*left*), for example, she wrote: "I have been learning Beethoven's G major Concerto lately, and it is the most horribly difficult thing I've ever attempted. I have practiced the first movement a whole month, and I can't play it any more than I can fly. . . . Kullak gave me a regular rating over it at my last lesson, and told me I must stick to it till I *could* play it. It requires the greatest rapidity and facility of execution, and I get perfectly desperate over it. Kullak took advantage of the occasion to expand upon all the things an artist must be able to do, until my heart died within me. 'What do you know of double thirds?' said he. I had to admit I knew nothing of double thirds, and then he rushed down the piano like lightning from top to bottom in a scale in double thirds, just as if it were a common scale."

Later, in contrast, she worked with Liszt (*right*): "Liszt hasn't the nervous irritability common to artists, but on the contrary his disposition is the most exquisite and tranquil in the world. We have been there incessantly, and I've never seen him ruffled except two or three times, and then he was tired and not himself, and it was a most transient thing. When I think . . . how cuttingly sarcastic Kullak could be at times, I am astonished that Liszt so rarely loses his temper. He has the power of turning the best side of every one outward, and also the most marvellous and instant appreciation of what that side is."

Compounding the parent-child relationship that develops between most music teachers and their students, the bond between Leopold Mozart and his son Wolfgang was also biological. Mozart's best biographer, Alfred Einstein, described the result: "As soon as Leopold recognized the unusual musical gifts of the boy he sought to develop them, 'even while the child was at play', as it is put in the most reliable source about Mozart's youth. . . . Leopold has been reproached with having forced his son's talent like a plant in a hothouse, and for having commercialized it. But Leopold was not being altogether hypocritical, or indulging solely in secret self-justification, when he emphasized repeatedly that he held it to be his duty before God and the world to further the inconceivable talent of Wolfgang as a gift sent from above. It is fairly certain that without the early travels, with their hardship and exposure to infection—to all of which Wolfgang fell a victim: scarlet fever, small-pox, etc.—he would have lived much longer. But his development would also have taken place at a different tempo. And Leopold was justified by the great willingness of the child, the boy, and the youth. Mozart was twenty-two years old before he slipped out from under his father's control."

Musically concerned as Libermann was, he was also deeply involved with piano technique as a worthy subject of study in itself. Thorough pedagogue that he was, he had devoured the extensive literature on matters digital, and by the time I worked with him he had long since developed an organized and coherent system based on grabbing and relaxation. Freed from Shorr's tension-and-poking pedagogy, I was soon learning flashy music, mostly Liszt, and playing it with an ease and brilliance I

had not thought possible for me.

In gaining the freedom to move my fingers, I suppose I lost something valuable as well. Musically profound though the Busoni-Petri school undoubtedly was, in Libermann's hands the result often seemed cool and even sometimes artificial. Gone from my playing was the warm, Slavic musicality that Shorr at his best produced in his students; it was replaced by Teutonic sobriety and dryness. Perhaps more important, I consequently

Sergei Rachmaninoff's teacher, Nikolai Zverev, with his class in 1886. Scriabin is seated on the left; Rachmaninoff is standing, second from right. Rachmaninoff, who worked with Zverev from the ages of twelve to sixteen, finally stopped his lessons (and living in Zverev's house) because of his teacher's desire to have him play the piano rather than compose. As Rachmaninoff's memoir attests, Zverev's daily routine was spartan indeed. In the words of another student: "Practice had to begin at 6 a.m., and we took turns in being the one who had to get up at that hour. No excuse was ever allowed—if a pupil had been at a play or concert the night before, or had not gotten to bed until 2 a.m.—nothing could change this schedule. . . . And woe to him if any sleepiness was betrayed in his playing—Zverev would storm in, a frightening figure in his underwear, with a horrible shout and sometimes a hard smack. The sleepy pupil would instantly wake up and play with new attention."

Pierre Monteux (*right*) and Darius Milhaud (*above*, in his studio). These two teachers, who were not pianists, showed me that much if not most of music lay outside the domain of the keyboard. Monteux's surface geniality, so prominent in this photograph, was accompanied by a phenomenally acute ear, a vast knowledge of repertoire, a rapier wit, and that most vital of a conductor's attributes—complete self-interest and self-absorption, expressed at its purest when dealing with other people. Milhaud's music—because of the very facility with which he wrote it—remains underestimated to this day. His ability to solve the most arcane problems of strict counterpoint with artistic grace remains in my mind as the most awe-inspiring musical demonstration I have ever witnessed.

lost some of the involvement with the audience (and the audience's involvement with me) that had marked my public success as a child.

Still, the new atmosphere of freedom, ease, even humor at my lessons was tremendously gratifying to me on a personal level—and probably a large part of the reason my fingers at last began to flow over the keys. Passionately fond of jokes in half a dozen languages and a brilliant raconteur, Libermann liked to quote his own adage inspired by the girls he taught at Mills College: "The only body in the world that doesn't grow older is a student body." He even seemed to like talking with me! He never shrieked, and he rarely became envenomed.

Heinrich Barth (*left*) and his then teenaged student Arthur Rubinstein. Barth, like Nikolai Zverev, who taught the young man Rachmaninoff, saw his responsibility as more than the mere impression of his own musical personality on the student. In the first volume of his memoirs, *My Young Years*, Rubinstein describes Barth's attitude toward him: "After some time I noticed that he actually became fond of me. A tender look in his eyes and a shy, boyish smile would appear now and then in his usually sad, stern face, especially after a satisfactory performance. But God help me if I arrived unprepared for a lesson! I would begin, and as soon as I hit wrong notes, I would notice with horror how his long beard rose bit by bit into a horizontal position, which meant that he was drawing up his lower lip and biting it with rage—and then hell would break loose! He would jump to his feet, shout insults at me, bang his fists on the piano, and disappear for a while. After calming down, he would dismiss me sullenly, without a word."

Alexander Libermann, *top left*, with his musical and pianistic progenitors: *top right*, Felix Blumenfeld (a teacher also of Vladimir Horowitz); *center*, his teacher Theodor Stein, a member of the St. Petersburg Conservatory faculty after 1872; *bottom left*, Egon Petri, whose assistant Libermann eventually became and remained for many years; and, *bottom right*, Petri's revered master Ferruccio Busoni. Of Blumenthal I heard little from Libermann, save his association with Horowitz. Of Stein I heard nothing. Libermann always talked of Petri in my lessons, usually admiringly but sometimes disparagingly as well. In the early years of my work with Libermann I played for Petri often. Libermann's great admiration, like mine, was both for Petri's extraordinary musicianship—he, like Monteux, seemed to know and to be able to hear all the notes of every piece ever written—and for his quickness of mind. Libermann's stories about Busoni (with whom he had not studied) were the kind of tales one hears about a saint—in this case a saint with the vision of a prophet and the fingers of a devil.

S.L., in a picture taken in 1954 by a sidewalk tourist photographer on Central Park South in Manhattan. I was on my way back to San Francisco from Pierre Monteux's school in Maine, where I went every summer from 1951 to 1957. The bow tie, worn under the influence of Libermann, was one of a group of six I had ordered, sight unseen, from the Libermanns' relatives in Paris.

Gone were the days of Shorr's attacking me for every moment spent away from the piano; Libermann actually recommended to me books on non-musical subjects—German military history was one—that particularly fascinated him.

Under this welcome new dispensation I blossomed pianistically and personally. I went to college, studying political science, and then to graduate school, again in political science. I played many times with the San Francisco Symphony, gave two recitals in Town Hall in New York, and appeared at Lewisohn Stadium with an orchestra drawn from the New York Philharmonic. But even this happy story was not without strains. At the urging of a patron who had come into my life as part of the local German-Jewish philanthropy, I had begun studying, still in my teens, with the great French composer Darius Milhaud and the increasingly famous conductor Pierre Monteux.

This alienation of my loyalties didn't sit well with Libermann. It is hard to blame him for feeling miffed, for the problem wasn't that he didn't respect Milhaud and Monteux, but that they didn't think much of him. The subtle yet clear pressure I felt from these two international artistic personalities caused Libermann to seem provincial in my eyes, a local piano teacher. Libermann, as any dedicated teacher would, must have felt this keenly. At any rate, he engaged in uncharacteristic sniping, telling me how unimportant I was to my newfound mentors.

Even without my experiences of Milhaud and Monteux, I would still one day have left Libermann. Twenty-two years of study and playing had exhausted northern California's musical life for me without at the same time giving me a viable career. To me, New York seemed a beacon of hope at the end of the 1950s. I still felt I needed a piano teacher, and there was no choice more natural than that famous trainer of championship pianists, the instructor of Van Cliburn himself: Rosina Lhévinne, the widow of the fabled virtuoso Josef Lhévinne.

In fact I had known Madame Lhévinne since the end of my days with Lev Shorr; my parents had taken me to Los Angeles to play for her when I was thirteen in the hope that she could provide a magic way out of the cul-de-sac in which I found myself with Shorr. At that time she seemed to me a slightly disheveled, benevolent, altogether grandmotherly figure. She was impressed with my talent if not with my playing and wanted me to come back to New York with her. Though my parents were invited to migrate with me, my father wisely demurred, and the matter ended there. I next saw her at my Town Hall debut in 1955, when she came

Above, Rosina Lhévinne with Van Cliburn in the mid-1950s, before his 1958 Tchaikovsky Competition triumph. She seemed to have more faith in Cliburn than in anyone else she ever taught; yet while she gloried in his (and her) success, it is my impression that she watched the unfolding of his household-name career with much disquiet—not because she minded so the musical result, but because she feared the consequences for the elegance of his pianism. *Right*, a snapshot of Rosina with me at her side, which perhaps demonstrates the stiffness of much of our relationship. Though I was seeing her almost daily in the period during which this picture was taken—the summer of 1960—neither my increasing familiarity with her nor my gratitude for her pianistic interest in me could obliterate the fact that I had come to her at the age of twenty-five with a preexisting, almost fully developed musical life.

to the after-concert party and pressed me to come to Juilliard to work with her. This time, because I was still in college and on my way to graduate school, I backed off. Four years later, my interest in political science at an end, I reconsidered, and finally I made the break with California.

Though I had committed myself to attend Juilliard in the fall of 1959, I decided to begin my studies with Rosina, as she was widely called—not, of course, to her face—in Aspen the preceding summer. The old woman I started to work with regularly there was hardly the kindly crone I had previously known. No longer cute and cozy, the new (to me) Madame Lhévinne was energetic and irascible, often rigid, and opinionated on just about every musical issue. At my first lesson I played the Beethoven *Pathétique* Sonata, to which she reacted with a certain coolness and distance. When I played it almost immediately thereafter in a student concert, she didn't come, but sent instead her immensely gifted and strikingly attractive young assistant. (The assistant gave me high marks, as I did the assistant; we were married four years later.)

The next lesson—my second—was a disaster. I brought her the Tchaikovsky First Piano Concerto, because she had promised me the coveted opportunity to play it in her master class at the end of the summer. From the first crashing chords through the first slow passage she was implacably critical. Everything I did was wrong; nothing fit with what, in her own words, "Tchaikovsky told Mr. Lhévinne." What had passed one faraway day in Moscow before the turn of the century was now present in unfortunately only a vague way in the living room of a tacky little house high up in the Colorado Rockies. It promised perhaps a better model than Shorr, but I could only wish that I had been provided a clearer picture of what it was I was supposed to copy.

On a level rather less metaphysical, it soon became clear that Madame Lhévinne had been so hard on me because of a need to extricate herself from a promise she had made to another student that he, too, would play the Tchaikovsky in the master class. A reason had to be found so that we might share the performance. What she heard as the weak-

Above, Rosina Lhévinne, ca. 1950, demonstrating the garb and bearing of a great lady pianist of the old school. *Facing page:* The important influences in her artistic life: *top left,* her teacher Vassily Safonov, a fixture on the faculty of the Moscow Conservatory, its director from 1889 to 1905, and the predecessor of Gustav Mahler as the vastly successful conductor of the New York Philharmonic from 1906 to 1909; *top right,* Safonov's teacher Leschetizky, with whom he studied in St. Petersburg; *bottom left,* the three Brassin brothers, Gerhard, Louis (standing), and Leopold. Safonov studied with either Louis or Leopold—the standard reference books are vague on the matter. Louis was the author of a transcription of Wagner's *Magic Fire Music,* much played by Russian piano virtuosos. Leopold was a pupil of Ignaz Moscheles (*bottom right*), the German pianist, teacher, and composer (d. 1870). As a pianist, Moscheles charmed all by his virtuosity and nobility of personality; as a composer, he wrote much trivial, now forgotten music.

Above left, Josef Lhévinne, a pianist respected and loved by his colleagues. As a performer he seems to have lacked both an exciting platform personality and the kind of intellectual curiosity that finds an outlet in new or hitherto undiscovered repertoire. He continued to play the music of his hero, Anton Rubinstein, long after it had fallen out of fashion. *Above right*, Alexander Villoing, the teacher of Anton and his brother Nicholas. It was the true student of Anton Rubinstein, Josef Hofmann (*right*, a portrait of Hofmann and Rubinstein), who was to make the great pianistic career of Lhévinne's generation. Though neither Hofmann nor Lhévinne recorded very much, it was Hofmann's curious combination of demonic dexterity and musical waywardness that was to impress the cognoscenti of piano playing; by contrast, Lhévinne's quiet elegance seemed all too easy to honor and at the same time to discount.

ness of my first movement—before she had heard the other movements—made the compromise possible. When the class came the other student began; I finished. Rosina's smiles of satisfaction and relief showed how much the matter had troubled her.

Our relationship improved immediately after the Tchaikovsky lesson. But though the personal mood was excellent—I even worked as an unpaid secretary and ghostwriter for her—I could never forget that she was entirely dedicated to the past, both of piano playing and of music. She was hardly unselective in her loyalties. She was quite willing to give up such bypassed relics of other years as her teacher Vassily Safonov, who in his day had been important as both pianist and conductor; even the great Anton Rubinstein, whose mantle Josef Lhévinne had inherited, she honored and revered only for his playing, not for his rejected and sentimental music. It was vastly different, however, with Scriabin and especially with Rachmaninoff. She had known both in Russia before the turn of the century as schoolmates and as figures in the musical life of Moscow. She spoke of these men with awe; Rachmaninoff's was the only playing which for her approached that of her husband.

The great cause of her life was naturally her husband; for her, Josef Lhévinne was both spiritual saint and artistic genius. She was aware of his flaws; she herself talked—in decorous terms, it is true—of his continual philandering, of his childish unwillingness to work as hard as she thought he should, and of his irresponsible attitude toward money and his family's security. Coming from someone else, it would have been a damning indictment. To Rosina, however, these many shortcomings were only the patina on a classic sculpture. What counted was his fabled sweetness of disposition, his gentle musicality, and his golden fingers.

I couldn't, of course, testify to his disposition; though Rosina remained convinced that I had played for him in 1944, in fact I had neither met Josef nor heard him in concert. I was, however, somewhat familiar with his playing, if only at second hand; his few but elegant recordings were hallowed objects on every Rosina Lhévinne student's phonograph. The performances enshrined on those disks were of romantic works, short in length, pleasing in mood, and frequently ferocious in technical difficulty. I could only admire, as everyone always did, the perfect technical mastery and the lovely tone he was able to convey despite the handicap of wretched, antiquated shellac originals. There could be no doubt that Josef's pianistic achievements were stupendous.

But what his musical achievement was always seemed to me to be rather a different matter. My impression of his art was that, consistent with the Russian approach to classical art, all the considerable risks he took in performance were technical, not musical. He played with marvelous speed, lightness, and evenness; everything was, to use a favorite word of Rosina's, "orderly." The music he chose to play on those records was well served by such an approach—if one could persuade oneself that all there is in music is easy virtuosity and restrained loveliness.

Those qualities were in fact Rosina Lhévinne's goals for her students. She hated harsh tone, musical exaggeration, heightened contrasts of both tempi and dynamics, and all kinds of irregularity and uniqueness. All these were "disorder." Unfortunately, what seemed disorderly to her often seemed to me hallmarks of originality in performance and interpretation. Her preferred sound image was of running water—cool, soothing, diverting, and decorative. I rather thought in terms of torrents and even floods. What I did always seemed to her too much; what she urged on me always seemed to me much too small.

So, despite the fact that I respected her and that she (I think) liked me, we fought for most of the three years of our work together. Finally I removed myself from our weekly struggles, pleading first one and then another excuse for not scheduling any lessons. In the last ten years before her death in 1976, at the age of ninety-six, I saw her only infrequently, and when I did I always regretted that our musical sympathies had not been closer.

I certainly did learn much of value from her, and I never could imagine having another teacher after her. She was, after all, a historic personage, a personal witness to the silver age of European music

A picture of the family Lipman in 1974. My wife, the pianist and teacher Jeaneane Dowis, continues to suggest to me in her daily practice that a humane approach to students is not only possible but also rewarding. Our son Edward, here shown tormenting a violin, has now switched to the oboe, for which he displays a sizable talent. His tolerance of the necessary drudgery seems greater than his father's was; it is our hope that he will find his way to accomplishment without the severe measures my wife (who has her own experience of being a child prodigy locked away in her heart) and I know so well from our own lives.

at the end of the nineteenth century and the golden age of Russian music before the 1917 revolutions. Once, two or three years after I had stopped studying with her, I had a chance to see just how much she still lived in the splendid past. About 1965, when she was well into her eighties, I attended one of Rosina's semipublic classes at Juilliard. A student was playing the opus 119 *Klavierstücke* of Brahms to Rosina's rapt attention. When he finished, she seemed lost in an intimate personal reverie. As the students waited silently for an opinion, she remained under the spell of her thoughts. Finally she breathed out, as if for herself alone, "Listen to the dissonances!" What dissonances? I thought. Then I realized: the pieces had appeared in 1892, when she was twelve years old. Those were *her* dissonances, and for me to have lived and played in her world, I would have had to hear them as mine. That I couldn't, I suppose, meant that at long last I was on my own.

As I look back across more than forty years in music, I now can see clearly that despite all the ways in which my teachers were different, in one way they were the same. All of them, through the varying prisms of their own characters and personalities, expressed a common nature: at heart they were all prisoners of the past. They all taught me what they had been taught, just as they had been taught it. They wished for me what had been wished for them, and they judged me as they themselves had been judged. More than that, none of them were the kind of successes they had spent their early lives trying to emulate and their later lives urging upon their students. Part of this descent from glory can, I suppose, be explained by the rare talent of such figures as Essipoff (and Leschetizky), Busoni, and Josef Lhévinne. Geniuses have always been few and far between, and followers have always tended to be epigones.

Of course, the piano itself is a prisoner of its past. Its great heroes—men like Rachmaninoff, Hofmann, Schnabel—all belong to yesterday; even the most famous pianists of today—Rubinstein and Horowitz—seem like survivors of an epic age. No longer is the piano evolving in sound or construction; the most talked-about new pianos of today emphasize their old-fashioned tone and their unchanged methods of construction. Even more basically, the idea of the piano as the central instrument of music making, the one with a whole musical world potential in its eighty-eight keys, is gone.

Not surprisingly, the current plight of the piano merely reflects that of art music in the years since World War I. By the end of the first two decades of our century, the great repertoire of music had in large measure been written. Since then we—performers and composers alike—have been living on its capital. There is no change for the better in this regrettable situation anywhere in sight; until such a change occurs, we have hardly any choice but to retreat further into our richly hung museum.

Given the world in which I grew up and the backgrounds of those who taught me, I could reasonably have expected nothing but what I got from my life as a piano student, save a few more kind words. Even the hard times I went through seem in retrospect just about par for a rocky, hilly, and long course. If I learned nothing about the future—and precious little about the present—I certainly learned a great deal about the past. At least it can never be said about me that I am a creature without a history.

Serkin and Horszowski, in a scene that demonstrates the repose and remove they sought at Marlboro.

VIII

RICHARD SENNETT

Pianists in Their Time

A Memoir

My own musical career was disastrous. I studied the cello as a child and continued to work, more seriously, in college. Whatever my gifts, I could not perform in public; I fainted or vomited during performances. At the age of nineteen, in 1962, I decided to give up the cello, but I did not want to abandon music. I began to study conducting, left the University of Chicago, and moved to New York, where I prepared for the classes of Pierre Monteux. Our demons, however, do not leave us, no matter how much we change circumstances, and I found it no more possible to conduct than to play in public.

During the time I spent in New York I became close to the pianist Murray Perahia, and through him the pianists Peter Serkin and Richard Goode. When I went to Harvard for graduate study, I bought a house in Vermont near the Marlboro Music Festival, where they played every summer, and my friendship with these three and with other pianists our age deepened. Apart from my sterling character, wit, and charm, what attracted them to me was the fact that I was someone who had quit.

These "Marlboro school" pianists of the 1960s formed a distinct group because of something beyond a common age, a shared love of chamber music, and an urban, mostly Jewish background. They were ambivalent about having careers as pianists. They loathed the show biz of music. They felt that, as pianists, they faced unique dangers in being seduced by success.

A scene stands out in my mind which demonstrates the length to which this loathing of public life, so close for a musician to a loathing of oneself, could be taken.

It was in 1967, I think, that we were seized by the mania for organic farming. Peter Serkin lived about ten miles from me in the country, both of us near the festival that his father, Rudolf, had established with some other refugee musicians after the war. The land in southern Vermont is rocky but in patches fertile, a teasing sort of landscape in which to farm. Rudi himself had succumbed to the urge in his self-deprecating sort of way. He had a tractor that he would ride on his own property, smiling with embarrassment but firm about which controls

to use when. Thanks largely to Rudi's efforts with the Marlboro Festival, southeastern Vermont was an outpost of Bohemia—the Bohemia of the mind, although the landscape does somewhat resemble the Central European Bohemia from which many of the musicians living there had come. By the middle 1960s neat new wooden houses with skylights, with Chinese gongs on the front porches, with sensible, energy-efficient foreign cars in the driveways, were dotted among the ramshackle cabins of the old Vermonters. An herb-and-grain store had begun a thriving business in Brattleboro; the local liquor store had taken to stocking claret. In the 1950s summer visitors to the Marlboro Festival had begun to enrich the tourist business, which had struggled along before on skiers and hunters. By the 1960s, some of the summer people had become year-round outsiders, reveling in the snow, flickering electricity, and acrimonious town meetings which the locals bore patiently as part of the normal affliction of existence. So when the gospel of organic vegetable farming began to be preached, the old Vermonters dismissed it as too much trouble, and we embraced it as a logical step in our quest to become at one with nature.

Peter and I and our then wives began planting on his back land leeks, chicory, and a variety of vegetables to be used in Indian cuisine. The advantage of this was that the vegetables united our love of nature with our interest in Indian mysticism; the disadvantage was that none of these plants—with the exception of the leeks—loves an alpine climate. So we had to work very hard over them. And that work entailed the rough use of tools with our hands, tools such as scythes, trowels, and knives which might damage a muscle or sever a nerve our teachers had taken a decade to develop.

Facing page: Top, a class at Marlboro. Richard Goode is the pianist on the far right, Peter Serkin is the pianist on the left, and Rudolf Serkin is behind them. *Bottom left,* Pablo Casals. The concerts at which he conducted were legendary. In the fewest and most rudimentary words he managed to convey an enormous amount, whether in class or conversation. *Bottom right,* my favorite picture of Peter as a younger man. It could represent him at a concert, at a rehearsal, or at dinner.

The scene I remember is Rudi quietly standing on the edge of the field, watching us wield with no great skill the dangerous tools of our trade, frowning. In the way of these things, he said nothing to his son, a great artist even in his early twenties, but asked me, who no longer had anything to lose, if it was wise to take such risks. We all knew some older musicians who put their hands in danger; Mischa Schneider, the cellist in the Budapest Quartet, did woodworking, but there were few as rash as he. And I think Rudi knew that there was some secret desire in Peter that an accident should occur, and so Peter would be excused from ever having to perform again, like a brilliant student no longer obliged to recite in front of the rest of the class. Rudi knew this, not only because he knew his son, but because every summer he saw others like Peter, if not quite so gifted—boys and girls who loved to play but hated to perform. "You are all beatniks," Casals once remarked to me (the Catalan pronunciation of this American word is something like "be-*at*-nish"). He meant more than the fact that we had long hair, wore jeans on the concert platform, and the like. "What you have, you don't give to others." But what if all the machinery of giving in music—managers, tours, lunches with society ladies who sponsor concerts, the politicking and hustling involved in competitions—what if all this machinery kills the gift? That was the fear of my friends. In their "beatnik" moments they spoke of free "alternative concerts," or of "reciprocal concerts" for which the audience would pay in goods rather than cash (a friend of mine once played both books of Chopin Etudes at such a concert and wound up with about two bushels of organically grown tomatoes in return). The more intelligent musicians thought about ways to develop their art and play for friends, while making a living at something else.

In reflecting on these and other incidents in subsequent years, I've come to think they represent something other than the usual adolescent follies. They are instances of the odd relationship of musical performers to the dominant modern image of the artist: the artist as rebel. A young man can throw down the gauntlet to his family by over-

The emblem of the 1960s was the Woodstock Festival. It was an event Franz Liszt would have well understood. Some of my friends, like Peter Serkin, were attracted to the unbuttoned ambience. On the other hand, the star system built out of these concerts represented all that my friends loathed.

throwing his legal studies and announcing he is going to become a poet. But a young musician has been in the hands of special teachers since the age of eight or nine; he or she has started adult work ten or fifteen years earlier than his or her peers, practicing at least three hours a day. By the time the musician reaches late adolescence, he or she is too deep into the art for it to be a surprise, or a fresh weapon, to anyone else. Moreover, the essence of a performer's art is seducing others rather than confronting them. A composer might take a sort of grim pleasure when a piece of his is booed; that pleasure is not available to a pianist performing a Mozart concerto. When the juices of adolescence begin to run, as they did for Peter and others of our generation, it seemed possible to revolt against the world only by turning against what we had been made ourselves. Our rebellion was in using hand tools that might sever a nerve, hard work in nature that did not succor artistic thoughts but obliterated them, calling one away from practicing and tiring the hands.

My friends grew up in a rebellious generation, and they loathed the show biz of the music "industry." Yet the paths of rebellion against the world often seemed to lead to self-destruction, to rebellion

This is not the Liszt whom the public knew. Liszt became, in fact, so appalled at his own public life that he finally went into retreat as a monk.

against their own art. And because my friends were pianists, this dilemma was particularly provoking. For more than a century pianists had been developing a special relation to the public, one that offered enormous possibilities both for gratification and for corruption.

The public life of the modern pianist has been shaped by two historical forces dating back to the nineteenth century. On the one hand the pianist as a public figure became someone who was expected to make a virtuoso display; technical improvements in the sound quality, volume, and damping of the piano made it an instrument capable of such display. And on the other hand the pianist played to audiences among which were many who also played, thanks to the industrial manufacture, relative cheapness, and popularity of the instrument in the home. Because of his ever-expanding powers and his audience's familiarity with the instrument, the pianist occupied a special place among musicians.

The history of piano design and manufacture can be found in such excellent studies as E. M. Rosamund Harding's *The Piano-Forte: Its History Traced to the Great Exhibition of 1851* (reissued by Da Capo

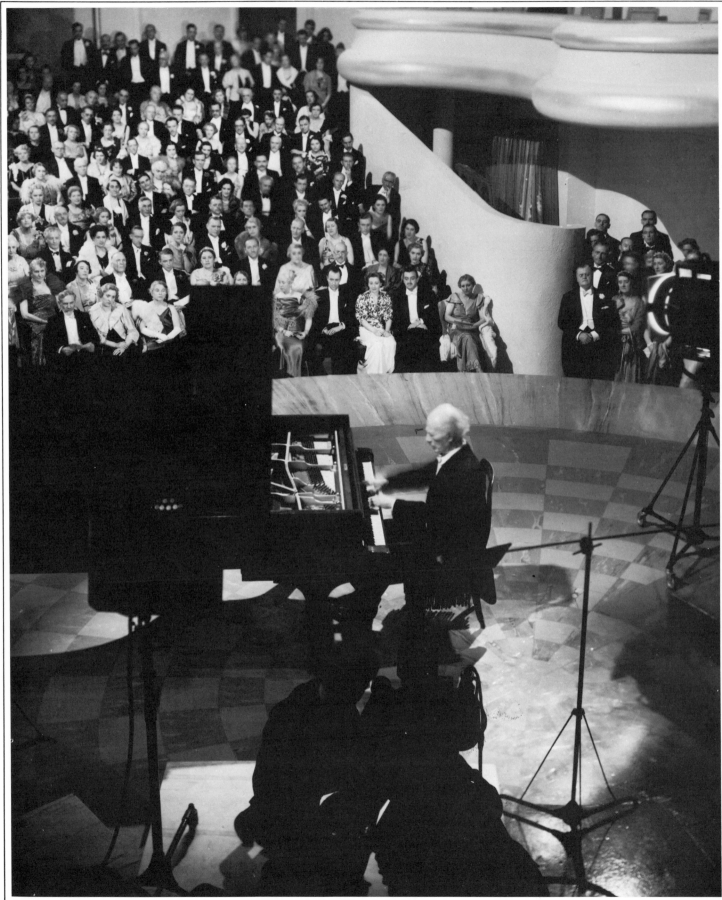

Paderewski, the most public of pianists, in the 1938 film *Moonlight Sonata*.

Press, New York, in 1973) and Philip James's *Early Keyboard Instruments from the Beginnings to the Year 1820* (New York: F. A. Stokes, 1930). Basically, the instruments made by Cristofori are the modern piano in germ because they work by something akin to escapement action (the hammer falls back from the strings even as the key remains pressed down). The German Johann Stein began improving the piano action in the 1770s, followed by his son-in-law Johann Streicher, by Anton Walter, and by J. Wenzel Schanz, at the end of the eighteenth century. The English piano maker John Broadwood was also experimenting at the end of the century with improving volume by increasing the number of strings on the piano. The end of the Napoleonic era signaled the end of harpsichord making and the total dominance of the piano, which in the 1820s and 1830s began to be manufactured, to standards of the highest quality, in great quantity.

The technical perfection of the instrument coincided with a new appreciation of sheer technique in music. The first great name associated in the nineteenth century with virtuosity as an end in itself was the violinist Paganini. His half-adoring, half-revolted protégé on the piano was Liszt. We find in the public career of Liszt a marriage made between technical virtuosity and the artist's personality. Paganini's famous declaration, "The concert is—myself," was transformed in Liszt's career into the notion that exceptional virtuosity is coupled with exceptional sensitivity. The artist's capacity to astound others was taken as a sign of his inner emotional powers.

In music, the belief that technical power and personal power are one changed the musician's relation to the musical text, and thus to the composer. Liszt, like Paganini, believed that musical notation was simply inadequate to render music. A score is at best a rough guide to what a performer should do. Schumann's belief that a performer should subordinate himself or herself to the text, should be an invisible medium between composer and listener, simply made no sense to these very different romantics. The performer had, for them, to make music with inadequate indications from the composer; the performer had to take a much more active

role, to be much more present as a human being, for the notes to come to life at all. And to Liszt, the key to bringing music to life was to possess such superlative technique that anything the performer felt at the moment of playing could be expressed.

Virtuosity, the expression of personality, the creation of living sound out of dead printing: this trinity perfectly suited the emergence of a solo instrument uniquely self-sufficient in tone color, dynamic range, and volume. The result was that the pianist came to seem a special sort of performer. Here, for example, is how Henry Reeves described the end of a Paris concert by Liszt in 1835: "As the closing strains began I saw Liszt's countenance assume that agony of expression, mingled with radiant smiles of joy, which I never saw in any other human face except in the paintings of Our Saviour by some of the early masters; his hands rushed over

Felix Vallotton's portrait of the contemplative Schumann captures the spirit of those musicians, like my friends, who were interested in arousing something other than public ecstasy.

Arthur Schnabel represents a transition from the anti-heroic musicians in the nineteenth century, such as Schumann, to the modern pianists of the Marlboro school.

the keys, the floor on which I sat shook like a wire, and the whole audience was wrapped with sound, when the hand and frame of the artist gave way. He fainted in the arms of the friend who was turning over the pages for him, and we bore him out in a strong fit of hysterics" (quoted in Sacheverell Sitwell, *Liszt* [New York, Philosophical Library, 1955]). This made perfect sense to an audience in the 1830s. Only a great man could make great music. The signs of his power lay not in his modesty, his self-effacement in rendering Mozart, Chopin, or Beethoven, but in the intrusion of his own personality to re-create what the markings of the score so inadequately indicated of theirs. It was only logical, therefore, that he could literally overwhelm himself while overwhelming others.

The credo of the virtuoso has been written most dramatically by Liszt himself. This is how he put it: "The virtuoso is not a mason who, chisel in hand, faithfully and conscientiously whittles stone after the design of an architect. He is not a passive tool reproducing feeling and thought and adding nothing of himself. He is not the more or less experienced reader of works which have no margins for his notes, which allow for no paragraphing between the lines. Spiritedly-written musical works are in reality, for the virtuoso, only the tragic and moving *mise-en-scène* for feelings. He is called upon to make emotion speak, and weep, and sing, and sigh—to bring it to life in his consciousness. He creates as the composer himself created, for he himself must live the passions he will call to light in all their brilliance. He breathes life into the lethargic body, infuses it with fire . . . " (quoted in Arthur Friedheim, *Liszt and Life: The Recollections of a Concert Pianist* [New York: Taplinger, 1961]).

From the time of Liszt, down into our time, in the playing of Horowitz, Michelangeli, and other self-consciously virtuoso virtuosos, this credo has persisted. It is not unique to the piano, but because the piano is uniquely fitted to be a solo instrument, it is a strong tradition in piano playing, matched perhaps only by the attitudes of and toward opera singers.

It was against this tradition that my friends were in revolt—or rather they were the latest generation to revolt against it. One of the aphorisms Schumann appended to his *Album for the Young*, opus 68, was "As you grow older, converse more frequently with scores than with virtuosos!" Later in the nineteenth century, even when the romantic excesses of Lisztian performance went out of fashion, their foundation remained among those pianists and teachers who believed that the performer was the music. And this approach to the piano continued to generate revolt. Here, for example, is Artur Schnabel's criticism of Theodor Leschetizky, a great teacher and performer who aimed at lyric dignity rather than lyric passion. Schnabel says of his teacher, "Leschetizky's limitations showed in his comparative indifference to, or even dislike of, the kind of music in which the 'personal' becomes just an ingredient of the universal. He had, for

An extreme example of the popular diffusion of the piano: the delivery of a Steinway to turn-of-the-century India. Given the climate, the piano's chances of survival were not great.

instance, not much use, or love, or curiosity, for the second half of Beethoven's production. The more glory the music itself emanates, the less it leaves for the performer. It was such transcending music which he seemed to evade, by instinct. . . . He saw music as a, so to say, public function. For him it was not music itself which gave to the musician, who took. For him the musician, as a person, was the giver, and he who listened took . . . " (from Artur Schnabel, *My Life and Music* [New York: St. Martin's Press, 1963]).

My friends were, as I've said, only the latest generation of performers to revolt against the centrality of performing—an idea that even in its purest form encourages egoism and in its more usual, impurer forms permits all the corrupting show biz surrounding the virtuoso to flourish. If there was

something that distinguished young pianists of the late 1960s from Schnabel's generation, it was the coupling of the revulsion against egoism to a revolt against bourgeois culture. Schnabel rejected a tradition of performing in the name of preserving what was best and purest in Central European culture, literary and philosophical as well as musical. Pianists plunged into giving "alternative concerts," were engaged in something cruder and more extreme. To rebel against musical show biz, one had to revolt against business and by extension against society as a whole. Rather than a question of preserving musical standards, it seemed a matter of wiping the slate clean. The idea of starting fresh, starting all over again, was the *idée fixe* of our time. Obviously an infantile idea—but then, we were young.

A more typical document of the piano's diffusion, Renoir's *The Daughters of Augusta Holmes.* In the nineteenth century the piano, above all other possessions, represented Culture in the home.

The other historical force in the development of the piano which my friends had to come to terms with concerned their audience. In the course of the nineteenth century audiences developed a strong affinity for the piano; many listeners themselves played, played well, and used the piano as the means of knowing the chamber, orchestral, and operatic literature, as well as the literature for other solo instruments. Firms like Bechstein, Steinway, Pleyel, and especially Knabe produced large numbers of high-quality instruments; volume production put the price of good pianos within the reach of ordinary families. (Although there were attempts to mass-produce string instruments in the nineteenth century, the results were unsatisfactory. Reasonable-quality woodwinds and brasses could be mass-produced, but they never caught on as pianos did.) The sociologist Max Weber called the piano the "bourgeois instrument" *par excellence*. The piano was a complete harmonic and melodic instrument whose price allowed even a family of modest means to experience a great deal of music in the privacy of the home. Moreover, the piano became a symbol of status for ordinary people: possessing one showed that the family was cultured.

One result of the massive diffusion of pianos in the nineteenth century was that the professional pianist faced audiences who felt an elementary kinship with what he did on stage. The pianist, as pianist, seemed comprehensible to his listeners— the most comprehensible of nineteenth-century artists—because his was the art so many practiced in their homes.

And they practiced it well, "they" being women. Good piano playing was one of the few feminine accomplishments that the Victorian world was willing to encourage. A young woman who played well did not frighten men; on the contrary, this particular accomplishment added to her attractions. And the time at the disposal of young women for practice was great.

The emphasis on the piano as a feminine accomplishment meant that, ordinarily, young men were steered toward different instruments or into singing if they showed a love of music. Gide records that his parents resisted his learning the piano for plea-sure because it was not quite manly. A young man had to show, early, very exceptional talent indeed to be encouraged to play the piano. I don't mean to emphasize too much this sexual division, because certainly many young middle-class men did learn to play. Undeniably, though, for women the piano occupied a special place; no young girl was encouraged to play the french horn or trumpet, as these seemed distinctly "unfeminine" instruments. Even in the string family sexual prejudices held sway. The cello, for instance, was considered absolutely unsuitable, because the player's legs must be spread. The piano did not compromise a girl's femininity. And thus was a group of concert goers formed who were unusually well equipped to judge the professional artists they heard.

Finally, a peculiar bond between the pianist and his public was established because piano transcriptions were the gateway for many people, especially those living in small towns or in the country, to experience other forms of music. In the pre-phonograph era, the performing pianist might similarly be asked to play in concert transcriptions of music his audience was unlikely to hear in other forms.

It would be easy to imagine that pianists in revolt against the virtuoso, show-biz world could adopt the most familiar mask of the modern artist: the artist as rebel. But these developments deterred the pianist from imagining himself or herself as an estranged being.

The conviction that an artist *ought* to be estranged from society is another romantic legacy that persists to the present day. It first appeared in its modern form among romantic poets, especially Wordsworth, Victor Hugo, and Novalis. Painters came to believe it rather later in the nineteenth century; Manet is one of the first great painters of that century to think of his rejection of society as something like wearing a badge of honor. Rejection and being rejected were of a piece. In what Lionel Trilling calls the "adversary culture" that writers and painters developed in the nineteenth century, technical and artistic innovation seemed naturally to be in advance of public taste; public rejection confirmed the fact that an artist was truly innovative.

Estrangement from the public formed an alter-

This engraving of Lord Byron epitomizes the romantic view of the artist who had withdrawn from public life in the nineteenth century. The artist, taking leave of his contemporaries, lives in nature; the only society that arouses him is the society of the past, whose noble traditions are now in ruins.

native image of the great artist to the image projected by the virtuoso. An estranged artist had freed his capacity to create by freeing himself from the morals and beliefs of his age. The artist has become great because he has rebelled. Such an idea does not appear in Dante, or in French and Italian poets of the Renaissance. It is the aesthetic version of nineteenth-century individualism: a human being must uproot himself from his contemporaries, cut himself off, in order to release the creative energy within him. When his work is greeted with hostility, it is a sign that the creative uprooting has succeeded.

These ideas are so familar to us because during the course of this century they have taken a powerful hold among the public as well as among artists themselves. They have made the ordinary, intelligent person come to think of the history of both painting and poetry in terms of an avant-garde which colonizes the future and to whose level the general public rises after a generation or two of misunderstanding. And they have led to the modern belief that a great artist deals with the values of his time principally by challenging them.

Musical life since the romantic era has been as touched by these general ideas as any of the other arts. But performing musicians, because of the nature of their work, have not comfortably assimilated them. In part this is because, as I have said, the performer is constantly engaged in seducing the public. In part it is because the technical innovations that since the romantic era have occurred within the performer's sphere have been enthusiastically received by the public. Playing or singing in tune, rapidity of execution, precise large masses of sound in orchestral work, have been greeted as signs of progress in art. Thus Liszt himself could proclaim in his letters that the artist must always live in noble isolation, disdainful of the sentiments of the rabble, and in the next breath describe with great glee his public acclaim and financial success, ascribing them (quite accurately) not only to his nobility of feeling but also to the fact that nobody before him was able to play the piano as well. Innovation in the means of performing did not in the nineteenth century lead to public rejection. The musical performer could not therefore understand himself by linking rejection, rebellion, and creativity, which his poetic or painterly colleagues did.

Even for the pianist who eschewed the virtuoso's role, the industrial production of his instrument, its mastery among a section of his audience, its use as a vehicle, through transcriptions, for experiencing a wide variety of music, all meant that the pianist could not easily think of himself as an outcast artist. I do not mean, of course, that a pianist getting bad reviews didn't in the last century, or doesn't today, harbor the natural defensive reaction that the public has failed to appreciate his genius. But a painter faced with bad reviews has a refuge in the "adversary culture": this is what happens generally to creative people; it's not really personal. The history of the piano in the last century barred the pianist from this refuge. Good pianists are not rejected generically. A particular person is.

And I don't mean to imply that good poets or painters have sought rejection, or sought to cut themselves off from the ordinary run of humanity. Like any cultural form, the adversary culture is a road map; it allows you to know where you are, if you feel lost and need to consult a guide. It was certainly true that my friends felt lost, but while some of them, like Peter Serkin, were consciously bent on becoming estranged, others, like Richard Goode or Murray Perahia, simply wanted to avoid the dangers of corruption, to protect the purity of

The Chopin monument in Paris represents a typical attitude of nineteenth-century audiences toward musicians. The audience expected the performer to transport them outside themselves.

their art—a protection that required that they establish in their dealings with the world a wary solitude.

The striking thing about these young pianists of the 1960s, the thing that allows me to speak of them, for all their individual differences, as a group, was that they managed to contrive for themselves a life in New York during the winter and at Marlboro during the summer which provided them with a good measure of protection from the world as well as companionship with one another. They managed to come to terms, I think, with the social history of their art.

The world we inhabited in New York was anything but picturesque. We couldn't afford Greenwich

The playing of Michelangeli most of us found somewhat disturbing. He is a pianist of dramatic gesture rather than a musician bent on seeking out the secrets of a musical text.

Village, which was even in the 1960s expensive. Besides, the apartments in the Village tended to be small and have thin walls, making practicing a nightmare to neighbors. We lived instead on the Upper West Side of the city, in the old bourgeois apartment buildings that line West End Avenue and Riverside Drive. Twenty years ago the good middle-class families were leaving this neighborhood as fast as they could for the suburbs or the more luxurious East Side. The abandoned apartments were filled with cockroaches, which felt so much at home that they acted more like household pets than pests. But the walls of these deserted bourgeois apartments were thick. Put down a Turkish carpet (these were cheap, thanks to the rush to chrome, leather, and glass among the former tenants), put some Indian print cotton hangings on the wall, move in the piano, a naugahyde couch, a wide plastic table for the kitchen, and some wooden chairs (all these household items, save the piano, could be bought at a store on upper Broadway where people were as likely to be discussing concert programs as whether the torn white naugahyde couch was a better buy than the pristine sewage-colored one)—the result was the Musician's Home, circa 1962.

The neighborhood was a racial and ethnic inferno. Blacks and Puerto Ricans lined the side streets and occupied Columbus and Amsterdam avenues. The young among them were sunk in an angry misery which they relieved by attacks on the elderly Russian and Polish Jews who held onto their cheap apartments. During the day the benches on the traffic islands in the middle of Broadway were lined with these elderly people, seeking a bit of sun at the cost of breathing car and bus fumes. We were the Nice Young People; that is, we were white and cultured. On the other hand, we kept late hours and were not entirely clean. We shopped at supermarkets on Broadway where the cockroaches also felt uninhibited.

Most of the Upper West Side pianists I knew taught or had studied at the Mannes School, over on the East Side. The Juilliard School, then still housed near Columbia University, was viewed with aversion, as a place where pianists who wanted to be stars rather than musicians were likely to go. The aversion to the "careerism" of the Juilliard people was one strongly felt way in which my pianist friends tried to define the ground rules for a pure musical existence. Sometimes my friends called Juilliard "Horowitz-land." Consistently they spoke of the Juilliard students as so besotted by ambition that the little prodigies of Horowitz-land lacked any general musical, not to say literary or historical, culture. The Mannes School, by contrast, seemed artistically serious. As dingy and dirty inside as one's apartment across the park, it was filled with teachers who had devoted themselves to music itself and to their students, rather than to concert careers. The music historian and theorist Carl Schachter had an immense influence there; the conductor Carl Bamberger taught Murray Perahia and others. Recitals at Mannes tended to be programs of music that people were unlikely

Above, Horowitz greets fans after a Carnegie Hall concert in 1965. The Horowitz "phenomenon" is a fate my friends feared, even though they wanted a reasonable amount of worldly success. *Left*, Horszowski, who appeared as a heroic figure to the Marlboro school pianists. He was not a pianist's pianist but a musician's musician.

The sign (*top*) tells half the truth. Marlboro was also an annual opportunity for musicians to doubt themselves, to feel they ought to be better and purer than they were. The music shed at Marlboro (*bottom*) is the face the festival turns toward the public.

to hear in any commercial concert hall; I remember, for instance, a concert Peter Serkin gave which consisted of hours of Takemitsu, Messiaen, and Bach. The concerts by young people at Juilliard, in contrast, were displays of the sort of thing the budding pianist might give if awarded a contract by an agent, and the talk at intermission was desultory as people looked around to see if any agents, in fact, were present.

The Upper West Side pianists I knew in the 1960s were reacting with some difficulty to the fact that most of them had shown early and exceptional promise as children. This may account for their extreme dislike of some Juilliard students, whom my friends imagined were merely continuing a kind of childhood slavery in the obsessive pursuit of career. This reaction to developing so quickly, so early, pushed Murray Perahia, for instance, into the study of conducting; I remember his frequently telling me, "You've got to be a musician, rather than a pianist," and I think he was afraid that if he kept on formally studying the piano he would be both artistically impoverished and humanly imprisoned in the world of his childhood. Others, like Henry Shapiro, sought to develop dual professions—Henry became a literary scholar while continuing his piano work.

The little prodigy pushed by avid adults is a stock figure, of course, in musical history. This stereotype misses the experience of my friends. Whatever their family background, they were children of that era, one in which dropping out of bourgeois life was equated with authenticity. But these pianists had already, so to speak, dropped in. By their late teens they had so developed that they were able to give artistically compelling performances. They absorbed the culture of their generation in believing not that they were about to compromise themselves as adults, but that they might have already been caught up in compromise by winning the approval of adults. Moreover, they viewed the culture of the young at that time as partially a psychological reproach to themselves. People spoke about "missing out" on living a "real life," by which these particular young people meant that the discipline and absorption in music during their childhood had put them out of touch with the sense of possibility, adventure, and starting everything entirely fresh which other people seemed to feel. When, therefore, we took drugs, we did so with the sense of making up for something we had missed. When we played farmer or woodsman in Vermont, it seemed more a matter of being just like everyone else our age than warding off the evils of adulthood.

There was also the matter of being Jewish, which gave my friends of those years an aversion to narrow careerism. It is true that since the middle of the nineteenth century a disproportionate number of musicians have been Jewish. I think the reason for this is fairly simple. Performing has been one of the few careers outside the ghetto that have been open to Jews without much resistance. But Jewish musical culture in the past hundred years has not been steadily, uniformly, of a piece. Jewish musicians of Heifetz's generation left the culture of the ghetto in becoming successful musicians. For the Jews of my generation some kind of assimilation had already taken place, in our parents' generation. This was particularly true in New York, where, thanks to the presence of a large Jewish population dating from before the First World War, and the addition of great musicians who were Jewish during the 1930s, the culture of the city and our culture had merged.

In reacting against music as a career, we went back to something that had been lost in this history of assimilation. We went back to the value placed in traditional Jewish culture on study and reflection. Once an older cellist said to me, "You Marlboro boys act like rabbis: you dress badly; you

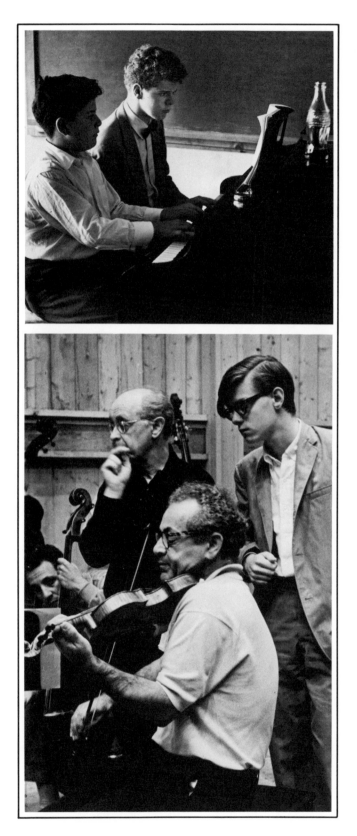

If James Levine (*top*, at left, with Van Cliburn) had put this Coke bottle on my piano, I wouldn't have been able to listen to him play for fear the Coke would spill into the piano. Marlboro, however, was littered with food. I once found a pastrami sandwich in the bottom of my cello case. *Right*, Rudolf and Peter Serkin listen as Alexander Schneider leads a chamber music class. In New York Schneider helped young musicians whom he had met at Marlboro by playing chamber music concerts with them and by arranging orchestral performances at which they could perform the concerto literature.

Left, Horszowski, flanked by Rudolf Serkin and Ruth Laredo. Their performance of the Bach D Minor Three-Piano Concerto is legendary. *Below*, a rehearsal with Eugene Istomin, Arnold Steinhardt, and Madeline Foley, who represents another Marlboro phenomenon. She is a great cellist who is virtually unknown to the general public. There were several musicians like her whom Serkin sought to bring in contact with the young.

don't drink; you don't have fun; and you're full of yourselves." All true. Sunk in the naugahyde sofas, drinking water or tea, we were terribly serious. We were purposefully spiritual. We went to concerts by Mieczyslaw Horszowski—a great pianist never given his due—and during intermission gave one another silent, penetrating looks which showed that We Were Moved. But in our defense it should be said that this Talmudic seriousness about the sacredness of music was also genuine, and that it was part of our generation's reaction to the showiness, seduction through virtuosity, and glitter that had been the recipe of so many pianists since Liszt.

It was the great virtue of Rudolf Serkin's Marlboro Music Festival to give this seriousness a focus and to make it more than an attitude. The essence of Serkin's art is its intensity. In musical terms, this means that an immense effort is made to make each musical phrase expressive; attacks, ritards, and accents receive great care in his piano playing; the propulsion of the music is built upon the accumulation of these intense musical moments. Rudolf Serkin is not a relaxed pianist, nor is he a sloppy romantic. Rather, he plays like a man in great pain who disciplines himself by focusing on the expressive possibilities of each chord, each melodic fragment under his fingers. It was this way of playing that he communicated to others. It served as a model especially for those young pianists of my generation who were bent on playing *innerlich*, avoiding surface display—even when they disagreed with a particular interpretation of Serkin's.

The Marlboro Festival was organized in a way that directly reflected Serkin's intensity. Technically there were no teachers or students, only older and younger colleagues working together. The initial emphasis in the festival was on playing chamber music for two months in the summer. The chamber music work was particularly valuable to the pianists as a discipline in cooperation, rather than virtuoso self-display. Concerts were subordinate in the first years of the festival to the real musical work, which went on in rehearsals. None of the older musicians expected to be paid.

The Marlboro Festival was organized in Vermont after the Second World War by Serkin and others as a breathing space for themselves, as a place to work on the most demanding sort of music in the least commercially pressured circumstances. By the 1960s necessity and the very success of the festival had somewhat weakened the initial atmosphere of being in a musical retreat. A large music shed had been built for concerts; the costs of the keep of the younger musicians had grown; the festival had a touring company known as Music from Marlboro, which gave chamber music concerts around the country.

These changes meant the young led a double existence at Marlboro. On the one hand they were under the eye of a master whose intensity, honesty, and self-effacement more than matched their own. On the other hand, Marlboro had become an institution that could give a young pianist's career a unique momentum. He or she worked as a colleague with the best older musicians; the concerts played to select and influential audiences. There were the Vermont hills in which the festival was set, bread fights in the dining hall, incessant comings and goings sexually—but there was also tension. People worried about what Rudi really thought of them, whether they would be invited back a second year, whether they would get to tour. It was worst for the pianists, and Rudi was aware of this. "Do you know that we are called the 'Marlboro Mafia'?" a friend of his once said to me. "And do you know that in the real Mafia the young ones are always the greatest schemers?"

I suppose this could be said of most of the artists of my generation. Loudly declaiming the evil of worldly success, with a genuine commitment to recovering a sense of purity in art, they nonetheless had to survive in the world, and survival comes only to those with a desire to dominate.

The Marlboro school pianists were not representative pianists of their generation in one way: they were not super-technicians. There has developed among certain American pianists, such as Grant Johannesen, a completion of the technical work begun by Liszt. Pianists like him have total mastery, seemingly, of anything of which the piano is technically capable. This is what one thinks in listening to them play Chopin or Schumann: "What amazing technique!" The Marlboro school pianists were bent on erasing that reaction from the listeners' consciousness; they wanted to make the technical feats undetectable and arouse in the listener a sense of the beauty of the music itself. Moreover, the Marlboro school pianists wanted to play music with the maximum of inner feeling and the minimum of surface finish: Schumann rather than Liszt, never Rachmaninoff, seldom French music like Ravel's *Gaspard de la nuit*, which they imagined (quite wrongly, in my view) to be thin musically. Their sensibilities were tuned to the demanding and convoluted literature of the romantic era, rather than to its bravura literature.

The goal my friends set for themselves in public was probably most clearly defined by Richard Goode. He once said to me something like this: "Imagine a concert in which the audience is moved by the performance in such a way that they want to hear one of the pieces played again, rather than a new piece as an encore. Imagine a review of this concert which only talks about the structure and quality of the music, in which compliments are paid me only through a renewed love of music that had seemed stale."

This ideal not only requires that the musician transcend the role of virtuoso. It requires also that the very familiarity of the piano and its literature be somehow suspended in the performance. And this act of simultaneously disappearing as the performer and making the music sound as though it had just been composed requires that the pianist feel himself in the closest contact with the audience: not estranged withdrawal, not the self-consciousness which isolates, but rather a presence that is at once intense and modest. What Richard Goode envisions is romantic music played without either of the romantic artist's masks.

In the last decade the Marlboro school pianists have realized this ideal in different ways, to different degrees. The ones who grew up emotionally have become less judgmental about others yet better defended against them. Armed openness is the condition of any adult, it is true; for my friends who are pianists it has taken specific forms. I notice it in Murray Perahia, for instance, in little things:

he can now receive compliments in good grace after concerts from society matrons swathed in furs and return them. Ten years ago the glittering ones frightened him. He has developed a sense of humor about whispering in the audience while he plays—"Sometimes I'm bored too and try to listen in." Ten years ago he would have blamed himself for causing their inattention. My friends will never become pianists who love the audiences to whom they play so passionately. Their solution to the relation between the artist and his public has been in part to cultivate neutrality. It shows, for instance, in the encores they play, which are in the case of Murray, Richard Goode, and Peter quiet small pieces that let the concert fade away, rather than brilliant miniatures that milk every last possibility of enthusiastic applause.

This relaxed, protected presence in public has allowed them to develop the musical sensibilities they possessed as adolescents. That, I would say, is the most striking thing about them. Nothing fundamentally new has happened to their playing in the last decade. Prematurely knowing, they have deepened that knowledge; approaching middle age has not led them into new fields of understanding. For example, my friends, with the exception of Peter Serkin, still do not make much of an effort to play French music; when occasionally they try Fauré or Debussy, they make both sound like Brahms. Peter never played Chopin well as a boy; his recent attempts to play him remain failures. One can't reproach an artist for the fact that his or her art must have limits in order to have character. What impresses me is rather the fidelity to a certain vision of the piano. Line built out of dramatic moments, great attention to the often disruptive inner

---

Facing page: Top, a rehearsal for *Pierrot Lunaire* in 1969, with, from left, Paula Robison, Felix Galimir, Richard Stoltzman, Murray Perahia, and Ronald Leonard. Galimir had a profound influence on Murray and other of my friends—a modest perfectionist, self-effacing in public, demanding of himself and others during rehearsals. *Bottom,* Richard Goode in a performance of the Brahms Horn Trio. It is a remarkably difficult work musically and it is remarkable that a man could have so deep a conception of it so early in his life.

I think this picture gives some suggestion of the intense concentration Rudolf Serkin could give to the formation of the young, in this case his son Peter.

voices that appear in romantic music, great attention to the darkness in Mozart, a search for what lies behind the exclamatory rhetoric in Beethoven— at seventeen or eighteen my friends felt these things. Now they feel them more.

This fidelity to the art which they so early possessed is a fidelity to Rudolf Serkin. No matter how quarrelsome the younger Marlboro pianist can be about a specific interpretation he gives, no matter how much the force of his personality has at times felt like a great weight to them, none has rebelled against him by rejecting his kind of playing. His credo that every single moment counts expressively, his urgency, his lack of peace, is theirs.

The rebellious culture of their adolescence, for all its silliness and for all the danger it posed in turning them against themselves, had at least the positive effect of deflecting them from the pursuit of virtuosity, so much more efficient in its economic organization today than in the time of Liszt, so much more brutal in its artistic consequences. My friends were lucky in their time. They built a community for themselves in New York, and a community was built for them in Vermont. If they felt estranged from their more successful contemporaries, they did not need to feel estranged from one another. The ideology of the 1960s put a certain damper on the competitiveness all performers need in order to survive; it proposed certain ideas of the purity of the self, infantile when stated badly, but valuable given the state and nature of the art my friends practiced. All this has made it possible for them to act as pianists of the type Schumann envisioned: in the world but not of it, dedicated to finding what lies below the surface of sound by dedicating themselves to a study of the composer's written intentions; they have become his "invisible presences." I think it fair to say that the Marlboro pianists have become as close an approximation of Schumann's musical ideals as any of us is likely now to hear.

187, *188*, 189, *203*, *204*, 205, *208*
Sessions, Roger, 133, *138*, 163
Shakespeare, William, 9, 11
Shapiro, Henry, 202
Shaw, George Bernard, 41
Shorr, Lev, 163, *164*, 165, *166*, 168, *169*, 171, 174, 178, 180
Shostakovich, Dmitri, 165
Shudi, Burkat, 45, 54
Silbermann, Gottfried, 11, 50, 51
Sissle, Noble, *151*
Sitwell, Sacheverell, 194
Smit, Leo, 137
Smith, Willie "The Lion," *152*
Sowerby, Leo, 122
Stark, John, 159
Steele, Richard, 47
Steibelt, Daniel, 17, 19
Stein, Johann A., 54, *55*, 56, 59–60, 63, 64, 193
Stein, Theodor, *177*
Steinhardt, Arnold, *204*
Steinway, Henry Engelhard (Heinrich), 50, *65*, 70
Steinway, William, 101
Stern, Isaac, 163
Stern, Lucie, *118*

Steuermann, Eduard, 137
Stoltzman, Richard, *207*
Strauss, Richard, 122
Stravinsky, Igor, 27, *34*, 35, 73, 117, 122, 128, 133, *138*, 157, 158
Streicher, Johann Andreas, 64, 193
Swanson, Howard, 118

Tailleferre, Germaine, *138*
Tannenbaum, Belle, 115, 122
Tatum, Art, 145, 158
Tchaikovsky, Peter Ilich, 21, 22, 180, 183
Thompson, Agnes, 116, 117
Thompson, Kathleen, 116
Thomson, Virgil, 123, *125*, 128, *133*, 134–35, 158
Thorne, Francis, 137
Tomaschek, Johann, 17
Tourel, Jennie, 135, *139*
Trilling, Lionel, 197
Tureck, Rosalyn, 113
Turner, Walter J., 73

Vallotton, Felix, *193*
Van Horne, Harold, 122, 123

Verdi, Giuseppe, 117
Victoria, Queen, 19, 21
Villa-Lobos, Hector, 165
Villeroi, Duchesse de, 67
Villoing, Alexander, *182*
Viñes, Ricardo, 133
Visconti, Luchino, 36

Wagner, Cosima, 68
Wagner, Richard, 25, 36, 134
Waldstein, Count, 63
Walter, Anton, 193
Weber, Max, 197
Weisgall, Hugo, 139
Wells, H. G., 25
Wiener, Frances, 165, *169*
Wild, Earl, 128
Wilson, Teddy, 145
Wittgenstein, Paul, 39, 133
Wordsworth, William, 197
Wright, Cedric, *162*, *164*
Wuorinen, Charles, 137

Zoffany, *10*
Zumpe, Johann, 51, 52, 54
Zverev, Nikolai, *174*

ANTHONY BURGESS was born in Manchester, England, in 1917. He attended the Xaverian College, Manchester, and Manchester University, where he studied languages. He had intended to take a degree in music, but failed the qualifying physics examination. Nevertheless, he regards himself as a composer who turned late to literature and in old age is turning back to musical composition. His Symphony in C was performed in Iowa City in 1975; his *Waste Land* and song cycle *The Bridges of Enderby* were given in 1980 at Sarah Lawrence College; and his ballet suite *Mr WS* was heard on BBC radio early in 1981. As a novelist he became widely known in 1962 for *A Clockwork Orange* and, in the seventies, notorious when Stanley Kubrick turned the novel into a film. Burgess's other fiction includes *Napoleon Symphony, MF,* and *ABBA ABBA.* He has also published criticism and Joyce exegeses and a primer on linguistics. He lives with his wife in Monaco.

ANNALYN SWAN was born in Biloxi, Mississippi. She began to study the piano at the age of six and made her orchestral debut at sixteen with the Gulf Coast Symphony. She won numerous awards in district and state piano festivals and performed widely during high school, occasionally as a duo pianist with her brother George. In 1973 she was graduated summa cum laude, Phi Beta Kappa, from Princeton University, where she was the first woman editor in chief of *The Daily Princetonian.* A Marshall scholar, she subsequently studied at King's College, Cambridge University, and earned an honors M.A. Formerly a staff writer for *Time,* she is now music critic and general editor of *Newsweek.* Her articles and reviews have appeared in various publications, including *The New Republic.* She lives in Manhattan with her husband, Mark Stevens, an art critic and writer, and plays her Steinway for pleasure.

ANTHONY LIVERSIDGE is a British journalist and critic who has published widely in the United States and Europe; his articles have appeared in *The Economist, Fortune,* and the *Village Voice,* among other publications, and he writes a monthly column, "Keyboard Topics," for *Ovation* magazine in New York. He holds an M.A. with honors in economics from the University of Edinburgh and is the author of *The Book of the Piano (and Other Keyboards),* to be published in 1982 by Harper & Row. He lives in New York.

DOMINIQUE BROWNING began to study the piano when she was four years old. She is a much-awarded veteran of the high school piano-competition circuit and a graduate of Wesleyan University in Connecticut, where she earned a degree from the College of Letters in philosophy, literature, and history. After several years as an editor at *Esquire,* she moved in 1981 to *Texas Monthly* and now resides in Austin, Texas.

NED ROREM was raised in Chicago and attended Northwestern University, from which, many years later, he received his first honorary doctorate. He also studied at the Curtis Institute and at Juilliard, where he was awarded his M.A. degree in 1948. Soon after, Rorem moved to Morocco and then to France, where he lived until 1958. These years as a young composer among the leading figures of the artistic and social milieus of postwar Europe are portrayed in his *Paris Diary* (Braziller, 1966) and in ensuing diaries and essays. He has composed three symphonies, three piano concertos, six operas, several ballets and other music for the theater, choral pieces of every kind, and an array of orchestral works including the suite *Air Music*, for which he won the Pulitzer Prize in 1976. Rorem has been the recipient of a Fulbright Fellowship (1951), two Guggenheim Fellowships (1957 and 1978), three Ford Foundation grants, three grants from the National Endowment for the Arts (two for music, one for prose writing), a grant in 1968 from the American Academy and Institute of Arts and Letters (of which he was elected a member in 1979), and commissions from the major orchestras of the United States. His instrumental pieces have been conducted by Bernstein, Mitropoulos, Ormandy, Paray, Mehta, Reiner, Steinberg, and Stokowski, among others; his songs have been programmed by such eminent recitalists as Leontyne Price, Phyllis Curtin, Donald Gramm, Eileen Farrell, and Shirley Verrett. He lives in New York.

WILLIAM BOLCOM, associate professor of composition at the University of Michigan, is a composer and pianist. His principal musical studies were on the west coast and in Paris, where he worked with the late composer Darius Milhaud. His extensive works for the theater include two operas for actors, the first of which (*Dynamite Tonite*) was produced at the Actors Studio Theater, at Yale, and at several other theaters in the United States and Europe. His orchestral works have been played by the Chicago, Los Angeles, and other major orchestras. He has been composer in residence at the La Rochelle (France) and Aspen music festivals, and his chamber works are performed worldwide. As a pianist he has recorded extensively on Columbia, RCA, Nonesuch, and other labels. With his wife, singer Joan Morris, he tours throughout the United States and Canada in programs of classic American popular song (their most recent recording is a double album of Rodgers and Hart, released by RCA in the fall of 1981). Bolcom and Morris (as they are billed) reside in a lovely farmhouse outside Ann Arbor, Michigan, and a minuscule apartment in New York.

SAMUEL LIPMAN was born in California in 1934. He received a B.A. in government from San Francisco State College in 1956 and an M.A. in political science from the University of California at Berkeley in 1958. He was a National Woodrow Wilson fellow in the academic year 1956–57 and a special student in piano at the Juilliard School in New York from 1959 to 1962. His piano teachers were Lev Shorr and Alexander Libermann in San Francisco and Rosina Lhévinne in New York. He studied counterpoint and orchestration privately with Darius Milhaud and general aspects of music with Pierre Monteux. He has concertized widely in the United States, appearing in recital and with major orchestras under such conductors as Abravanel, Comissiona, Fiedler, Fricsay, Horenstein, and Monteux. In 1975 he gave the New York premiere of the Elliot Carter Piano Concerto (1965) in Carnegie Hall with the American Symphony Orchestra. He has been a member of the artist faculty of the Aspen Music Festival since 1970 and was a founding member of the Waterloo Music Festival in New Jersey, where he has been on the artist faculty since 1976. He has been a regular contributor to *Commentary* since 1975 and its music critic since 1976. He is the recipient of three ASCAP-Deems Taylor Awards, for his writings in *Commentary* and for a collection of his essays entitled *Music after Modernism* (1979). He is married to the pianist and teacher Jeaneane Dowis. They live in New York with their twelve-year-old son Edward.

RICHARD SENNETT is a sociologist who writes most often about family life in cities, the development of urban culture, and more general issues of social psychology. He used to be a cellist. He was born in Chicago in 1943, educated at the Breck School and the University of Chicago, and took his doctorate from Harvard University in 1969. He is the author of *Authority* (1980), *The Fall of Public Man* (1977), *The Hidden Injuries of Class* (1972), *The Uses of Disorder* (1970), and *Families Against the City* (1970). In addition to serving on the boards of several scholarly journals, he writes regularly for *The New York Review of Books*, *The New Yorker*, and *The Partisan Review* in the United States; the *Times Literary Supplement* in Great Britain; and for *Le Monde*, *Tel Quel*, and *Minuit* in France. He is presently University Professor of the Humanities at New York University and Directeur d'Etudes at the Ecole des Hautes Etudes in Paris. Sennett has been the recipient of numerous honors and awards, among them a Guggenheim Foundation award (1973), a senior research fellowship from the National Endowment for the Humanities (1976), and two visiting fellowships at the Institute for Advanced Study (1973–74, 1979). He has been guest scholar at Clare Hall and King's College, Cambridge University (1976); delivered the Sigmund Freud Memorial Lectures at the University of London (1977); and been a resident scholar at the Villa Serbelloni Study Center in Bellagio, Italy. In 1980 he was Visiting Professor at the Collège de France in Paris.

JAMES R. GAINES was born in Dayton, Ohio, where he studied piano with Donald C. Hageman. Later, while attending the McBurney School in New York, he continued his studies with Julian de Gray, McNeil Robinson, and Donald Rock and sang in the professional choir at the Church of St. Mary the Virgin. While earning his bachelor's degree in English at the University of Michigan, he studied harpsichord with Anthony Newman in New York. Gaines has been an editor and critic at *Saturday Review* and a writer on national affairs at *Newsweek*, and he is currently a senior editor at *People* magazine. His articles have appeared in numerous other publications, including *Smithsonian* and *The New York Times*, and he is the author of *Wit's End: Days and Nights of the Algonquin Round Table* (Harcourt Brace Jovanovich, 1977). His most recent project has been teaching his daughter Allison to play the piano; so far she is putting up with it. They live in Brooklyn Heights, New York.

ILLUSTRATION CREDITS

P. 2: The Bettmann Archive, Inc.; p. 5, top and bottom: Culver Pictures; p. 6, bottom: The Bettmann Archive, Inc.; p. 8, left: Culver Pictures; right: The Metropolitan Museum of Art, The Crosby Brown Collection, 1901; p. 9: Music Division, The New York Public Library at Lincoln Center, Astor, Lenox and Tilden Foundations; p. 10: Property of the Honourable Lady Salmond, Sussex, England; p. 12, top: Courtesy of The New-York Historical Society, New York City; bottom: Courtesy, Museum of Fine Arts, Boston, M. and M. Karolik Collection, 47.1227; p. 14, top left and right: The Bettmann Archive, Inc.; bottom: Culver Pictures; p. 15: Smithsonian Institution, Photo No. 56,414; p. 16: Music Division, NYPL; p. 17: The Metropolitan Museum of Art, Purchase, Joseph Pulitzer Bequest, 1943; p. 18, top: Culver Pictures; bottom: Courtesy of the Fogg Art Museum, Harvard University, Bequest of Grenville L. Winthrop; pp. 20–21: The Bettmann Archive, Inc.; p. 22: Music Division, NYPL; p. 23, top: Music Division, NYPL; bottom: Culver Pictures; p. 24, top and bottom, and p. 26: Music Division, NYPL; p. 27 and p. 29, top and bottom: The Bettmann Archive, Inc.; pp. 30, 31: Culver Pictures; p. 32: The Bettmann Archive, Inc.; p. 33, top: The Bettmann Archive, Inc.; bottom: Steinway & Sons; p. 34: Music Division, NYPL; p. 37, top: Universal Pictures; bottom: Creative Film Society; p. 38: Photo by William P. Gottlieb/EJG Collection; p. 39: Courtesy of *Musical America*; p. 40: The Metropolitan Museum of Art, Anonymous Gift, 1944; p. 43, top: The Metropolitan Museum of Art, Gift of Mrs. Eva Mali Noyes, 1927; bottom: Bibliothèque Nationale, Paris; p. 44, top: The Metropolitan Museum of Art, Pulitzer Bequest Fund, 1953; middle: The Metropolitan Museum of Art, Gift of B. Han, 1929; bottom: Smithsonian Institution, Photo No. 56,341D; p. 45: The Metropolitan Museum of Art, Harris Brisbane Dick Fund, 1933; p. 46: Culver Pictures; p. 48, top: The Metropolitan Museum of Art, Gift of Mrs. Susan Dwight Bliss, 1944; bottom: The Metropolitan Museum of Art, The Crosby Brown Collection of Musical Instruments, 1889; p. 49, top and bottom left: The Metropolitan Museum of Art, The Crosby Brown Collection of Musical Instruments, 1889; bottom right: Music Division, NYPL; p. 51: Smithsonian Institution, Photo No. 56,499; p. 52, left and right, and p. 53: Music Division, NYPL; p. 54, top: Smithsonian Institution, Photo No. 74285; bottom: Smithsonian Institution, Photo No. 74283; p. 55, top: The Metropolitan Museum of Art, Gift of Professor Stoddard Lincoln, 1972; middle: The Metropolitan Museum of Art, Gift of Curtis Freshel, 1958; bottom: Courtesy, Museum of Fine Arts, Boston, Leslie Lindsey Mason Collection; p. 56: Yale University Music Library; p. 57, top right: Music Division, NYPL; bottom: Culver Pictures; p. 58, all: Music Division, NYPL; p. 59, top: John Broadwood & Sons, Ltd.; p. 60: Photo by David Bannister, Regent Gallery; p. 61, top: The Bettmann Archive, Inc.; bottom: Smithsonian Institution, Photo No. 56,371; p. 62, top: Smithsonian Institution, Photo No. 56,455A; bottom: Smithsonian Institution, Photo No. 56,445; p. 65, top: Culver Pictures; bottom left and right: Steinway & Sons; pp. 66, 68: Culver Pictures; p. 69, top right: Steinway & Sons; bottom: Culver Pictures; p. 71, top: Music Division, NYPL; bottom: Concert for Piano and Orchestra, by John Cage, © 1960 by Henmar Press, Inc. Used by permission of C. F. Peters Corporation; p. 72: Baldwin Piano & Organ Company; p. 74 and p. 76, top and bottom: Courtesy of L. Bösendorfer Klavierfabrik, A.G.; pp. 78–99: Photos by Peter Lehner; p. 100: Photo by Henry Grossman;

p. 102: Steinway & Sons; p. 104: Photo by Fritz Curzon, Courtesy of Harry Beall Management, Inc.; pp. 106–13: Photos by Henry Grossman; p. 117: Courtesy of *Musical America*; p. 118: Curtis Institute of Music; p. 119, left: Music Division, NYPL; right: Culver Pictures, Inc.; p. 121, top: Courtesy of Gerald Cook; p. 125: Photo by Jim Benton; p. 126, bottom left: Curtis Institute of Music; bottom right: Courtesy of CBS; p. 127: Photo by Eugene Cook; pp. 129, 130: Courtesy of Santa Fe Chamber Music Festival; p. 131: Music Division, NYPL; p. 132, top left: The Bettmann Archive, Inc.; top right: Photo by Sheila Rizzo, Courtesy of *Musical America*; bottom: Music Division, NYPL; p. 134: Property of Mme. Jean Seringe, Paris; p. 135: Photo by Victor Parker, Courtesy of *Musical America*; p. 136, top: Courtesy of CBS; p. 138, top: Photo by Don Hunstein, CBS; bottom: The Bettmann Archive, Inc.; p. 139: Photo by Don Hunstein, CBS; p. 140, left: Photo by Don Hunstein, CBS; right: Frank Driggs Collection; p. 141: Photo by Man Ray; p. 142: Stanley Dance Collection; p. 144, left and right: Music Division, NYPL; p. 145: The Chrysler Museum, Norfolk, Virginia; p. 146: Nick Perls Collection; p. 147: Photo by John Gruen; p. 149, top left and right: Frank Driggs Collection; bottom: Stanley Dance Collection; p. 151, top: Steinway & Sons; bottom: Frank Driggs Collection; p. 152: Stanley Dance Collection; p. 154, left and right, and p. 155, all: Music Division, NYPL; p. 156: Baldwin Piano & Organ Company; p. 157: Photo by William P. Gottlieb/EJG Collection; p. 158, left and right, and p. 159: Music Division, NYPL; p. 160, top: Music Division, NYPL; bottom: Courtesy of *Musical America*; p. 162 and p. 164, top: Photos by Cedric Wright; p. 167, top left: Steinway & Sons; top right, bottom left and right: Music Division, NYPL; p. 169: *San Francisco Examiner*; p. 171, bottom: Photo by Rondal Partridge, Courtesy of Mills College; p. 172, left: Music Division, NYPL; right: Courtesy of *Musical America*; p. 173: Culver Pictures; p. 174: Reprinted by permission of New York University Press from *Sergei Rachmaninoff: A Lifetime in Music* by Sergei Bertensson and Jay Leyda. Copyright © 1945 by New York University; p. 175, top: Courtesy of *Musical America*; bottom: Photo by Fred Fehl; p. 176, left: From *My Young Years*, by Arthur Rubinstein. Copyright © 1973 by Aniela Rubinstein, Eva Rubinstein Coffin, Alina Anna Rubinstein, and John Arthur Rubinstein. Reprinted by permission of Alfred A. Knopf, Inc.; p. 176, right: Music Division, NYPL; p. 177, top left: Courtesy of Mills College; top right: Music Division, NYPL; center: Leningrad Conservatory of Music; bottom left and right: Music Division, NYPL; p. 179, top, and p. 180: The Juilliard School of Music; p. 181, all: Music Division, NYPL; p. 182, top left: The Juilliard School of Music; top right: Leningrad Conservatory of Music; bottom: Steinway & Sons; p. 186: Photo by Woodrow Leung; p. 188, all: Marlboro Music Festival; p. 190: Wide World Photos, Inc.; p. 191: Music Division, NYPL; p. 192: Culver Pictures; p. 193: Music Division, NYPL; p. 194: Culver Pictures; p. 195: Steinway & Sons; pp. 196, 198: The Bettmann Archive, Inc.; p. 199: Music Division, NYPL; p. 200: Courtesy of *Musical America*; p. 201, top: Wide World Photos, Inc.; bottom: Colbert Artists Management, Inc.; p. 202, top and bottom: Marlboro Music Festival; p. 203, top: Photo by Clemens Kalischer, © 1956, Image Photos; p. 203, bottom: Marlboro Music Festival; p. 204, top: Photo by Fred Plaut; bottom: Marlboro Music Festival; p. 207, top and bottom: Photos by J. M. Snyder; p. 208: Marlboro Music Festival. Grateful acknowledgment is made to Mrs. Helen Hollis of the Smithsonian Institution and to the Music Division librarians at the New York Public Library for their assistance in finding pictures.